"This book is a must-read not only for ACT therapists with an interest in brief therapy, but for any ACT therapist who wants to improve their efficiency and effectiveness with the model. Low on theory and high on practicality, this book is choc-a-bloc full of new tools and techniques for brief but powerful ACT interventions. You'll be amazed at how simple and easy it makes the trickier aspects of ACT, such as self-as-context and creative hopelessness. If you want to get better results in less time with more clients, then you need to read this book right now!"

—Russ Harris, author of *The Happiness Trap*

"If you are looking for a rapid way to help people reduce their suffering and make positive changes, this book can show you the way. The four questions Strosahl, Robinson, and Gustavsson provide can give you a quick handle both on what's going on with clients and on how to help them change. A nice variation on the ACT method with some new insights and additions to make it compatible with clients' and third-party payers' demands for efficient and effective treatment."

—Bill O'Hanlon, author of *Change 101, A Brief Guide to Brief Therapy,* and *The Change Your Life Book*

"Brief therapy alert: This book is valuable reading for anyone interested in time-sensitive 'brief' therapy. It provides theory, methodology, research evidence, and numerous clinical examples for how to help clients rapidly make significant changes. It is also an excellent introduction to the larger field of acceptance and commitment therapy, offering concepts and techniques that clinicians can adapt to their own practices. Strongly recommended!"

—Michael F. Hoyt, PhD, author of *Brief Psychotherapies* and *Interviews with Brief Therapy*

D0912748

Brief Interventions *for* Radical Change

Principles & Practice *of* Focused Acceptance & Commitment Therapy

KIRK STROSAHL, PhD
PATRICIA ROBINSON, PhD
THOMAS GUSTAVSSON, MSc

Distributed in Canada by Raincoast Books

Copyright © 2012 by Kirk Strosahl, Patricia Robinson, and Thomas Gustavsson
New Harbinger Publications, Inc.
5674 Shattuck Avenue
Oakland, CA 94609
www.newharbinger.com

Cover design by Amy Shoup
Acquired by Catharine Meyers
Edited by Jasmine Star

Printed in the United States of America

14   13   12

10   9   8   7   6   5   4   3   2   1

First printing

To all the courageous clients I've seen over the years, who have taught me so much about what is humanly possible. Your words of wisdom permeate this book. To my wife and soul mate, Patti, and my three lovely daughters, Regan, Frances, and Joanna. You help keep me in the present moment and call me on it when I'm not there!

—Kirk Strosahl

To Ryland Day, my grandson, and Regan, Ezra, Frances, and Joanna May, my children, with the hope that your walk on the Good Red Road will be one of respect and trust and that your own true north pulls you, again and again.

—Patricia Robinson

This is my first book, and I hope it helps people who are in caregiving roles in all kinds of settings. I would like to thank my coauthors, Kirk and Patti, for being such great teammates, and my teachers, supervisors, colleagues, and clients over the years, who have taught me so much. I also extend gratitude to Cecilia, for many years of companionship and for being a friend; to my dog, Ella, who keeps me in shape with one thousand walks a year; and most of all, to my lovely children, Edith and Alice. You are the ones who make this all worth doing.

—Thomas Gustavsson

To Jasmine Star, your positive energy, inquisitive nature, wonderful interpersonal skills, and superlative editing and writing skills made this book not only possible to write, but fun to write. You are the greatest!

—All of the authors

Contents

Part 3
Case Examples

Part 4
FACT with Couples and Groups

Introduction

When we are no longer able to change a situation...
we are challenged to change ourselves.

— *Viktor Frankl*

This book is designed to help you, the clinician, help people who are struggling, sometimes desperately so, to experience rapid, life-altering change. When people lack the skills to be flexible in their approach and are unwilling to change strategies that aren't working, many of life's most difficult moments can seem emotionally overwhelming, and it is easy to get stuck, or frozen in place. Interestingly, some individuals, when confronted with these types of difficulties, "get large" and seem able to transcend the situation. We know that this can happen even under the most horrifying life circumstances—just read Viktor Frankl's *Man's Search for Meaning* (1992) as one example—so there is no reason to believe it can't happen in the normal course of everyday living. The quest to develop a model for promoting rapid, lasting change starts with this question: How does one person recruit the inner resources to accept what has happened and move on in life, while another is all but annihilated by the same type of life challenge?

In Frankl's case, he witnessed horrible atrocities on a daily basis and struggled to make sense of the barbarism he observed. His transformation involved accepting that he might never see his wife again (and in fact he never did) while still finding ways to experience and express his undying love toward her. This ability to transcend horrible circumstances is not logical; it is the human version of the quantum leap in physics. Our basic proposition is that any person, no matter how far down in the hole he or she is, can experience radical life changes in exactly this way.

What Is Focused Acceptance and Commitment Therapy?

Focused acceptance and commitment therapy, or FACT, is a new model of brief therapy that is a highly condensed version of a well-established, longer-term treatment called acceptance and commitment therapy (ACT; Hayes, Strosahl, & Wilson, 1999, 2011). FACT uses acceptance and mindfulness strategies to help clients transform their relationship with unwanted, distressing experiences, such as disturbing thoughts, unpleasant emotions, painful memories, or uncomfortable physical symptoms. FACT does not attempt to change the content of such private events; indeed, it is efforts to change, suppress, eliminate, or control these events that FACT views as problematic. When clients become preoccupied with managing their emotions, avoiding painful memories, or trying to replace negative thoughts with positive thoughts, they can't attend to the immediate needs of their life situation. In effect, they become rigid, ineffective problem solvers. FACT teaches clients to instead simply observe and accept the presence of these experiences. This new perspective allows them to see emotions as just emotions, memories as just memories, thoughts as just thoughts, and sensations as just sensations.

A second feature of FACT is its emphasis on helping clients connect with personal values and engage in committed actions that are consistent with those values. Instead of focusing on emotional control, FACT helps clients focus on regaining a desired quality of life. Since we have no ability to control the arrival of emotions, thoughts, traumatic memories, or the unpleasant physical symptoms that are often associated with them, we must focus energy on what we can control: our immediate behavior.

The term "commitment" in the name focused acceptance and commitment therapy refers to taking actions that are values-based, flexible, and ever-expanding in scope.

A Unified Model of Human Suffering and Resiliency

A unique feature of FACT is that it is based in research showing that a limited number of mental processes explain both human suffering and human vitality. We will examine these processes much more closely in the remainder of this book and for present purposes will simply say that there are three basic dimensions that determine both level of suffering and level of vitality: awareness of the moment, openness to private experience, and engagement in valued activities. FACT explicitly holds that *all* human suffering, regardless of its form, is caused by deficits in one or more of these core processes. This means that FACT is a transdiagnostic approach; it is not a treatment specific to certain diseases, disorders, or conditions. You can apply FACT to virtually any human problem you encounter. To demonstrate, think of a person who is able to experience both pleasant and painful private experiences directly, without struggle or defense; who at the same time can stay in the present moment and be mindfully aware of self-narratives that might interfere with effective action; and who can also connect with core personal values in life and direct problem-solving efforts in line with those values. Would you ever see a person like this in therapy? We think not!

Evidence for FACT

Acceptance and commitment therapy has recently been designated an evidence-based treatment by the Substance Abuse and Mental Health Services Administration (SAMHSA). A recent review (Levin, Hildebrant, Lillis, & Hayes, in press) found forty studies on ACT components, alone or in combination, with an average weighted effect size of $d = 0.70$ (95% CI: 0.47 to 0.93) on targeted outcomes. Another review

(Ruiz, 2010) found twenty-five outcome studies in clinical psychology areas ($N = 605$; eighteen randomized trials), twenty-seven in health psychology ($N = 1,224$; sixteen randomized studies), and fourteen in other areas, such as sports psychology, stigma, organizational development, and learning ($N = 555$; fourteen randomized studies). Across all studies, between-group effect sizes appear to be around 0.65 (Hayes, Luoma, Bond, Masuda, & Lillis, 2006; Öst, 2008; Powers, Vörding, & Emmelkamp, 2009; Pull, 2009). ACT has also been applied to many "nontraditional" problems, such as epilepsy, chronic pain, pediatric pain syndromes, obesity, smoking, and diabetes, to name a few. Many ACT studies involve brief, time-limited interventions, perhaps consisting of two to four sessions of therapy or a half-day or full-day psychoeducation class. The fact that even brief ACT interventions seem to produce long-term results was a big factor spurring the development of FACT.

To our knowledge, FACT is the only brief therapy that has been studied in a controlled way after being disseminated in a mental health delivery system setting (Strosahl, Hayes, Bergan, & Romano, 1998). The study compared a group of therapists who received training in FACT with another group of therapists who received training in solution-focused brief therapy (SFBT; de Shazer, 1985). Analysis of data from a large sample of clients revealed that FACT-trained therapists achieved the same clinical outcomes as SFBT-trained therapists but had significantly fewer clients drop out of therapy, had higher client satisfaction ratings, were more likely to terminate therapy by mutual agreement with the client, and were less likely to refer clients for psychiatric evaluation and treatment. Both SFBT and FACT therapists took about four sessions on average to complete treatment.

How Is FACT New?

There have been few true innovations in brief therapy models since the late 1980s, and the few studies of the effectiveness of those new approaches have been inconclusive. None of the existing brief therapies currently practiced in mental health settings can be considered an evidence-based treatment at this time. At the same time, the health care world is changing. Community mental health agencies and managed behavioral health organizations require clinicians to use time-limited, evidence-based treatments. Often these treatments come in the form of treatment manuals that can be dense and hard to follow. Therapists are asked to treat clients in fewer sessions without compromising outcomes. This places the contemporary clinician in a very difficult position. So many evidence-based treatment manuals, so little time! What is needed is a simple, consolidated, uniform, and evidence-based approach to human behavior change that allows the clinician to apply the same treatment principles across a broad range of problems. FACT is just such a treatment model.

About This Book

Part 1 of this book, Principles of Brief Intervention (chapters 1 through 3), is designed to give you a solid understanding of the origins, defining characteristics, and evolution of brief therapy; to examine how people get stuck repeatedly using the same patterns of unworkable behavior; and to illustrate the core principles of how people develop the personal flexibility needed to make radical behavior change a reality.

In chapter 1, we offer a quick primer in brief therapy and make the case that many and possibly most clients prefer briefer treatments for their problems. We review the research on client preferences in seeking therapy, how clients utilize therapy, patterns of change in therapy, comparisons of brief and long-term therapies for the same problem, and the phenomena of rapid change in the initial sessions of therapy. We also review the evolution of brief therapies and describe the most dominant modern approaches to brief therapy. We conclude with a review of contemporary issues in the field of brief therapy.

In chapter 2, we examine the question of how humans get stuck in unworkable patterns of behavior. We describe the core assumptions of FACT and introduce the central tenets of relational frame theory, an exciting new approach to human language and thought. Our intent is to show that human suffering originates in the very same processes of language that produce our most notable human achievements. We describe the two modes of mind that are largely responsible for producing suffering and vitality, respectively: problem-solving mind and wise mind.

In chapter 3, we introduce a set of ideas and principles describing how people succeed at promoting radical change. We also examine how the FACT clinician can both model and teach basic skills designed to increase clients' psychological flexibility.

Part 2, Practice Tools and Methods for Brief, Focused Interventions (chapters 4 through 6), offers a structured interviewing strategy that helps create a context for rapid change and presents interview and case assessment tools and techniques that will allow you to quickly and effectively intervene with the problems your client is seeking help for. Throughout this part of the book, clinical case examples and in-session dialogues are used to highlight key principles and strategies.

In chapter 4, you will learn a set of focused interviewing techniques that can be used to quickly get the individual in contact with the costs of using unworkable avoidance strategies. You will learn how to create motivation for change by engaging clients in an assessment of their life direction and whether the direction they are headed in is consistent with their personal values.

In chapter 5, we introduce several practical tools for assessing clients' psychological flexibility and analyzing the available leverage points for making a brief intervention. We also introduce a method for case analysis and treatment selection that will help you decide when, where, and how to intervene.

In chapter 6, we describe how to build psychological flexibility using brief interventions. We examine specific clinical strategies for promoting awareness, openness, and life engagement. FACT makes extensive use of metaphors, analogies, and direct experiential exercises to help develop flexibility. Clinical case examples demonstrate how these strategies are applied in therapy.

Part 3, Case Examples (chapters 7 through 10), demonstrates the application of FACT with children and families (chapter 7), people with substance abuse issues (chapter 8), people with trauma and post-traumatic stress symptoms (chapter 9), and elderly people with mood problems and demoralization (chapter 10). In each chapter, a case example drawn from actual clinical practice is used to show how FACT can be applied with that particular type of problem. Therapy dialogues are used to show how FACT interventions are set up and delivered in the clinical conversation. At the end of each chapter, we offer some general guidelines for treating individuals with that type of problem.

Part 4, FACT with Couples and Groups (chapters 11 and 12), describes how to use FACT as a couples therapy and how you can modify FACT for delivery in a group or classroom format. Again, we use case examples to highlight ways that FACT assessments and interventions can be tailored to each of these special circumstances.

On a Final Note

This book is written to help you increase the psychological flexibility of your clients in a focused and consistent way. If you are to do this, you must be willing to step back and look at some widely shared and perhaps treasured assumptions about how people change and what your role is as a helper in that process. You may have to reconsider your notions of how people get stuck in unworkable patterns of behavior. You may have to think more broadly about the general problem of human suffering and why it is so prevalent. We will ask you to adopt what we call the eagle's-eye view of the human condition. Once you see the big picture of human suffering and learn what to do about it, you will be in a position to intervene in strategic and powerful ways. We hope you find this approach as liberating, powerful, and promising as we do.

Part 1

Principles of Brief Intervention

Chapter 1

A Brief Review of Brief Therapy

Remember, kids, it's not secondhand smoke that kills;
it's secondhand thoughts.

— *George Herms*

This may be the first book you've read on the topic of brief therapy, or it may be the fiftieth. In either case, we think it will be useful to begin with a general orientation (or reorientation) to the theory and practice of brief therapy. Here is what we aim to accomplish in this chapter: First, we provide a general framework for determining what does and doesn't qualify as brief therapy. Second, we examine some common myths and misconceptions about how people change, how therapy produces change, and what clients hope to gain by seeking therapy. Third, we give you a brief history lesson on the origins of the brief therapy movement and how it has evolved up to the present day. Finally, we review significant issues in brief therapy that may be limiting its acceptance by the wider mental health community. If, by the end of this chapter, you are interested in learning more about the theory and practice of brief therapy, there are many useful texts to choose from (for example, Hoyt, 2001, 2009; O'Hanlon & Weiner-Davis, 2003).

Defining Brief Therapy—Not as Simple as It Sounds

A long-standing conceptual problem is how to define "brief therapy." In part, this is because "brief" is in the eyes of the beholder. For a psychoanalyst used to seeing clients two times a week for years, seeing a client for only one year might be considered brief. Indeed, many published studies of "brief psychodynamic therapy" involve twenty-session protocols, exceeding the length of many full-bore cognitive behavioral treatments. A clinician used to treating depressed patients with a sixteen-session cognitive therapy protocol might consider eight sessions brief. To complicate matters, several terms are often used as if they are interchangeable: brief strategic therapy, time-limited therapy, short-term therapy, time-effective therapy, and brief intervention, to name a few. We thus have an alphabet soup of terms that can potentially create a lot of confusion, on top of the difficulty inherent in pinpointing a definition of brief therapy.

Let's start the clarification process by taking on the issue of time. *Time-effective* treatment is an approach emphasizing getting the most bang for the buck out of each therapy session. If a client is seen twelve times and the maximum clinical impact is obtained by virtue of those twelve sessions, that is time-effective treatment. If, on the other hand, maximum benefit for the same problem could be achieved after only four sessions, the use of twelve sessions to achieve the same outcome would not be considered time-effective treatment. The terms *time-limited* and *short-term* refer to therapy in which a preset and limited number of sessions are delivered as part of a treatment program; for example, an eight-session group intervention designed to develop personal problem-solving skills. *Brief intervention* usually refers to a one- or two-session protocol for addressing high-risk behaviors like smoking, drinking, or substance use. This type of therapy is often delivered in settings such as primary care venues, hospitals, jails, or crisis programs, where the ability to meet with clients over time is extremely limited.

A different approach to this issue is to think of therapy in general as a horse race between what the treatment model requires and what the client is willing to accept. Whereas the client's motivation for therapy decreases steadily over time, many therapeutic approaches sequentially introduce concepts and skills over the course of treatment. Unfortunately, those clients who drop out of treatment won't benefit from strategies slated for later stages of treatment. The average number of sessions completed by a typical client during a single episode of therapy in the United States ranges from four to six (Brown & Jones, 2005; Olfson et al., 2009; Talmon, 1990). Our view is that a brief therapy is one designed for completion before reaching this natural breaking point. In this definition, brief therapy really represents, in part, the clinician's philosophical acceptance that the amount of time available to help a client is going to be limited, that the therapy process needs to be client driven, and that the clinician's mission (should he or she choose to accept it) is to help the client achieve meaningful behavior change during the time available.

Myths and Misconceptions about Change

In this section, we examine some myths and misconceptions that have led many behavioral health clinicians to discount brief therapy as a legitimate form of treatment. Although research on traditional brief therapies is sparse, the research on psychotherapy in general, and cognitive behavioral therapy in particular, offers a wealth of scientific data pertinent to this discussion.

Myth: Clients Want Lots of Therapy

Clients enter therapy because of heightened levels of psychological distress, and as their distress dissipates, they are increasingly less inclined to return for additional therapy sessions (Brown & Jones, 2005). This suggests that clients' primary motives in seeking help are emotional reassurance and practical problem solving. These two outcomes are easily achieved for most clients within the first few sessions of therapy. It is important to remember that, although a therapy session consumes only one hour of the therapist's time, it consumes far more time for the client. The client may have to hire a babysitter, take unpaid time off from work, commute to and from the therapist's office, and pay for gas on top of it all. In reality, and unfortunately, therapy is an inconvenience for most clients.

Research shows that most clients will end therapy quickly, with or without the agreement of their therapist. While estimates vary somewhat, it's probably safe to say that 30 to 40 percent of clients drop out of treatment without consulting their therapist (Olfson et al., 2009; Talmon, 1990). In a naturalistic study of over nine thousand clients in therapy, a large majority ended treatment by the fifth session, and the modal number of psychotherapy visits was *just one* (Brown & Jones, 2005). Imagine the implication that this single finding has for traditional mental health practices. The first session is usually devoted to taking an extensive history of the client and preparing a treatment plan. Interventions are often put on the back burner for later sessions due to the time-consuming intake process. Meanwhile, the most likely scenario is that the client won't return for a second visit! One brief therapy model, called single-session therapy, takes this client tendency very seriously; it is based on the assumption that the therapist and the client will see each other only once and therefore has the goal of making as much impact on the client's life as possible in the first session (Talmon, 1990).

All of that said, there remains a relatively small group of clients who prefer long-term therapy and consume a disproportionate amount of the total therapy services provided in the United States (Howard, Davidson, O'Mahoney, Orlinsky, & Brown, 1989). Interestingly, what predicts clients staying in therapy is continued high levels of psychological distress (Brown & Jones, 2005). In other words, they aren't staying in therapy because it's working; they are staying because it *isn't working.*

Interestingly, a client satisfaction survey that one of us (Strosahl) conducted showed no differences in therapy outcomes among clients who stopped therapy on their own versus clients who stopped therapy by agreement with their therapist. This same survey of several hundred clients also indicated no outcome differences between clients seen once versus clients who had multiple therapy sessions. The only difference was that clients who dropped out of therapy reported lower levels of satisfaction with their care. The take-home message is that what drives clients' preferences for therapy and how much therapy they are willing to tolerate has been virtually ignored by the mental health community. If we are to be guided by the data, it appears that most clients prefer brief therapy.

Misconception: Degree of Change Is Dependent on Amount of Time in Therapy

A commonly held belief in the mental health community is that the benefits of therapy accrue over time; hence, the longer clients are in therapy, the more benefits they will experience. Research has been conducted on the dose-effect relationship between number of therapy sessions and the amount of change clients experience. The seminal study in this area was published about twenty-five years ago but seems to have been largely ignored (Howard, Kopta, Krause, & Orlinsky, 1986). That study had a number of important findings that warrant discussion. First, approximately 15 percent of clients have experienced clinical improvements before they arrive for the first session. It appears that the act of deciding to get help is actually helpful in its own right. Further, 50 percent of the total gains from therapy are achieved by the eighth session. After the eighth session, progress in therapy slows significantly. At least twenty-six sessions are required to achieve 75 percent of the total benefits. A more recent study of dose-effect relationship showed that clients who underwent brief treatments experienced relatively rapid rates of change compared with clients who received longer-term treatment. Interestingly, the number of therapy sessions was not a significant predictor of clinical change, leading the authors to conclude that change is a nonlinear process (Baldwin, Berkeljon, Atkins, Olsen, & Nielsen, 2009).

Myth: The Longer the Therapy, the More Powerful the Effects

A related but slightly different myth is that longer-term treatment produces superior outcomes compared to shorter-term treatment; for example, that sixteen sessions of cognitive therapy for depression should produce longer-lasting reductions in depression than eight sessions of the same treatment. In a test of this idea (Molenaar et al., 2011), results indicated that the degree of symptom reduction and long-term improvement in social functioning was just as great in an eight-session treatment as in a sixteen-session treatment. Similar results have been found in studies comparing short- and long-term family therapy for anorexia (Lock, Agras, Bryson, & Kraemer, 2005), short- and long-term family-based treatments for childhood behavior problems (Smyrnios & Kirkby, 1993), brief and longer-term cognitive behavioral therapy for post-traumatic stress disorder (Sijbrandij et al., 2007), and a brief, intensive two-day treatment for panic disorder (Deacon & Abramowitz, 2006). This finding has also been observed with depression and a wide range of anxiety disorders (Cape, Whittington, Buszewicz, Wallace, & Underwood, 2010). Overall, recent research suggests that brief treatments are just as effective as longer-term treatments for the same disorder.

Misconception: Brief Therapy Is a Superficial Intervention with Few Long-Term Benefits

A key issue in the delivery of any kind of psychotherapy is the long-term impact it has on the client's life functioning. Treatments that only reduce transient symptoms of distress but don't affect longer-term patterns of maladaptive behavior will create a revolving-door problem. Specifically, clients have to seek therapy repeatedly to address new problems created by long-standing behavioral issues. One theory of change in psychotherapy, called the phase model, holds that clinical response occurs in three discrete phases that are assumed to be time dependent (Howard, Lueger, Maling, & Martinovich, 1993): The first phase, termed "remoralization," involves a sense of subjective improvement as the client starts to do something about the problem. In the second phase, termed "remediation," clinical symptoms are reduced to low levels. In the final phase, termed "rehabilitation," stable improvements in functioning begin to appear. Since rehabilitation is thought to be a longer-term process, one could argue that brief therapies will do little to promote this type of functional improvement.

In a recent study examining this prediction, 338 consecutive clients participating in a brief consultation program in primary care were administered a measure based on the phase model at each visit. The average number of intervention sessions per client was one and a half, with the mode being one. Among clients receiving two or more sessions, results suggested that clinically and statistically significant changes occurred in all three phases of change (Bryan, Morrow, & Appolonio, 2009). Another recent study examined the effectiveness of a two- to four-session cognitive behavioral intervention for regular amphetamine users and found a significant increase in the probability of abstinence among clients receiving at least two sessions (Baker et al., 2005). These results suggest that the process of therapeutic change is not yet well understood and may in part be influenced by the subtle or not so subtle communications and expectations of the therapist. If the client hears that some specific personal issue is going to take a long time to deal with in therapy, the client may dutifully, if unconsciously, comply with that suggestion.

Myth: Rapid, Large Clinical Gains Are Rare in Therapy

For over a decade, two of us (Strosahl and Robinson) worked in a brief therapy center where, together, we led many groups for depressed clients. Many of these clients had depression scores in the severe range and had been depressed for a long time. While leading these groups, we noticed a curious thing: After one or two group sessions, a certain percentage of these clients exhibited large, sudden reductions in depression that endured for the rest of the group intervention. Even severely depressed clients sometimes exhibited this pattern.

As it turns out, we were not alone in seeing this effect. It is estimated that 40 to 45 percent of depressed clients exhibit sudden large gains within the first two to four treatment sessions (Doane, Feeny, & Zoellner, 2010; Tang, DeRubeis, Hollon, Amsterdam, & Shelton, 2007). Similar observations of clients making rapid progress in the initial sessions of cognitive behavioral therapy have been noted for post-traumatic stress disorder (52 percent of clients; Doane et al., 2010), binge eating (62 percent of clients; Grilo, Masheb, & Wilson, 2006), and irritable bowel syndrome (30 percent of clients; Lackner et al., 2010). What is equally intriguing is that rapid response is associated with long-term improvements in functioning, as well as a reduction in relapse rates (Crits-Christoph et al., 2001; Lutz, Stulz, & Kock, 2009; Tang et al., 2007). This tendency of rapid responders to show better longer-term functioning was also found in a sample of depressed adolescents (Renaud et al., 1998). The evidence for sudden gains is growing steadily, as is demonstrated by the first published meta-analysis of this interesting clinical phenomenon (Aderka, Nickerson, Boe, & Hoffman, 2012). At this point, we can safely conclude that rapid gains in therapy are not evidence of a "flight into health," but rather are demonstrations of radical change in action!

History 101: Evolution of Brief Therapy

Now it's time to look back at the roots of the brief therapy movement in the United States. There were two principal early schools of brief therapy, both of which continue to have large numbers of dedicated followers: Ericksonian hypnotherapy and problem-focused brief therapy.

Milton Erickson and Clinical Hypnosis

Milton Erickson was a psychiatrist who is regarded as the founder of modern-day hypnotherapy (Rosen, 1991). Afflicted with a nearly fatal case of polio as a child, crippled and in pain for much of his life, Erickson developed a unique approach to accessing nonverbal learning processes via therapeutic interventions. He believed that verbal self-knowledge was as harmful as it was helpful and spent most of his career developing nonverbal methods for inducing change.

Erickson mastered the use of paradoxical interventions, confusion, indirect suggestions and encouraging resistance. A paradoxical intervention is one in which the client is instructed to "practice the problem" more intently, or do more of it. The concept underlying such interventions is that most clients feel they have no control over whether a particular problematic behavior or emotion occurs. Therefore, instructing them to generate the problem is a paradoxical demonstration that they do have control.

Another core element of the Erickson approach is the use of confusing language practices. The motive behind creating confusion in therapy is to draw clients out of a familiar frame of reference—the well-worn and ineffective mental model they bring into therapy about "the problem." Drawing clients out of their frame of reference initiates a mental operation in which they attempt to integrate the confusing information into their existing frame of reference. Since this isn't possible, their frame of reference must expand to include the inconsistent or confusing information.

Indirect suggestion was a defining feature of Erickson's clinical approach. Indirect suggestion can involve embedding a nonspecific, positive suggestion in the dialogue (for example, "I'm looking forward to hearing about the other ways you notice yourself reacting when you get into this situation again"). Indeed, clinical hypnosis arguably is the art of making indirect suggestions that subtly influence the client's subsequent behaviors. Erickson also developed nonverbal strategies to make clients more susceptible to suggestion. One of the better known is a tactic called pacing. In pacing, the therapist mimics a particular feature of a client's verbal or nonverbal behavior (for example, head nodding, foot tapping, or frequent use of a phrase, such as "you know"). Whether verbal or nonverbal, indirect suggestion strategies are thought to increase the client's receptivity to change by accessing mental processes that are not under the direct control of language.

In addition, Erickson was the first to explore the notion of encouraging resistance, a technique designed to offset the natural tendency of clients to get into a push-pull relationship with the therapist. Erickson's approach involved riding with resistance, allowing clients to withhold any information deemed irrelevant or too emotionally threatening. This tactic is really a paradoxical intervention in reverse; the more it is suggested that the client certainly won't want to discuss some painful issue, the more the client might be tempted to bring that issue into the therapy conversation.

Erickson's work remained largely unknown outside of the clinical hypnosis community until the publication of *Uncommon Therapy*, by Jay Haley (1993). Haley's book brought Erickson's unique perspective and clinical methods into the mainstream of the brief therapy community.

Even today, proponents of his methods continue to wield considerable influence on the theory and practice of brief therapy (see O'Hanlon, 2009). In addition, the Milton Erickson Foundation (erickson-founda tion.org) continues to be a leading force in the development of novel strategic therapy approaches and sponsors an annual conference devoted to advances in brief therapy and hypnotherapy.

Problem-Focused Brief Therapy

The second major force in the evolution of brief therapy was the development of a new brief therapy model at the Mental Research Institute (MRI) in Palo Alto, California. Founded by anthropologists Gregory Bateson and Donald Jackson in 1958, MRI began a long-term study of cross-cultural communication practices using cybernetics theory. One of the most famous findings of this project was the double bind theory of schizophrenia (Bateson, Jackson, Haley, & Weakland, 1956), which stimulated research (which continues to this day) into the communication practices of families of people with schizophrenia. The notion that communication practices within a family could promote the onset of schizophrenia triggered a major resurgence of clinical and research interest in interventions for family systems. Arguably, MRI is responsible for the family therapy movement in the United States, and indeed, it offered the first formal family therapy training program in the world. Informed by the work of John Weakland (Weakland & Ray, 1995) and Paul Watzlawick (Watzlawick, Weakland, & Fisch, 1974), the MRI Brief Therapy Center opened in 1966 and developed a unique form of brief therapy called problem-focused brief therapy.

One of the seminal concepts of this approach is that it is not the "problem" that is the problem; the "solution" is the problem (Watzlawick et al., 1974). This simple but counterintuitive idea has become a cornerstone of almost every brief therapy. It implies that the client's strategies for solving what is perceived as the problem are either creating or amplifying the problem. Another major contribution attributed to Watzlawick is the concept of type 1 versus type 2 change. In type 1 change, small changes in perspective might occur but the client is still locked into a system that is dysfunctional on a larger scale. In type 2 change, the client's perception suddenly shifts, such that the existing worldview is replaced by an entirely new perspective. FACT seeks to promote type 2 change by altering the client's relationship with distressing emotions, thoughts, and memories.

Contemporary Approaches to Brief Therapy

In recent decades, two important schools of brief therapy have capitalized on the emerging health care philosophy of providing briefer, lower-cost therapy: solution-focused brief therapy (SFBT; de Shazer, 1985, 1988, 1991) and narrative therapy (White, 2007; White & Epston, 1990).

Solution-Focused Brief Therapy

Early in his career, Steve de Shazer was a member of the MRI brief therapy team. He noticed that the more clients talked about a "problem" in therapy, the more self-deprecating and rigid they became. He theorized that systematically directing the therapeutic conversation to focus on client strengths and solutions would enable clients to change more quickly. This led de Shazer to develop his now widely practiced approach.

A key tenet of SFBT is that "problem talk" creates a shared assumption between therapist and client that the client is stuck and nothing can change. Clients enter therapy with the belief that talking about their "problem" will help them discover ways to fix it. From an SFBT perspective, the more clients engage in this kind of talk with the therapist, the more the "problem" is magnified. Therefore, the goal of SFBT is to shift the therapeutic conversation to "solution talk." This is accomplished by focusing on client strengths and successes, rather than on deficits. There are many SFBT interventions strategies that are designed to shift focus to what clients are doing right. This helps clients imagine what a better life might look like and what steps they can take to move in that direction. SFBT might be thought of as an approach that focuses on the impacts of small positive changes. Second-generation advocates of SFBT continue to develop novel, client-centered methods for inducing rapid, positive change (see Miller, Hubble, & Duncan, 1996).

Narrative Therapy

Narrative therapy was developed by Michael White in Adelaide, Australia (White, 2007; White & Epston, 1990). We describe this approach as a brief therapy with some trepidation because the only existing clinical study of the approach used an eight-session protocol to treat depressed clients (Vromans & Schweitzer, 2010). According to the definitions we outlined above, this would qualify as a time-limited or time-effective treatment, but not as a brief therapy. However, many clinicians utilizing brief therapy note that they integrate narrative therapy concepts and strategies into their practice, so we briefly review this approach just to be on the safe side.

White was heavily influenced by the philosophy of postmodernism. A highly simplified description of this philosophy is that humans create reality through their mental constructions of it—that there is no objective reality. Thus, the same situations, events, and interactions can be interpreted in endless ways. Human narratives are made up of events linked by a theme occurring over time and organized according to a plot. A story emerges as certain events are selected over other events as more important or true. As the story takes shape, it invites people to select only certain information while ignoring events that don't fit the story line.

When clients seek therapy, they are often being dominated by problem-saturated stories. These stories can also exert a powerful influence on the self-concept of clients (for example, *I've always been a social misfit*). Thus, narratives can shape the way people see their lives and capabilities. Narrative therapy focuses on destabilizing the personal narratives that clients hold as reality. A classic narrative intervention is to externalize the narrative by writing it down, by having an external witness (often a friend or acquaintance of the client) be present to hear the client's narrative, or by giving the narrative its own properties or motives that are at odds with the client's goals and desires. The goal is to allow more compassionate narratives to compete with harsh, critical, and self-rejecting narratives.

Brief Therapies: Barriers to Buy In

Over the years, the popular appeal of brief therapy within the larger mental health and health care community has waxed and waned. It would be fair to say that most practicing clinicians have had at least some level of exposure to one or more brief therapy approaches. However, widespread adoption of brief therapy as the preferred approach to mental health care has been met with several criticisms, some practice-based, some theoretical, and some empirical.

Managed Care Conspiracy?

There is little doubt that the rise of managed care has been a major boon to the field of brief psychotherapy, so much so that some practitioners incorrectly equate brief therapy with the exploitative goals of managed care. However, the history outlined above indicates that brief therapies were in existence for decades before the managed care era. Nevertheless, critics argue that managed care networks were conveniently quick to adopt brief therapy as a preferred practice model with the intent to deprive clients of needed longer-term therapy services and to make money for the insurance company by doing so. This link between managed care and brief therapy has engendered unnecessary resistance to the expansion of brief interventions and therapies in settings where these are the only viable treatment approaches, such as in primary care, emergency rooms, crisis programs, and school-based programs.

Hazy Theories of Clinical Change

Since their inception, brief therapies, such as the MRI and SFBT models, have been renowned for their catchy sayings and techniques, and they have taken a rather iconoclastic stance with respect to the sacred assumptions of more traditional therapeutic approaches. The nontraditional feel of these approaches appeals to many clinicians looking for new ways to help their clients. The relative simplicity of brief therapies has also helped promote their dissemination. The downside is that brief therapies often are based on vague or poorly articulated models of intervention and change. The result is that it is difficult to conduct dismantling studies of brief therapy approaches to isolate their active ingredients. For example, we would have trouble identifying which solution-focused techniques are the core ingredients that produce change because what is described is not the change process itself, but the techniques used to induce change. There is a big difference between simply describing the intervention methods of a particular treatment and articulating how those methods work to produce change.

Lack of Evidence

A common criticism that has been present for decades is that brief therapy approaches lack scientific support for their clinical effectiveness (Jacobson, 1985). The world of mental health is changing and, whereas it was fashionable a decade ago to blast the notion of evidence-based treatment as unachievable in the mental health field, it is now considered the gold standard. Mental health centers, and the clinicians who practice in them, are now required to use treatments that have some scientific evidence. It is no longer trendy to argue that mental health outcomes cannot be quantified, measured, and used to improve the quality of treatments offered to clients.

It is indeed ironic to, on the one hand, point out the abundant evidence for rapid change in therapy and, on the other, state that none of the traditional brief therapy approaches discussed in this chapter would make the cut as an evidence-based treatment. Solution-focused brief therapy has received the most scrutiny, but the studies are limited in number, are often post hoc in nature, and lack essential methodological controls (such as random assignment to control groups or the use of wait-list controls or comparison treatments). There are two published meta-analyses of SFBT in the U.S. literature (Gingerich & Eisengardt, 2000; Kim, 2008). Both conclude that SFBT cannot be considered an evidence-based treatment at this time. The most recent meta-analysis calculated effect sizes for SFBT and found them to be in the range of 0.11 to 0.23. These would be considered only mild treatment effects. As a comparison, meta-analyses of acceptance and commitment therapy considered across a very wide range of clinical complaints have shown average effect sizes of 0.62, with several studies showing effect sizes of 1.2 or greater.

We were able to find only one outcome study for narrative therapy, which involved a cohort of depressed adults (Vromans & Schweitzer, 2010). It does not appear that there was a control group or comparison treatment used in this study, so the results must be viewed with caution. However, the treatment produced very impressive reductions in depression among clients who completed treatment. The calculated effect size was approximately 1.26, which would be comparable to most evidence-based treatments for depression. Unfortunately, it must be noted that this is the only scientific study of narrative therapy in the nearly twenty years since its introduction.

Summary: Brief Interventions Might Be the Best Interventions

We believe that most people are equipped with the psychological tools necessary to transcend their suffering and that they can do so rapidly given the right circumstances. When it comes to therapy, our review of the literature suggests that more is not necessarily better. The "insight" and "understanding" clients often gain from longer-term therapy can be a double-edged sword. As we often tell clients, understanding how you got into this mess has no bearing on how you will get out of it. If insight and understanding are not combined with meaningful, real-life behavior change, they have little practical benefit.

In reality, the scientific understanding of why and how people change is so limited that we would gladly exchange everything we currently do know for everything we don't know. This is an interesting paradox for a field that is over sixty years old and has generated literally thousands of research articles on the effects of therapy. As we shall see in chapter 2, focused acceptance and commitment therapy attempts to unravel portions of this unsolved mystery by proposing a unified, transdiagnostic approach in which human suffering and human vitality are linked to the same small number of core mental processes.

Chapter 2

How People Get Stuck

Reality is an illusion, albeit a persistent one.

— *Anonymous*

In this chapter, we will try to answer a question that clinicians of all types routinely ask: How is it that bright, caring, sensitive people can repeatedly engage in the same unworkable responses in important life situations, despite enduring negative consequences for doing so? How and why do people become so rigid at the very moment when their life situation demands flexibility? In the remainder of this chapter and, indeed, the remainder of this book, we will address this perplexing, exasperating feature of humans and what you, the clinician, can do to help people develop more flexibility in dealing with life challenges.

While life is precious, it is not easy. The journey from birth to death is full of challenges and transitions, both expected and unexpected. In the midst of this cascade of unending change, the "job" of the human is to stay connected with personal values and engage in ongoing patterns of behavior that embody those values. The challenges to living a vital life are as endless as the life situations that define humanity. Living a chosen life is therefore not a birthright; it is earned, often painfully. Perhaps one of the most unique aspects of human existence is how hard it is for us to be happy. The attributes of being human that make us singular (such as our ability to imagine the future so that we might problem solve, plan, and organize our behavior to achieve desired ends) also produce suffering (for example, we can imagine a better life, determine that it isn't achievable, and commit suicide). The same processes that can make us remarkably adaptive in the face of overwhelming adversity can also produce rigid and inflexible responses to seemingly trivial problems.

The Basic Proposition: Human Suffering Is Driven by Language

While we will spend the remainder of this chapter unpacking this problematic feature of human behavior, the short version of the FACT approach is as follows: Human suffering is not abnormal; rather, it is ubiquitous and is an unintended by-product of human language and thought. Humans use language and thought to both organize and regulate their behavior, but the ever-present nature of language causes this voluntary relationship to become involuntary. As we mature, we lose sight of the fact that this regulatory function is even there; it fades into the background of daily reality. One of the more dangerous features of language is that its regulatory functions can make humans unresponsive to the direct results of their behavior, particularly if these functions are extended into life areas where they don't belong. Because of language, people can literally start living in their heads, more or less out of contact with how things work in the real world.

Among its many facets, human language is embedded with socially transmitted rules specifying that health involves being free from distressing, unwanted private experiences like negative emotions, disturbing thoughts, painful memories, or uncomfortable physical symptoms. To achieve health, one must be able to control or eliminate this "bad" stuff. Paradoxically, it is the attempt to control or eliminate unwanted private experiences that makes them *more* dominant, intrusive, and uncontrollable. But instead of changing tactics, humans *intensify* the quest for emotional control. For example, they avoid participating in events, situations, or interactions that might trigger distressing, unwanted experiences. Other control strategies involve emotion-numbing behaviors, such as alcohol and drug abuse, overeating, bingeing and purging, cutting, ruminating, worrying, or even taking psychotropic medications.

As patterns of emotional and situational avoidance widen, people lose their bearings in life and fall out of contact with positive, vitality-producing behaviors. Their life space constricts as their emotional control agenda takes over. The life constriction itself begins to generate secondary distress as important personal problems, such as a bad marriage, an abusive relationship, or lack of social connectedness, go unaddressed.

It is the attempt to avoid distressing, unwanted private experiences, not the experiences per se, that is toxic. Note the similarity of this idea to one of the oldest principles of brief therapy: It is not the "problem" that is the problem; the "solution" is the problem. In FACT, we hold that emotional control isn't the solution; it's the problem. In order to gain the illusion of control over painful experiences, the client must sacrifice living a vital life. The irony is that painful experiences can't really be controlled or eliminated in the first place and that attempts at control are what actually make painful experiences even more painful. FACT teaches clients to make room for distressing private experiences, to stand in the presence of socially programmed rules and self-generated life narratives without being dominated by them, and to engage in values-based actions that produce a sense of vitality, purpose, and meaning.

In the remainder of this chapter, we are going to walk through the FACT model, starting with its basic assumptions, then reviewing the science pertaining to the role of human language and thought as a regulatory system for human behavior, and concluding with an examination of how certain core mental processes can play a role in amplifying or reducing the suffering associated with painful life experiences.

Core Assumptions of FACT

The core assumptions of the FACT model form the basis of the goals of clinical assessment and also directly contribute to a key subset of intervention targets. These ideas lead to a host of intriguing clinical implications, many of which have already been tested and supported by clinical research.

Human Behavior Is Contextually Determined

Behavior cannot be understood in isolation from its context. There are three principal contexts we deal with in FACT: sociocultural context, the ongoing processes of the mind, and the observing self.

Sociocultural context. Sociocultural context is the world outside the individual's skin. It contains a variety of influences, both positive and negative. For example, to understand a depressed client's reality requires that we understand the impact of the client's depressive behaviors on others and how the behaviors of others impact the client. Cultural practices are another powerful feature in the sociocultural context. Certain depressive behaviors might not be tolerated in one cultural milieu but may be actively supported and reinforced in another. If you are a fan of family systems theory, think of the family system as another type of context the client is both influencing and being influenced by.

Ongoing processes of the mind. To be more accurate, we should probably use the term "minding," rather than ongoing processes of the mind, because the mind is not a thing. The brain is a thing with known structures created by specific cellular material. The process of minding, however, is a dynamic, ongoing enterprise. The mind is running twenty-four hours a day, seven days a week. Wake up from a good night's sleep, and there it is. Fall asleep, and there it is in a different form. An analogy one client used says it best: "My mind is like an operating system on a computer. There is always processing going on, and there is always a message on my monitor when I look at it."

The observing self. If the mind is an operating system continuously processing information and displaying output on a screen, then who or what is looking at the screen? In FACT, we call that entity the observing self. It is the very foundation of consciousness. Like "the mind," consciousness is not a thing; it has no boundaries or edges. The qualities of consciousness are continuous, even if we experience consciousness in qualitatively different ways (for example, sleeping, intoxicated, or meditating). Ultimately, we inhabit consciousness, and it is from this perspective that we see the products of the mind as if we were observing them on a computer monitor.

This is the perspective from which we can see thoughts as just thoughts, feelings as just feelings, and memories as just memories.

A key principle of FACT is that humans actively relate to and interact with all three contexts more or less simultaneously. We interface with the external world, read output from the mind, and see through the eyes of basic self-awareness. When these three contexts are relating harmoniously, human behavior is incredibly flexible. When the relationships between them are distorted or imbalanced, behavior becomes rigid and ineffective. One important clinical implication of this principle is that a therapy itself is really the interaction of these three contexts for both therapist and client. For example, a FACT therapist might say, "There are really four of us in the room right now: you, me, your mind, and my mind."

All Human Behavior Is Organized and Purposeful

All human behavior is organized and purposeful. There is no such thing as random behavior. This is because human behavior is either inherited or learned; it originates in our genes or from our learning history. The significance of this assumption might be lost if you see this as a "not so profound profundity," but consider this: Even when clients say they don't know where they are going in life, they are going somewhere. The question they need to consider is *Where am I going, and is that where I want to be going?* Even when a client is withdrawing from others and doesn't want to participate in life, that is actually a form of participation that is highly organized and purposeful. The benefit to the therapist of this principle is that everything the client is doing has a purpose. If you can get the client to identify the purpose, you are in an ideal position to promote rapid change.

What Works for the Client Is a Pragmatic Matter

FACT holds that there is no right way to live life; there is no truth with a capital T. Instead, whatever works to promote the client's sense of vitality, purpose, and meaning is functionally true. It doesn't matter how one gets to vitality; the important goal is getting there. If suppressing every memory of a traumatic childhood allows a client to achieve important life outcomes and experience a sense of vitality, then suppression is a functionally workable strategy for that client. This assumption directly defines the job of the FACT therapist: In essence, we must find out where clients are trying to go in life and then work with them to develop strategies that help propel them in that direction. Every client, no matter how chronically dysfunctional, is dealing with two central issues: One is where he or she wants to go in life, and the other is how to get there.

A Look inside the Word Machine

A central tenet of FACT is that all forms of human suffering and behavioral rigidity originate as a by-product of human language and thought. Our goal in this section is to show you how the human mind can produce suffering and behavioral rigidity. Kelly Wilson, one of the founders of acceptance and commitment therapy, once described the human mind as a "word machine" in a touching dedication to his brother, who committed suicide (Hayes et al., 1999). This is an apt analogy, because it points to a process that is mechanical, governed by cause-and-effect sequences, and inhuman in its motives. This way of thinking about the human mind may seem overly grim, but consider this: Humans are the only species known to commit suicide. We are also the only species known to feel stigma, experience prejudice, and hate others simply because of a difference in skin color. Humans deliberately kill other humans who have different religious practices or beliefs. On a smaller scale, our clients are being ground up by the same basic language tricks that have produced the world's greatest atrocities.

Relational Framing: The Basis of Language and Thought

Many of the clinical concepts underpinning FACT are based on a scientific model of human language and thought called relational frame theory (RFT; Hayes, Barnes-Holmes, & Roche, 2001). When we use the term "language" in this book, we are not simply referring to verbal behavior, such as speaking, but rather to the entire symbolic system that creates both language and thought (an internalized version of language). RFT holds that humans sequentially acquire symbolic abilities beginning in infancy and that as an individual's language system evolves over time, it directly regulates ever-enlarging patterns of behavior. Very young children need their behavior regulated by external means, but by the time they are in middle childhood, they have acquired social rules that help them self-regulate their behavior.

In RFT, relational frames are the cornerstone of human symbolic abilities. An example of a relational frame is "I-you." Very young infants cannot acquire this symbolic frame, so when they see a parent crying, they cry too. Other basic frames define relations, such as "if-then," which allows us to predict a future outcome based on a conditional event. The relational frame "then-now" allows us to understand time. It turns out that a quite limited number of basic relational frames can produce an incredibly complicated symbolic system, such as human language. The RFT model further proposes that human language is not a thing, but rather a generative, dynamic, ongoing process. When we think, we are framing. This allows us to incorporate immediate experience, link it to past experience, and use it to predict future experience.

How the Mind Regulates Behavior

RFT proposes that verbally derived behavior-regulating rules are the main output of the language system. Collectively, these rules organize and regulate most, if not all, human behavior. Language regulates behavior in two primary ways: contingency-shaped learning and rule-governance.

Contingency-Shaped Behavior

Behavior that is shaped by direct consequences is known as contingency-shaped behavior. In general, human behavior is more flexible and adaptive when it is shaped by direct consequences. For example, suppose you go outside in freezing weather with no coat or gloves on. You quickly realize that this isn't a good idea, and from that point on, you remember to think about the outside temperature before going out and then dress yourself accordingly. This is an example of effective contingency-shaped behavior. Contingencies can sometimes shape maladaptive but temporarily useful behaviors, like speeding in order to get to work on time, but ineffective behaviors tend to have results (like getting a $100 speeding ticket!) that cause them to quickly be modified so that more workable responses are used. Our social world is filled with such contingencies. You don't utter an expletive to a complete stranger unless you're looking for a fight. If you go to work without any clothes on, you will quickly be out of a job. The list goes on and on, all the way down to very subtle social contingencies (for example, the best way to make someone like you is to smile, make eye contact, and ask open-ended questions).

Rule-Governed Behavior

Language didn't develop to help us meditate or get in touch with our issues; it evolved as a system for ensuring survival. A singular feature of human language is that it allows behavior-regulating practices to be acquired symbolically, without the need to contact the real-world situation the rule refers to. Behavior that is initiated and regulated on the basis of symbolically derived rules is known as rule-governed behavior. For example, take the common instruction given to children: "Don't talk to strangers when you aren't with an adult." This rule essentially specifies a set of conditions in which the child is deemed at risk (encountering a stranger and being alone) and a specific behavior that is to be regulated (remaining silent, disengaging from the person). Note that both this rule and the behavior it will regulate are acquired symbolically, as if the child had learned this through direct experience. If the child does encounter a stranger, the rule will probably kick in and the child will leave. Therefore, the rule that strangers are inherently dangerous and not to be trusted might never be directly tested in the real world. This is a major feature of rule-governed behavior that is directly relevant to the types of problems clients seek help for. Rules not only regulate behavior; they also generate negative emotion states (fear produced by the possibility of encountering a "dangerous" stranger) that themselves produce behaviors designed to regulate those emotion states (run from or escape the situation).

Rule-governed behavior isn't inherently bad; what's harmful is the extension of this process into areas where rule governance takes people out of contact with real-world results. For example, the depressed person who ruminates endlessly doesn't make contact with the fact that rumination makes depression worse, not better. Instead, this "problem-solving" behavior is driven by rule-governed relations: Analyze what is causing your depression, eliminate the cause of your depression, and your depression will go away. In a technical sense, FACT interventions seek to reestablish a harmonious balance between rule-governed and contingency-shaped learning. We need to follow rules to survive, but we don't need to be dominated by rules.

The Hegemony of Language

Human existence is an intensely symbolic experience fueled by the ubiquitous presence of the mind. As mentioned earlier, the process of minding is an ongoing, dynamic process of forming relations. At the macro level, human language is equipped with some core functions that are responsible for what we perceive as existence. Unfortunately, there are some unintended by-products of minding that directly contribute to human suffering. Here's a brief overview of some of the core functions of language, highlighting their benefits and risks.

Self-Reflexivity

- **Operational definition:** Ability to be aware that we are aware

- **Purpose:** Cornerstone of conscious self-awareness

- **Upside:** Allows us to look inside to monitor private events and report states of being to others

- **Downside:** Can amplify negative states of mind and lead to preoccupation with negative private experiences

Comparison and Categorization

- **Operational definition:** Ability to compare and contrast things; ability to categorize and evaluate things based on similarities and differences

- **Purpose:** Allows discrimination between things; allows us to detect meaningful differences; supports discrepancy-based problem solving

- **Upside:** Critical to human problem-solving abilities; basis of human compassion

- **Downside:** Basis of prejudice, stereotyping, and self-loathing

Sense Making

- **Operational definition:** Ability to derive cause-and-effect relationships

- **Purpose:** Basis of reductive reasoning; allows behavior to be explained and justified

- **Upside:** Allows nearly any problem in the external world to be understood in cause-and-effect terms; basis of human mastery of the external world

- **Downside:** Can be applied to link one or more life events in a causal chain; creates the impression that negative "causes" must be directly manipulated to produce better results

Self-Narrative

- **Operational definition:** Ability to produce a coherent report of self-experience over time, linked to abstract and overarching themes

- **Purpose:** Allows advanced social behavior between humans; functions as a form of social control over individual members of a clan

- **Upside:** Facilitates social relationships; helps promote shared purpose; allows us to know one another; allows need states to be expressed and addressed

- **Downside:** Can devolve into justifications and explanations for ineffective living; can regulate behavior and produce self-defeating results; can be rigid and screen out important information

Prediction

- **Operational definition:** Ability to create a mental picture of a future occurrence based on different causal factors

- **Purpose:** Allows anticipation of and planning for future events; basis of the ability to protect oneself

- **Upside:** Useful in preventing threats to survival or personal comfort; helps organize and motivate problem-solving behavior

- **Downside:** Allows predictions to be generated about subjective well-being or important life outcomes; when negative, has been implicated in suicide; can result in behavior being unduly influenced by the content of predictions

Cognitive-Affective Scripts

- **Operational definition:** Ability to use thinking to identify and regulate primary emotions and associated behavioral impulses

- **Purpose:** Basis for cognitive regulation of emotions; allows organized social behavior between humans; forms the basis for moral order and cooperation rather than competition

- **Upside:** Useful in allowing emotions to be experienced, reported, and shared without destructive consequences to individuals or clans

- **Downside:** Can carry social programming that emotions are dangerous, that there are "bad" and "good" feelings, and that feelings cannot be trusted and must be controlled; leads to emotional avoidance and artificial, destructive methods of emotional control

With this mixed bag of positive and negative impacts, it is indeed remarkable that most humans implicitly trust the output of their minds and that therapeutic suggestions to the contrary—that the mind isn't always to be trusted—are often met with a mixture of surprise and disbelief.

Language Is Our Friend

Language organizes and regulates our behavior from minute to minute. This is an incredibly valuable function in everyday living. When you get ready to cross a busy intersection, your mind scans the immediate environment for moving objects, estimating speed and predicting safety margins. It then tells you to walk or stay put. You'd better listen to your mind in this situation, or you'll end up in the morgue. Most of us go through hundreds of symbolic, language-based transactions like this every day and, in many cases, we have no reason to question the utility of just letting the mind do the work. This leads people to develop an unquestioned belief in the usefulness of their symbolic abilities. We learn by repeated examples that the mind is central not only to survival but also to the way our behavior is organized and controlled and that this is generally for the better. Thus, it is hard for people to reverse course and to question the strategy of using the mind to solve every problem.

The Operating System Is Invisible

When clients enter therapy, most of them are not aware that their behavior is rule governed. This is because people tend to see the world through the eyes of language. The notion of the mind as a computer operating system truly is a fitting analogy. As end users, we only see what appears on the screen; we don't see the program that organizes what we see and how we see it. Once again, there are literally hundreds of examples each day where it is beneficial to allow the mind to "do its thing" without much concern about how the system works. In fact, it would be cumbersome to deliberately interrupt this rather automatic process in the course of normal everyday living. The fact that the system works is sufficient reason for most people to stop inquiring about how the system works. The result is that, for the sake of speed and efficiency, the process of minding is put on autopilot. We rely on the mind's representations of reality because it's useful to do so in day-to-day living, but this overreliance can become toxic when we unquestioningly accept subjective mental products like self-evaluations, memories, emotions, and self-narratives. When these issues are on the table, as they frequently are for clients in therapy, the first goal is to establish that defining what is real is not the sole province of the mind. FACT helps clients see the inner workings of the operating system by stepping back from it and observing its products.

The Two Modes of Mind

It is important to remember that not all forms of human knowing are linear and analytical. Nonverbal forms of knowing, such as intuition, compassion, empathy, inspiration, and prophetic vision, are the cornerstone of many great human accomplishments. Most humans experience the mind as a dynamic interplay between its verbal, analytic, reductive functions and its inductive, nonverbal forms of knowing. In FACT, we call the former the problem-solving mind and the latter wise mind.

A basic assumption is that clients suffer because they are attached to or overidentified with the problem-solving mode of mind. Thus, the goal of treatment is to decrease the domination of the problem-solving mind and to increase the client's ability to voluntarily make contact with wise mind. FACT interventions like learning to be an observer of private experiences, learning to accept what is present without evaluation or struggle, learning to be mindful and values oriented, and learning to engage in actions that embody personal beliefs are geared toward helping clients learn the skills needed to connect with wise mind.

Problem-Solving Mind

Simply put, the main function of the problem-solving mode of mind is to reduce the discrepancy between where we are and where we want to be. The ability to first detect and then reduce or eliminate discrepancies is the cornerstone of human verbal knowledge. When a discrepancy is detected, the problem-solving mind analyzes its potential causes and then organizes behavior to reverse the causes. This type of mental process is ubiquitous in everyday existence. For example, it's time to go to work in the morning and you have ten minutes to get out of the house. You aren't out of the house yet, but that's where you want to be. Your mind gives you a set of behavioral tasks to complete that ends with you being in your car or at the bus stop at the target time. The mind's job is to create a solution in which there is no discrepancy between where you are and where you want to be.

This simple, fundamental process can be applied to an almost infinite set of problems. Suppose you are depressed, and where you want to be is "normal," like others. The problem-solving mind will analyze why you are depressed and create a solution that reverses the cause (for example, *Try to act happy; substitute positive thoughts for negative ones*). The problem is that in the world between the ears, following this strategy actually makes emotions more intense, memories more intrusive, upsetting thoughts more dominant, and uncomfortable physical sensations even more invasive. But rather than self-correcting in response to negative results, the problem-solving mind will advise the human to try the same strategies again, only harder! There are two major by-products of the problem-solving mind's agenda that consistently produce suffering: emotional avoidance and rule following.

Emotional Avoidance

One of the consequences of treating human emotions, memories, thoughts, or sensations as a problem to be solved is that the task shifts from learning to use private responses as important pieces of information to finding ways to stay out of contact with them. For example, a client might confidently state, "I will be better when I'm not always feeling sad." From that perspective, sadness isn't seen as a signal that something is amiss in the client's life—an important sign. The agenda has shifted to killing the messenger because the news is painful. Almost without exception, clients enter therapy because they have used a variety of strategies to kill the messenger without success. They are hoping the clinician can help them succeed in this mission.

Rule Following

Earlier in this chapter, we discussed rule-governed behavior as one of the two essential mechanisms that organize and control behavior. For clinical purposes, we will use the term "rule following" to describe a situation in which the individual's behavior has become excessively rule governed. Rule following isn't always conscious or voluntary. Many of our most basic social rules are embedded in language acquisition; we "inhale" them as we develop the ability to use language. This is one of the chief social and evolutionary functions of language. We can transmit cultural practices and motifs without having to directly train each human in those practices. There are several culturally transmitted rules that help shape the problem-solving agenda when painful, unwanted experiences are at hand:

- Negative feelings are unhealthy.

- To be healthy, we must control or eliminate negative feelings.

- To control negative feelings, we must determine what is causing them and then reverse the cause.

- Negative feelings are causes of behavior.

- A bad history is the cause of current dysfunction.

Wise Mind

The notion of wise mind, which is as ancient as Buddhism, has recently been incorporated into a variety of cognitive behavioral treatments. Indeed, what has been called the third wave of behavior therapy is characterized by the increasingly widespread integration of mindfulness and acceptance techniques into treatment. One way of viewing wise mind is as an observing stance that allows us to shift attention from problem solving to the *process* of problem solving. This increases our ability to make choices based on values rather than on avoidance-based rule following. Particularly in Western cultures, wise mind seems to be dormant much of the time, probably due to the relentless social training we receive to rely on the problem-solving mind.

In contrast to the problem-solving mind, wise mind can only be utilized in the present moment and only in nonverbal ways. Wise mind awareness is nonjudgmental and detached from the literal meaning of immediate experience. Wise mind does not participate in the future before the future gets here. It accepts whatever is present in that moment when we become aware that something is present. It is a perspective in which critical narratives about oneself and others give way to compassion for others, acceptance of oneself, and even amusement. Wise mind allows us to see the interconnectedness of all beings and species. In most mystical or meditative traditions, making contact with wise mind is thought to produce a sense of detachment from worldly concerns, as well as a profound sense of well-being.

Competing for Bandwidth

For most people, daily existence isn't completely dominated by the problem-solving mind. Most of us experience moments, however brief, of wise mind and its broader perspectives. The problem is that contact with the two modes of mind is usually out of balance. There is too much self-analytical, evaluative, rule-governed thinking and not enough contact with the present moment and the bigger self that originates in the wise mind. As Table 1 shows, the messages from these modes of mind about common challenging situations can produce dramatically different approaches to living.

Table 1. Key Life Themes and Messages of Problem-Solving and Wise Mind

Aspect of life	Life theme	Problem-solving mind	Wise mind
Personal pain	What to do when unwanted distressing stuff shows up inside	Avoid making contact with it at all costs. Suppress awareness or distract yourself. Don't think about it.	Allow it in without struggle. This is part of you even if it is distressing.
	What is the meaning of distressing stuff	It is toxic and must be eliminated if you are to be healthy.	Personal pain is a signal and will guide you to make changes. It is healthy for you.
Daily living	Where you should put your attention on a routine basis	You gain the most by analyzing your past so you can understand yourself and think about what's going to happen next in life.	Live in the present because that's where life is.
	How to experience being you	Verbally analyze who you are and how you got to be that way. Explain yourself to others to justify your situation.	You are bigger than your experiences. You are the vessel that contains all of your experiences. You are interconnected with all things.
Life goals	How to guide your life journey	Find out what matters to other people, follow the social rules, and seek others' approval for what you do.	Connect with your values about what matters to you.
	How to address important life situations	Avoid actions that produce pain. Wait for others to change or for a lucky break.	Do things that embody your values and stand up for what matters to you.

43

Psychological Flexibility: The Path Out of Suffering

As explained, the functions and by-products of language suggest that the same processes that produce a sense of life vitality can also produce a rigid, ineffective behavioral style, depending upon which mode of mind is the dominant voice. In general, suffering and rigidity originate in an overly dominant problem-solving mind, whereas vital living originates in a more harmonious balance between wise mind and the problem-solving mind. We propose that there are three core processes that influence behavioral rigidity or its opposite—psychological flexibility: awareness, openness, and engagement (see Figure 1). We often describe these qualities as the pillars of human flexibility. When well built, pillars can collectively support vast amounts of weight; however, if one pillar is flawed in some way, the whole edifice can come crashing down. Note that FACT interventions often initially focus on promoting awareness, (sometimes referred to as "center" in the pillars approach), as being able to "show up" is often a prerequisite for remaining open and engaged. However, the decision about which core process to target should be based on the individual and the situation. Therefore, the order in which we examine these processes throughout the book will vary.

Figure 1. The Pillars of Flexibility

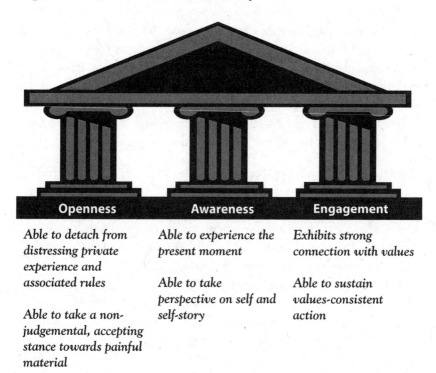

| Openness | Awareness | Engagement |

Able to detach from distressing private experience and associated rules

Able to take a non-judgemental, accepting stance towards painful material

Able to experience the present moment

Able to take perspective on self and self-story

Exhibits strong connection with values

Able to sustain values-consistent action

Openness. This core process refers to the ability to experience distressing unwanted private events directly, without evaluation or struggle. Open individuals tend to view these experiences as part and parcel of being alive, and their behavior is governed more by personal beliefs and values than by the amount of emotional pain they might be experiencing. People who lack strength in this area are not willing to experience distressing unwanted feelings, thoughts, memories, or physical sensations. They tend to follow rules that encourage suppression, control, or avoidance of these private experiences. Because of this, their behavior tends to be influenced by rules rather than by the real-world results of their behavior.

Awareness. This core process refers to the ability to "be here, now" and to take perspective on problems by stepping back from them and seeing them in a larger context. Aware individuals are able to experience life in the moment and, consequently, are able to adapt quickly to changing circumstances. They are able to step back and see even painful events in the big picture of life. People who lack strength in this area tend to ruminate about the past, chronically worry about the future, or both. They tend to engage in a lot of distracting activities because they feel anxious and uneasy just being in the moment. They tend to get lost in their self-narrative about their life, how they got to be the way they are, and, often, why meaningful change isn't possible. They process life events in terms of how these events fit into the self-narrative and therefore have difficulty learning new behaviors based on real-world results.

Engagement. This core process refers to the ability to engage in effective actions that are based in personal beliefs and values. Engaged individuals are connected with their values in important areas of life, such as work, relationships, leisure, self-improvement, and spiritual growth, and ground their daily routines in these values. When confronted with life challenges, they base problem-solving actions in their values. Thus, even difficult life events become opportunities for growth in the realm of values. People who lack strength in this area often complain that they feel lost or have no sense of direction in life. Their daily routines are based in a "have to" rather than "want to" mentality. When confronted with life challenges, they tend to either become passive and withdrawn or engage in impulsive, self-defeating actions, such as substance use, aggression, or escape. Consequently, they are often ineffective at solving problems and therefore accumulate more life challenges over time.

To summarize, rigid or inflexible individuals suffer because they try to suppress, control, or avoid unwanted private experiences (deficits in openness); they reside in their stories about the past or live in the future and thus are unable to capitalize on the vitality of the present moment (deficits in awareness); or they lose contact with their core values and fall into socially prescribed daily routines that don't contribute to their sense of life direction (deficits in engagement). Conversely, people with high levels of mental flexibility tend to be open to unwanted private experiences, have greater present-moment awareness, and engage in valued life activities even when doing so triggers painful experiences. In essence, flexible people don't generate suffering, even when confronted with painful life situations. The underlying goal of FACT is to help people develop psychologically flexible responses that will diminish their sense of suffering and create more of a sense of being fully alive, regardless of the life challenges they are confronting.

Summary: The Paradox of the Big Brain

Approximately one million years ago, nature began its grand human experiment. The brain mass of our ancestors began to expand exceptionally rapidly and, over the eons, this oversized brain and the advantages it bestowed distinguished humans from the rest of the animal kingdom. It is the reason we are at the top of the food chain and why, as a species, we were able to withstand radical climate change over and over again while our natural competitors died off.

But has something gone terribly wrong with this experiment? The big brain seems to have outlived its original purposes and is now running amok, so to speak. It is now talking to us about subjective realities in the same voice as it talks about objective realities. These subjective realities can be the source of immense suffering both for individuals and for our species. Religions originally arose to address this problem, but the big brain continued to evolve. We now have a whole lexicon focusing on internal states of mind. The big brain has evolved rules that specify which states of mind are desirable and which are to be eliminated, and it gives us a formula for how to produce desirable states and eliminate undesirable ones. It creates the impression that we know how other people are doing and how we compare to them. It gives us predictions about subjective future realities that can be so painful that they make suicide seem like a desirable option.

The biggest threat arises from two basic facts: that the big brain has cloaked itself so its machinations are nearly invisible and that we've become so dependent on it that it is considered airy-fairy to propose other ways of apprehending existence. The continued existence of *Homo sapiens* may be dependent on our ability to evolve ways to keep the big brain in check. While we are stuck with a big brain, we don't have to be dominated by its unworkable features. We can pull the cloak off the big brain and see it for what it is. We can make the process of minding visible and accessible and bring it under some degree of voluntary control.

In FACT, we believe that people have become prisoners of the functions of the big brain. They unknowingly follow rules formulated by the big brain that not only don't work, but actually create suffering. If we can somehow create distance between the human and the big brain, there's a chance the human will utilize other equally powerful forms of intelligence to pursue a different life course. The principles for how this distance between the human and the mind might be created, and for how to help the human set a new course, are the topic of the next chapter.

Chapter 3

The Process of Radical Change

Change is the only constant.

— *Proverb*

In this chapter, we will examine the FACT view of the core ingredients required for radical change. We have already established that extremely limited interventions can help people make powerful and sustained changes. Evidence for this is rife in the research literature. We have proposed that individuals get stuck in unworkable patterns of behavior because they follow language-based, culturally transmitted rules that encourage avoiding or attempting to control distressing private experiences in the name of achieving psychological health. And we've explained that following such rules over time produces behavioral and psychological rigidity and leads to a loss of contact with important values. But a question remains: How, then, can individuals escape this vicious cycle and transcend their struggle?

In a very simplistic sense, the FACT formula for radical change is illustrated in the following prototypical, fictitious dialogue.

Client: My problem is that I can't control what I'm thinking, what I'm feeling, what I'm remembering, and what is going on in my body. And it is really painful, all of it. Help me learn how to get rid of this pain so I can live a good life.

Clinician: What you think, feel, remember, and sense in your body isn't the problem. Those things are a natural part of who you are. They are healthy.

Client: If they aren't the problem, then what is the problem?

Clinician: Have you considered the possibility that trying to control this stuff, rather than simply accepting it as a natural part of you, is the problem?

Client: Why wouldn't I just focus on controlling this stuff, since it doesn't feel good?

Clinician: Because you can't actually control this stuff, no matter how hard you try. When you focus on that, you lose focus on something you can control: how you live your life. The distressing symptoms you are seeking help for don't mean there's something wrong with you; they are merely telling you that your life is out of balance—nothing more, and nothing less.

Client: So what should I do differently?

Clinician: Let's start by clarifying what matters to you in life and then how you can act in ways that are consistent with that. You can accept the thoughts, emotions, memories, or physical symptoms that show up as you do this, even though they might be unpleasant. You might have a story based in your past that says you can't do this, but you can also accept that story as just a story when it shows up. Over time, what's going on between your ears will seem less important than living the life you want to live.

This small example embodies a large number of theoretical and clinical implications that are the subject of this chapter: How do symptoms arise, what do they mean, and what is the desired outcome of an intervention in regard to symptoms? What are the basic assumptions about human suffering and transcendence that increase the likelihood of radical change? What intervention principles should guide the actions of the clinician? What role does the clinician-client relationship play in the process of change?

FACT Foundations: Symptoms and Their Meaning

The therapist's perspective on the symptoms the client brings into therapy directly determines the goal of therapy. The dominant model in Western countries has been to view symptoms themselves as the target of interventions. For example, we measure a client's depression symptoms and then declare treatment a success when the symptoms fall below a certain cut-off score. We are trained to view symptoms as signs of an underlying syndrome, and the task of assessment is identifying and counting up different symptoms and, on that basis, assigning a name, or diagnosis, that reflects an underlying illness. In FACT, we reject this biomedical approach as not only scientifically unsound, but also ultimately harmful to the client (see Hayes et al., 2011, for a more detailed discussion of this issue). Social labeling of this type has long been known not only to negatively impact clients' self-image, but also to motivate them to "live down" to the label. For example, a client who forcefully declares, "I am bipolar," is essentially communicating that his or her self-identify is fundamentally tied to being bipolar. We aren't doing people any favors by talking to them in these terms.

Stress and Coping Equilibrium

In FACT, distressing symptoms are viewed as a logical outcome of ongoing tension between the stressors that are impinging on the client's life space and the effectiveness of the client's coping responses. Living life requires us to confront stresses, however small, on a daily basis. We have a favorite FACT saying: "Life is one big symptom generator! When you stop having symptoms, that's the day you are declared DOA." A major requirement of daily life is to respond to the current level of stress with coping strategies that refresh and balance the person over time. Thus, the symptoms that lead clients to seek help may be produced by any combination of the following events:

- New stressors enter the client's life with no change in previously effective coping skills.

- Previously effective coping behaviors are abandoned due to normal life events like moving, changing jobs, becoming pregnant, and so forth.

- New stressors appear and the use of previously effective coping skills declines.

- New stressors appear that call for the use of somewhat different coping skills.

There are many extremely important clinical implications of this approach. First, symptoms are never wrong. If people are experiencing distressing symptoms, it is because there is a loss of equilibrium between the amount of stress they are under and the success of their coping strategies. Second, the types of symptoms clients experience are more a reflection of temperament, role models, and cultural practices than anything else. Severe symptoms don't necessarily mean severe problems. Small shifts in coping dynamics can produce big displays of symptom in some people. Similarly, long-standing symptoms don't mean clients are more "broken." They simply indicate that the imbalance between stress and coping responses has persisted over time. As long as the imbalance exists, the distressing symptoms will be present. Finally, the symptoms that people seek help for are almost invariably related to emotions. However, while the culturally promoted goal is to gain control of feelings in order to achieve health and well-being, emotions are actually a basic form of human intelligence that by far predates the development of language and thought. Unpleasant emotions are signals that life is out of balance; they aren't problems to be solved.

Living Vitally, Not Being Symptom-Free, Is the Goal

If experiencing symptoms is an integral part of being human, then using the absence of symptoms as a marker of psychological health is terribly misguided. One of the unintended and harmful effects of the bio-medically based approach represented by the *Diagnostic and Statistical Manual of Mental Disorders* (DSM) is the idea that the goal of treatment is to eliminate symptoms. If you see symptoms as originating in some insidious pathological process, it will necessarily lead to longer treatment—and not necessarily better treatment.

Ironically, treatments focused on eliminating symptoms have never been shown to actually eliminate them. A more accurate way to describe the results of these treatments is that they reduce symptom intensity below a level that is arbitrarily defined as the dividing line between what is normal and what is abnormal. These cut-off scores have never been empirically associated with any significant real-life outcomes, such as the likelihood of returning to work, improvements in relationship functioning, or better integration into the community. The notion that symptoms must be eliminated or radically reduced to pronounce someone cured has been heavily promoted by the pharmaceutical industry, which has artfully redefined the labeling of common human problems, framing them as diseases that need to be treated with expensive drugs. That's great for the corporate bottom line, but terrible for most people.

In FACT, the focus is instead on living life in accordance with personal values, even if doing so produces symptoms. The goal is to help clients exchange responses that aren't working, and that often are producing paradoxically negative results, for workable behaviors. In this view, symptoms are seen as indicators of the extent to which unworkable responses are being used.

FACT Foundations: Basic Assumptions That Support the Movement toward Radical Change

If symptoms are different than we have been trained to conceptualize them, then there must be corresponding shifts needed in how we think about the process of change itself. It's possible that the idea that symptoms are somehow the "problem" has also distorted our view of clients' dilemmas and what we must do about them to promote change. FACT has several unique, and specific, perspectives on this matter.

People Are Not Broken, Only Trapped

As long as people follow unworkable rules—no matter how much those rules are promoted by their culture—their coping strategies will fail and they will remain distressed. The goal in such cases is to get people to identify the rules they are following and the unworkable outcomes that result. This could apply as readily to a person with no mental health history who is dealing with a divorce by drinking the pain away as it does to a survivor of childhood sexual abuse with a ten-year pattern of drug addiction. Neither of these individuals is "broken" in the sense of needing years of therapy to correct personality damage. They are both pursuing the same agenda: controlling painful emotions, thoughts, or memories using strategies that ultimately will only promote more pain. The main implication of this stance is that every individual has the ability to learn how to step back from unworkable rules and adopt a different approach.

History Gets in the Way

People who are suffering often develop ornate explanations of their problem and how previous events in their lives have contributed to the problem. In FACT, we have a salient saying: "The most dangerous thing about your past is that it is about to become your future." The FACT therapist spends little time exploring and analyzing the client's history. The focus of the therapeutic conversation is on what the client is doing now, not what happened back then. This is not to say that history is irrelevant; it is very relevant. The history the FACT therapist is interested in is the stuff that shows up in the present and functions as a barrier to living in a vital way. Indeed, many FACT interventions trigger the appearance of clients' problematic history, which will then be the focus of interventions. In FACT, we believe that history is something we have to live *with*, not live *by*. Personal history creates our intelligence, but it can also make us dumb as stones if handled incorrectly.

Turn the DSM-IV Upside Down and It Might Work

In FACT, life functioning, not number and type of symptoms, is what matters in the long run. Quality of life is determined by footprints—where people are actually going in life—not by what's going on between their ears. Imagine, if you will, reversing the order of the multiaxial *DSM* system, making the client's functional status the first and most important axis. (Disregard the highly unreliable Global Assessment of Functioning, or GAF, Scale and instead think of this as a continuum ranging from nonfunctional to highly functional.) The second most important item becomes the stressors that are challenging the client. Third would be the client's general health status, health risks, and such factors as exercise, nutrition, sleep, and use of alcohol, drugs, nicotine, or caffeine. Instead of personality disorders, Axis II would reflect enduring response styles or traits that the client brings to bear on various life challenges. Lastly, what drops out of the chute would be the client's symptoms of distress, or the Axis I disorder the client is branded with.

Enter the River

When clients are stuck, they tend to withdraw from many important life activities; for example, they may stop seeing friends, quit going to church, exercise less, or spend less time with their partner or children. In FACT, the goal is to prod clients into action without having to be there to guide them forward or see how it all turns out in the end. If clients are living life in "approach mode," life itself will be their teacher. As a metaphor, think of taking a journey down the river of life on a raft. At first the river is gentle, snaking along at a comfortable pace, but then the current picks up and you hit a set of rapids. As you bump along and get bruised, you begin to feel fed up with the river and swim over to the bank. You stand aside and cuss and swear at the river because of all the rocks and the shallow, cold water. As you do so, the water keeps flowing past. The river doesn't reverse its course and start flowing upstream so you can start over again just because you're unhappy with it. And you will never change the nature of the river by screaming at it. By going ashore, you only postpone your journey to the ultimate destination. In FACT, we are trying to entice clients back into the river, with full knowledge that more rapids, shallow water, and rocks lie ahead. It is the entire experience of being in the river, both the calm, peaceful parts and the rapid, bouncing parts, that teaches you what a river is.

Change the Frame of Reference

When clients enter therapy, they have a particular view of the problem and what is causing it. FACT, like most brief therapies, is based on the belief that it is this view, or the client's frame of reference, that is the real problem. Almost without exception, clients seek help because they are unable to control or eliminate painful emotions, intrusive memories, or negative thoughts. They seldom express skepticism about the feasibility of trying to control or eliminate distressing private experiences. They usually believe that they simply aren't doing the control strategy right and that the therapist can help correct their errors so the strategy will work. It's almost as if they are socially programmed to believe that emotional control is the prime directive in life. In FACT, we want to change clients' frame of reference so they see that the problem is actually their attempts to control or eliminate emotions, thoughts, and memories.

Language Practices

FACT, like many brief therapies, attempts to play with both the client's use of language and the tone of the therapeutic conversation. This is because language and thought are the means through which people develop mental maps of their life situation. In order to reposition the client's perspective, existing maps must be destabilized and rearranged. This can be done through logical analysis, as in many cognitive behavioral therapies, but that approach is time-consuming. In addition, many clients have layers of maps that can be difficult to penetrate without months or even years of therapy. An instantaneous way to destabilize the client's view of the problem is to play with it. Such FACT interventions as metaphors, physical and experiential exercises, and odd uses of language are all designed to destabilize clients' belief systems and their confidence in the problem-solving mind. These tactics cannot be understood (and ultimately co-opted) in the conventional verbal sense, and this is exactly what makes them effective.

FACT Foundations: Intervention Principles

Intervention principles are high-level practice philosophies that shape how interventions are selected, implemented, and reinforced over time. Intervention principles have both orienting and filtering functions in therapy. First, they orient the clinician to the psychological processes that are deemed important to promote radical change. For example, the idea that the best time to intervene is now results in one set of clinician behaviors, whereas a principle emphasizing that the first objective is to collect a lot of information from the client, analyze it, and then, and only then, try an intervention, would result in a quite different pattern of clinician actions. The filtering function of intervention principles means they help guide the clinician through a laundry list of potential interventions and help determine which specific clinical tactics might be most effective. For example, a therapist following psychodynamic principles might have little interest in treating the client's unworkable responses from a skills-deficit perspective, resulting in little use of role-playing, guided rehearsal, and other skill-building strategies.

The Future Is Now

Many therapists are trained to use the first session to conduct a comprehensive assessment of the client's problem, life context, and pertinent history and ultimately to develop a diagnostic impression and treatment plan. In this approach, "treatment" often doesn't begin until the second visit. In contrast, experienced brief therapists believe the first session is by far the most important, in large part because it may be the only session (see Budman, Hoyt, & Friedman, 1992). The decision to seek professional help is a seminal event for most people. Normally, they have sought advice from friends or loved ones, analyzed the problem, read self-help books, used alcohol and drugs, prayed, meditated, engaged in expressive writing, and so forth. The fact that none of these strategies has worked gives you a distinct advantage. If things were working well—solutions included—the person wouldn't be seeking help. Another major reason first sessions are so important is that most people are naive about the problem they are experiencing. They feel emotionally distressed or have a vague sense that life isn't going well but often don't have a credible explanation for what's going wrong and how to fix it. This is an ideal environment for promoting radical change—indeed, it may be the best opportunity. In FACT, a guiding principle is that clients leave every session with a plan for behavior change that has the potential to radically change their quality of life.

Instigate and Assimilate

In FACT, we have two major approaches to offer people who are seeking help: We can help them instigate a new and possibly more effective behavior in a problematic life context, or we can help them assimilate feedback related to the impact of new behaviors. Some types of instigation take time to impact the surrounding contexts, and some make an impact immediately. The goal of intervention is to help clients instigate and assimilate repeatedly until they are self-instigating and self-assimilating. Asking questions like "What did you learn from this event or situation?" or "What showed up for you as you were trying this behavior? How did it feel? How do you feel now as we are talking about it?" can help clients assimilate and integrate the results of new behaviors. Sometimes, depending upon the type of instigation, it may make sense to wait for a month or two before seeing the client again, to allow the results of new behaviors to manifest themselves.

Behavior Change Is an Experiment

The hallmark of psychological flexibility is the ability to let experience serve as a guide. In FACT, we treat every intervention as an experiment. We help clients test the waters with new responses to old challenges. This can even be done in the therapeutic interaction with comments like "Would you be willing to experiment with just holding still when…[this feeling shows up, when you notice you are being pulled into the past, when you want to say something to your partner that might hurt your marriage, and so on] and just observe what happens inside and outside of you?" The truth is, we don't know what strategy will work for any particular client, so we have to get each person to experiment with different options.

Casting everything as an experiment removes pressure created by the belief that a chosen strategy *has* to work. (Flexible people don't end up in this kind of corner very often.) There is always another strategy that hasn't been dreamed up yet. This framework also allows both therapist and client to gracefully swallow a failed experiment. If the results of trying a new strategy are negative, the therapist can help the client assimilate this new information as a piece of positive knowledge. In FACT, we adopt the stance that real-life data is the client's best friend. We want to instill the notion that people learn as much from their failures as they do from their successes. At the end of each visit, it is important to say something along the lines of "When would you like to come back again? How long do you think it will take for you to see how this new strategy is working? Let's meet then to go over what you've learned."

Small Change Is Just as Powerful as Big Change

FACT, like most brief therapies, is based in the belief that small behavior changes can have a profound impact on people's contexts, both external and internal. Part of this impact involves the psychology of being stuck. When people feel defeated and demoralized, they are likely to believe that attempts at even limited behavior change are bound to fail. Simply having clients experience a success, no matter how small, can cut into this demotivating view. In addition, from a contextual perspective, getting clients to make a small change in some daily behavior doesn't just change what they might otherwise have done at that exact moment; it may also impact the social milieu such that the behavior of others changes too. For example, a spouse accustomed to seeing the client sit on the sofa and watch TV all day notices that the client is going outside to take a walk to the park. The spouse asks to go along, and a conversation ensues that creates an opportunity for the couple to address a relationship problem that has been causing distress but has been ignored. In FACT, we call this the principle of serendipity. If clients can just make that first behavior change, serendipity is likely to take over.

Small behavior change is far more likely to occur if it involves engaging in some type of new response in the external context. In FACT, the philosophy is "If you can't count it, it doesn't count." Behaviors, such as what we say or do, are the footprints we leave in the world. Thus, the most meaningful changes are tied to saying something different, or behaving differently. FACT therapists intervene by facilitating mental processes like staying aware and open, but only to the extent that strengthening these processes enables clients to take effective action in the real world.

Create Positive Valence

In chapter 2, we described how rule following generalizes to life areas and situations where it is ineffective. The ability of humans to create symbolic connections between seemingly unrelated events and situations is something that can create clinical problems, but it can also be used for positive clinical purposes. One way to use this native human ability is to create a positive valence around a proposed behavior change. The clinician might say something like "If you were able to go to church again starting this Sunday, would that tell you that you were beginning to turn the corner on this problem, even if it is in a small way?" This frames a linkage between a specific limited behavior (going to church) and a highly desired bigger life outcome (living life in a better way). Setting up an intervention in this way can have a powerful motivational impact and may lead to spontaneous change in other areas. After all, if going to church is a symbol of living life in a better way, there might be other small positive behaviors available that would have the same valence.

An additional component of creating positive valence is to get clients to state a behavioral intention, rather than simply agreeing in principle to do something different. An agreement like "You're right; I need to be more social, and one way to do that is to go to church more often" is not nearly as likely to produce a positive result as getting the client to say, "I intend to go to church this Sunday." When the clinician can get the client to publicly state a commitment, the odds that the client will actually follow through are vastly improved. This is key, because creating positive valence can end up being a double-edged sword if the client somehow fails to follow through.

FACT Foundations: The Clinician-Client Relationship

FACT places a strong emphasis on developing a healthy, psychologically flexible relationship between clinician and client. The relationship is intense, respectful, and horizontal. The therapist appreciates the difficulties associated with changing well-practiced behaviors, even those that are producing painful results.

The Therapist as Role Model

A unique element of FACT is that the therapist functions as a role model for acceptance, mindfulness, intentional choice, and committed action. The therapist models a stance of acceptance toward anything the client is struggling with. The therapist does not judge, condescend to, confront, or pressure the client. Instead, the therapist functions as a helper and uses questions to elicit the client's direct experience. If thoughts or memories show up for the therapist during an interaction, they might be honestly described in process terms (for example, saying, "I just had a memory of my father saying that to me when I was about your age. I noticed a painful little twitch in my chest when that memory showed up."). The clinician models staying present even when the emotional stakes are high, and he or she should consider discussing the difficulties of doing so (for example, "I found it hard to stay present while you were finding it hard to stay present. I wonder if there's something in the room that's pulling at both of us?") The clinician discloses personal values as they impact the relationship with the client (for example, "My value in being here is that I want to help you be able to choose the life directions that matter to you."). One of us (Gustavsson) once responded to a suicidal client with "Yeah, I know exactly what you mean. I do know the taste of gun oil. I was nineteen years old and depressed. I saw no future worth living for but didn't pull the trigger for some reason I can't recall. Do you know what showed up in my life many years after that?" Then he took out a picture of his kids and showed it to the client.

We Are in This Stew Together

As the previous example highlights, FACT consciously promotes the idea that client and therapist are in the same stew. Both are subject to the same social programming and cultural practices, and consequently, both are vulnerable to excessive dominance of the problem-solving mind. This horizontal stance can lead to very intense therapeutic relationships. Metaphorically, and sometimes literally, the clinician and client sit side by side, looking out at this thing called life and trying to figure out what to do. Life is baffling and confusing. It's okay to say this openly and even to commiserate about it. Sometimes moving your chair so that you are positioned right next to the client is a physical display of empathy, sympathy, and support. It gives the client a powerful message: *I understand what you're going through. It's tough and there are no easy answers. I'm on your team as we try to take this on. You can count on me to give 110 percent to help you.*

Stay Focused on the Client

When faced with people who are suffering, it's tempting to become directive and essentially tell people what to do. The problem is that what might have worked for the clinician in a similar situation may not work for the client. Instead, the clinician must hand control of the intervention over to the client. It is the client who must decide whether to try a new behavior or not. Choosing not to try something new isn't evidence of resistance; it's evidence that the client is making a choice not to experiment with a new behavior at that particular time. One of the most common errors in any type of therapy is overestimating clients' level of motivation and their skills for changing their behavior. In FACT, we take specific precautions to avoid this error. One is to always phrase potential behavior change as a matter of the client's willingness to engage in something new; for example, "Would you be willing to talk to your spouse about this particular issue? Would it be consistent with your values to have a conversation about this problem?" It is also wise to end each session with a question about clients' confidence that they will actually engage in the behavior change.

A Good Question Is Worth a Thousand Directives

To maintain balance in the contributions of the clinician and client, the therapist should use questions to make a point, rather than offering direct interpretations. Interpretations usually are spoken as directive statements, even if seemingly phrased as questions (for example, "You are sad right now, aren't you?"). Open-ended questions can achieve the same result but elicit more activity from the client (for example, "I just noticed some tears in your eyes. What just showed up for you? Would you be willing to stick with what just showed up so we can experience it together?"). Good therapists are usually skilled at constructing questions that lead clients in directions that will have a major clinical impact. Using questions frequently also forces the therapist to think of how to approach the client's reality with curiosity and genuine interest. This fosters clients' confidence that the clinician actually cares about what they are experiencing.

Why? The Forbidden Word

The one type of statement that should seldom, if ever, be used is a question beginning with "why." Asking a why question ("Why did you shout at your spouse instead of remaining calm?") will generally produce a programmed social justification ("I've always had an anger problem, ever since I was a kid") that leaves little room for any additional discussion. And in the worst case, it can lead to a downward-spiraling dialogue into irrelevant features of the client's history ("Why did you have an anger problem as a kid?" "My dad had an anger problem too."). The most effective questions start with "how" ("How did you feel when you spoke that way to your spouse?"), "what" ("What was your goal when you spoke that way?"), or "when" ("When are you more likely to react that way? When you're tired? When you're feeling frustrated?"). For all intents and purposes, "why" is a dead-end word when it comes to helping people change behavior.

Summary: Skills, Not Pills

The FACT model holds that symptoms are not abnormal; they are ubiquitous and arise in response to the challenges of everyday living. Suffering arises from rigidity, which is the result of an overly dominant problem-solving mind that has been programmed to follow socially sanctioned rules about health and how to achieve it. The same cultural messages that ensnare clients also trap clinicians because we are all participants in the same verbal community. It is therefore not surprising that many therapeutic approaches are nothing more than glorified versions of the same change agenda that is already suffocating the client: "You will achieve health when you no longer have painful emotions, distressing thoughts, or disturbing memories."

In FACT, we want to teach clients to stay in the present moment and not get lost in self-stories (awareness); to accept distressing private experiences in a detached, nonjudgmental way (openness); and to contact and act upon their chosen values (engagement). This requires that clients have courage to stick around when painful stuff shows up, and doing this reliably requires psychological skills. Standing still when painful thoughts or feelings show up is a skill. Staying focused on the present moment in daily life is a skill. Connecting with deeply held values and acting on those values, even though doing so is likely to produce some pain, is also a skill.

Unfortunately, little attention is paid to teaching these skills to children and adolescents. Kids are expected to be able to do trigonometry and algebra by the time they're in tenth grade, but no one teaches them how to sit with painful experiences, how to live in the present moment, or how to lead a values-based life—and most of us still haven't learned these skills by the time our fifth decade rolls around. In a very basic sense, FACT is a way to teach clients valuable life skills that can instantly make them far more flexible and adaptable. In part 2 of the book, we will examine the clinical processes that help teach people these skills and that, collectively, make up the FACT approach.

Part 2

Practice Tools and Methods for Brief, Focused Interventions

Chapter 4

Focused
Interviewing

If you do not change direction, you
may end up where you are heading.

— Lao-tzu

The decision to seek help is a seminal moment for most people. Often, they've tried a variety of solutions without success and, because of this, they might be open to trying something new. However, the decision to seek help in no way guarantees that people are ready for change. Often the opposite is true. Although they are emotionally distressed, at the same time they are trapped in the problem-solving mind's "control and eliminate" agenda for change. Thus, the initial conversation between client and clinician may involve the collision of two very different agendas.

The client believes that "bad" content must be eliminated in order to achieve health; however, in FACT, the therapist believes that the client's fixation on controlling or eliminating this content is actually the problem. Thus, from the FACT clinician's perspective, the most important outcome is to create a shared definition of the problem that seems credible to the client. This is not so much an intellectual confrontation as it is a carefully crafted exploration of the client's direct experience with the results of the "control and eliminate" approach to change. It is also important to help clients see the contrast between these results and what their mind has been promising. This is accomplished by helping clients get in contact with the costs of emotional and behavioral avoidance, in terms of how those strategies impact valued life outcomes, and by helping them consider what it would take to engage in a radical change in life direction.

These are lofty goals for an initial session, and they are far less likely to be realized if therapists are flying by the seat of their pants, so to speak. Spontaneity and innovation are great attributes to bring into an interview where change is the desired outcome, but they have their place. Structure, consistency, and a systematic interview approach are also important. We believe that the best way to establish a solid context for radical change is to combine spontaneity and structure. In this chapter, we will introduce some interviewing methods that will help you create a highly focused redefinition of the problem.

Focusing Questions

Clinical experience suggests that carefully crafted, sequentially arranged probes tend to produce highly useful information and help keep the interview focused on what matters. In addition, in many service settings there is limited time available to collect information, so it is imperative that most of the data you collect be highly productive. Perhaps most importantly, a well-designed interview sequence allows you to begin observing other aspects of the clinical interaction that you might otherwise miss. If you know what questions you are going to ask and in what order you are going to ask them, you can devote more attention to important client behaviors during the interview. In FACT, we employ a specific sequence of questions that typically produce a lot of useful clinical information:

1.   What are you seeking?

2.   What have you tried?

3. How has it worked?

4. What has it cost you?

1. What Are You Seeking?

Most clients have the same goal when entering therapy: to find strategies that will make their pain go away. The problem-solving mode of mind specifies a simple solution: In order for the individual to feel better, the pain must be eliminated. Thus, even if clients' painful emotions are perfectly appropriate given their life situation, the problem-solving mode of mind insists these emotions are the problem and must be removed or controlled. As the saying goes, "Begin with the end in mind" (Covey, 2004, p. 95). This means that very early in the interview, the FACT clinician must try to elicit what the client believes the outcome of successful intervention will be.

It's easy to engage the client's change agenda early in the therapeutic conversation, as exemplified in this dialogue with Hank, a depressed husband and father who's currently on leave from his job.

Clinician: Now that we've talked a little bit about your situation, I'd like to try an exercise that will help me better understand what you're seeking by coming to see me today. Try to complete the following sentence for me: "I'll know this therapy is working when…"

Hank: When…I can wake up and not be so depressed and I feel like I want to go to work and do other things during the day instead of just go back to sleep.

Clinician: So, your goal is to get rid of the depressed you and replace it with an upbeat and motivated you. Then you would be able to go back to work and do other things that you need to do.

Hank: Exactly. As long as my depression is this intense, I just can't get it together and do the things I need to do.

In this brief dialogue, several components of Hank's change agenda have emerged. Hank is pointing to depression as the reason why he can't go to work or perform daily activities, citing lack of motivation as the cause of this breakdown. Thus, Hank's goal is to control or eliminate his depression, which will allow him to return to his normal routine. This is a common and culturally promoted stance that most people adopt. The culturally transmitted message is that negative internal states are reasons why socially desirable behaviors are not occurring. Thus, by inference, the goal of therapy is to feel better (remove the cause of dysfunction) because then, and only then, can normal behaviors occur.

In therapeutic work with children and families, it is common for clients to blame others for their negative emotions. Consider the following dialogue from an initial session with Julie, a divorced mother, and Sylvia, her seventeen-year-old daughter, who has just been suspended from school for cussing at a teacher. Sylvia has a nineteen-year-old brother, Josh, who was a very successful high school athlete and honors student and is now a marine. Sylvia functions as the black sheep in her family. She styles herself as a goth, is flunking out of school, and is experimenting with drugs, alcohol, and sex.

Clinician: Okay, I've got a better feeling for the disagreements the two of you are wrestling with. Let me ask you, Julie, to complete this sentence for me: "I'll know the situation is better when…" *(Pauses.)*

Julie: When she stops doing things that she knows push my buttons and when she listens to my advice rather than doing exactly the opposite. Then I wouldn't be so angry, stressed, and anxious. I stay awake at night wondering what I did wrong as a mom. I feel like I didn't bring her up right.

Clinician: So, what I'm hearing you say is that in order for you to feel better, she needs to change her behavior because her behavior is causing you to feel all these negative emotions. It's causing you to review what you did as a parent and making you feel like a failure. Is that correct?

Julie: Absolutely, I care about her and I can't stand to see her make all these poor choices. My parents would never have let me get away with what she does. I just don't know what else to do.

Clinician: And you, Sylvia, how would you complete the sentence "I will know the situation is better when..."? *(Pauses.)*

Sylvia: When she stops telling me what to do and not to do all the time. It drives me crazy. Plus, no matter what I do, it's wrong in her eyes. It's never as good as what Josh would do. I think she hopes I'll fail because that will make Josh an even bigger hero. I'm sick of it. She wonders why I'm always in her face, and that's why.

Clinician: So, what would make the situation better in your eyes is if your mom would stop telling you what to do, treat you like you are your own person, and not compare what you're doing to what Josh would do?

As this brief dialogue shows, in an interpersonal conflict the problem-solving mind can create the impression that the other person's behavior is causing one's own negative emotions. From this perspective, if one is to get healthy, the other person must change his or her behavior so it doesn't produce those negative emotions. This stance, which is very common in the beginning phases of work with couples and families, is another manifestation of the basic change agenda: "I'm behaving the way I do because of the emotions I'm feeling." What is different is the locus of cause: "The negative emotions I'm experiencing are being created by the other person." This is an artifact of language and a classic trick of the word machine because, in reality, what is producing the emotions is our evaluations of the behavior of others, not the actual behavior of others. At this juncture in the interaction, it isn't necessary to intervene and point out or try to fix inaccurate cause-and-effect statements; there will be plenty of opportunities later in the interview to reshape the dialogue on what is causing what.

2. What Have You Tried?

The next step in the assessment is to explore the strategies the client has used to solve the presenting problem. Essentially, the question is "If the outcome you're seeking is to...[reduce your depression, get your mom to stop criticizing you, and so on], what have you tried to accomplish this outcome?" During this phase of the interview, it is essential to be non-judgmental and accepting of every strategy the client mentions and to avoid making any attempt to fine-tune a particular strategy or suggest other strategies the client might use. The stance of the FACT therapist is to display curiosity and interest, rather than being judgmental or giving advice. Let's take a look at how this might play out with Hank.

Clinician: It sounds like one strategy you've used to try to control your depression and feel more motivated is going back to bed and sleeping. It seems to make sense that if you could get more rest, your energy level might pick up, right?

Hank: Well, it's partly that, but I know that if I were to get out there, people would want to know how I'm doing, and then I'd feel on the spot. I wouldn't know what to say. I'm sure they can tell I'm depressed. I would feel like a weakling if they found out I wasn't working because I'm depressed.

Clinician: So, it sounds like another way to try to cope is to avoid situations like that—situations that might make your depression even worse. Are there any other things you've tried?

Hank: Well, I just try not to think about my problems and the fact that I'm not working or really participating with my family.

Clinician: How do you accomplish that?

Hank: I stay in my room a lot. I watch TV for hours, even reruns. I play video games on my computer. I really get into Internet games where I play against others.

Clinician: Cool. It sounds like you use a lot of different strategies to distract yourself from how you feel.

While it isn't necessary to examine all of the client's strategies, you need to gather enough detail to give you a good sense of what the client's basic approach has been. While people who are stuck engage in strategies that might seem different on the surface, these behaviors are, in fact, usually birds of a feather in terms of their functions. There are two main functional dimensions to consider that will be important in selecting an eventual intervention: First, you want to know the prevalence of the client's avoidance strategies (for example, not going to work, isolating, and playing video games). Second, you want to know what rules are driving these strategies (for example, *The way to cope with being sad and depressed is to just not think about it*). In general, the more prevalent the avoidance strategies and the more those strategies appear to be driven by rules rather than direct experience, the more invested the client is likely to be in needing to control, suppress, or avoid distressing private experiences. This might make it more difficult for the client to try an alternative approach.

3. How Has It Worked?

The concept of workability is central to the FACT model. Think of workability as the acid test of the client's strategies. The client has been trying various strategies with the goal of achieving a desired outcome. The question is, Is the desired outcome indeed being realized, or is a different, paradoxical result occurring? It is only by bringing clients into contact with the direct results of behavior that you can begin to drive a wedge between them and their mind. Although clients often get stuck following the rules of the problem-solving mind, they may not even be aware that these rules exist, or they might think there is no alternative. In this phase of the interview, the FACT clinician might slow the pace of the interview, paraphrase clients' answers more often, and allow longer periods of silence to occur as clients ponder the issue of workability. Again, we'll use the dialogue with Hank to demonstrate how this might unfold.

Clinician: It sounds like you've put a lot of effort into these strategies for controlling your depression over the past few months—things like distracting yourself, sleeping to preserve your energy, staying out of embarrassing situations, and even coming to see me. You've obviously tried to do these things to the best of your ability and have kept these efforts up over a long period of time. I have a question: If you think about your depression today versus six months ago, would you say your depression is better than it was, worse than it was, or about the same as it was before?

Hank: I don't feel any better, and I haven't for months. I don't think the medications are helping either.

Clinician: Would it be fair to say that, in some ways, you actually feel worse than you did before? That managing how you feel has become the main goal of your daily routines?

Hank: I hadn't thought about it that way before, but yeah, I pretty much think about how I feel all the time unless I'm busy with something else.

Clinician: If we could put a name to these strategies, it seems like they're all designed to control or improve your mood. Looking back over the last six months, do you feel these strategies have paid off? Have they actually helped you improve your mood over time?

Hank: Well, when you put it that way, it doesn't seem like things are getting better... Actually, they're getting worse.

Clinician: That's weird. I mean, what I'm hearing you say is that all these strategies you've used to help improve the way you feel have actually made you feel worse. Is that what your experience is telling you? Because that's the opposite of what your mind is telling you will happen. I mean, you've kept this up for months; you've done everything you can think of; you've done it about as well as it can be done from what I'm hearing. Yet here you are, feeling worse than ever. This is like some kind of strange loop or something. Is it possible that your mind is wrong and that doing what your mind tells you to do is actually making things worse?

Hank: I don't know. This is kind of strange. I never thought about it quite like this. Hmm.

Notice that in this dialogue, in a very roundabout way, the clinician is beginning to create some doubt in the client about whether the problem-solving mind's change agenda is achievable or workable. When reflecting what the client has said, it's crucial to stay closely connected with the client's self-reported direct experience and to avoid talking in generalities. Just repeat back what the client has been telling you and raise one simple question: "Could it be that following your mind's advice is the problem?" The goal is to get the client to generate the answer to this question, however poorly shaped the response might initially be. It's perfectly reasonable to ask some follow-up questions if the client seems to be on the verge of this discovery, but you should never tell clients what their experience shows. Understand that this isn't about helping clients develop insight; it's designed to help them make contact with the direct results of their behavior.

4. What Has It Cost You?

The paradoxical results clients are often getting aren't benign or even neutral in terms of important life outcomes. Generally, following rules that promote avoidance has costs, resulting in increasing restriction of life over time. To gain control over unwanted, distressing private content, people must sacrifice valued life activities, as engaging in many typical valued activities might trigger unpleasant emotions, negative thoughts, intrusive memories, or unpleasant physical symptoms.

As the pattern of avoidance widens, even activities with a low probability of triggering difficult private experiences get swept away. The saying "Avoidance begets avoidance" captures the essence of this problem. The more you avoid things, the more you get in the habit of avoiding things. Getting clients in contact with the costs of this expanding pattern is necessary to create the motivation for radical change. Clients must be in direct contact not only with the fact that their avoidance strategies aren't working, but also with the reality that the quest to gain control of painful stuff is causing them to lose control of life. Once more, we'll offer an example of how this plays out in the next part of the clinical dialogue with Hank.

Clinician: It seems like the more energy you put into trying to keep your depression in check, the more dominating it becomes. Is it possible that these strategies *are* depression—that this is exactly what your depression wants you to do?

Hank: Now you've got me confused. Are you saying that I'm depressing myself?

Clinician: Not that you're doing that on purpose. I've never met anyone who liked being depressed. But check out your experience with this: Is it possible that your attempts to control how you feel are resulting in you being more and more cut off from the type of life you want to live?

Hank: I definitely am losing out on my life, compared to before.

Clinician: So, what are you losing out on specifically?

Hank: I don't think I'm there for my kids, even though I'm home all day. I don't like it when they run around the house and make a bunch of noise. The noise makes me really short-tempered. My wife and I haven't had sex in months. She pretty much just tries to steer clear of me. I feel really cut off from her. I don't have anyone to talk to now.

Clinician: Wow, that's quite a heavy price tag. How about work, your friends, and things like that, outside the house?

Hank: People at work have been very understanding. They tell me to take my time and get to feeling better… But the reality is, I'm missing out on projects that I would be good at. If I'm not there, they have to give someone else those jobs. I have a couple of guy friends I used to get together with. We'd go to each other's houses, watch football, and have some chips and beer. I've been making excuses when they ask me to come over. Now it's playoff time, and we've always gotten together for those games. But they haven't called for a long time. They've probably given up on me.

Clinician: Okay, so another impact has been that you're losing out at work on things that in the past felt like important ways of contributing. And you're also noticing that your friends might be moving on without you. But we can't know for sure what they're thinking, right? They might just be cutting you some slack because they know you aren't feeling well. The main thing is that you've lost that connection for now.

Hank: Yeah, well, when you add all of this up, I don't have much to look forward to when I wake up: just another day of trying not to sit around and be bored.

Clinician: So, I hear you saying there's another cost: that you don't have anything that motivates you anymore—nothing that creates a desire to get up and get active.

Hank: Right. That's a good way to say it. *(Tears up.)*

Clinician: I can see that it's very painful for you to talk about this. You've done the best you can to try to deal with this. With the way you've been feeling, it takes a lot of courage just to live day to day. Coming in today is a huge first step, and I'm proud of you for taking that step. Talking about personal problems is kind of like going to the dentist. The dentist is going to poke and prod various parts of your mouth, and if there's a problem somewhere, you will feel some pain. But that poking and prodding is necessary for you to get healthy. It's the same here. We're just trying to figure out where the sore spots are, so we can fix them.

As this dialogue demonstrates, the costs of avoidance aren't always evident to clients. When people are in the middle of a highly avoidant pattern of living, they lose sight of how much their current way of living deviates from their values and the possibilities for life. Thus, the goal of this persistent, gentle type of questioning is to bring clients back into contact with the emotional costs of avoidance, including collateral damage as the costs themselves begin to produce additional negative stuff that is also avoided. For example, depressed clients frequently report feeling numb inside; in effect, their depression is functioning as an emotional avoidance strategy in its own right. Indeed, even the act of taking antidepressants and other "anti" medications that blunt emotions might be considered a form of emotional avoidance.

Clients often display tears of despair or express hopelessness during this phase of the interview. The clinician must be compassionate and at the same time reassuring when the client contacts the sometimes irreversible costs of avoidance. This phase of the intervention isn't about rubbing the client's nose in the consequences of avoidance; it's about helping the client develop a healthy motivation to try something new.

Setting the Stage for Radical Change: What Kind of Life Would You Choose If You Could Choose?

The main goal of FACT is to help clients make a fundamental change in life direction. When clients are stuck in the problem-solving mode of mind, they often lose contact with larger life goals and desires. If clients are going to let go of unworkable avoidance strategies, there had better be something important in life that will justify taking that risk. Ultimately, the goal is to help clients become aware that they have a choice between continuing to use avoidance strategies and trying something completely different: accepting what is present inside and still actively moving in valued life directions. This is at the heart of the process that promotes radical change. It starts with the distress the client is seeking help for and ends up as a discussion about core values, the costs of avoidance, and the possibility of living a different kind of life. Here's an example, again with Hank.

Clinician: I'm curious about the kind of life you dreamed you would be living at this point. If you could live your life any way you wanted to and there were no restrictions on what you could do, what would your life look like?

Hank: Well, I would be spending quality time with my wife; we would be close like we used to be. I'm afraid that won't happen because my depression keeps me from being the way I want to be.

Clinician: Okay, well, for right now let's just imagine that anything is possible. Let's wait a bit to look at barriers like depression. I just want to hear what kind of life you'd like to be living.

Hank: Well, with my kids, I'd like to be a better father than I am now.

Clinician: Okay. If you can, leave out the comparisons between what you'd like to be doing and what you are doing. We can come back to that stuff. What would you be doing as a father if you could be the father you want to be?

Hank: It's interesting that I keep going back to what I'm not doing. That's what I do all the time. Okay, I bet you're going to say to just put that aside and we'll talk about it later, right?

Clinician: Right on. Now, tell me about the father you'd like to be.

Hank: Well, I used to be very involved in my kids' sports. I coached their teams, and we practiced all kinds of sports in the backyard. I'd also like to be a role model for them, show them how to be organized about work, how to study, how to do the best you can do. I'd like to roughhouse with them and just be able to enjoy them growing up.

Clinician: What about work and your involvements outside the family?

Hank: I actually love doing the work I do. It makes a difference to people. I like a challenge. I like working with other people to figure out solutions to problems. As for friends, my wife and I had some friends who loved to camp. Our families used to go camping together all the time. And as I mentioned, there are also my football buddies. We're on a bowling team together in the city league, and I'd like to get back into that.

Clinician: This is very cool, Hank. Wouldn't it be something if we could get you back to living that kind of life? It sounds like it would be a really gratifying life to live.

This dialogue demonstrates how the clinician can shift the tone of the conversation from the oppressive feel of what isn't working to the uplifting quality of living a valued life. The mere fact that the clinician is interested in the client's vision of a valued life implicitly conveys the message *You can live this kind of life if you choose it.* We jokingly say that the FACT therapist suffers from "learned optimism disorder": the belief that any person can change course in life at any time. The main barrier isn't the client's psychopathology; it's that the client can't live a valued life while engaging in emotional avoidance. The two simply can't coexist. Also implicit in this discussion is the liberating idea that people can live a valued life without first having to clear out their emotional garbage. People can live a valued life and have emotional garbage at the same time!

Reframing the Problem

If there is an art to promoting radical change, it lies in the ability to recast clients' problems in a new light. The ability to convert what looks like a complicated problem into a simpler situation is the linchpin of brief interventions. Simple problems aren't necessarily simple to fix, but they do create a greater focus and help identify which behaviors need to change.

Reframing has long been considered a central feature of many brief therapy approaches. It literally means helping clients get out of an existing frame of reference—a systematic set of beliefs about what the problem is, what's causing the problem, why it has persisted despite the client's efforts, and what must be done to solve it. Helping clients question both the accuracy and usefulness of their existing system of beliefs is the underlying goal of reframing. Once clients become uncertain about this system, they naturally develop a powerful tendency to look for other explanatory systems. This motivates them to consider new information that they might previously have resisted. Hearing clients say things like "I hadn't thought about my situation this way" or "The way you're talking about my problem isn't what I expected" is a clue that reframing has been successful.

FACT includes a large number of reframing strategies, often delivered in the form of sayings, stories, analogies, or metaphors, that help create a highly focused and apparently solvable definition of the problem. These strategies often will double as core therapeutic messages that can be used again and again. This is frequently necessary because, in the initial stages of habit change, most people tend to vacillate between their old, unworkable strategies and newer, more workable approaches. In terms of skills, the process of change often involves integrating new responses on top of older, habitual ones. Here are some of the core FACT reframing messages frequently used at this stage:

- Controlling the way you feel is the problem, not the solution.

- You aren't hopeless; it's the strategies you're using that are hopeless.

- Which are you going to believe, your mind or your experience?

- You can gain control of your feelings, but to do so you must lose control of your life.

- Controlling your feelings is like holding a beach ball underwater. You can do it, but you can't focus on anything else.

- A rabbit has to stop running before it can figure out if it's safe.

- Going to the dentist hurts, but it hurts a lot worse if you don't go!

- It isn't about feeling good; it's about feeling *it good*.

Summary: Harnessing the Power of Direct Experience

In this chapter, we examined a specific set of FACT interview strategies that help focus the conversation with clients and set the stage for reshaping their view of the problem. Many single-session interventions essentially end after the focusing questions because these questions are so evocative and obviously relevant to the ends the client is seeking. After all, when clients recognize that their avoidance strategies aren't working and will never work, they often begin to spontaneously reorient away from their unworkable agendas. They might indicate an intention to engage in some valued activity in the immediate future without any prodding from the clinician. From a FACT point of view, focused interviewing is designed to reveal that, indeed, the emperor (aka the problem-solving mind) has no clothes.

However, for some clients more intervention is needed. The clinician might need to complete a more in-depth assessment of the client's strengths and weaknesses and use that information to formulate a case analysis that points to specific intervention targets and strategies. In the next chapter, we will introduce you to a set of case analysis methods and tools that will help you accomplish this important task.

Chapter 5

Strategies and Tools for Increasing Motivation

We can't solve problems by using the same kind
of thinking we used when we created them.

— *Albert Einstein*

Promoting rapid, sustainable change in just a few contacts requires the clinician to quickly distill information into some type of coherent framework that both engages the client and suggests a potentially life-changing intervention. To be effective, the FACT clinician must be able to identify issues that are salient to the client, engage the client in a dialogue about valued life directions, assess the client's skill deficits, and develop an intervention that integrates all of these fundamental ingredients for radical change. In this chapter, we first discuss how to use the client's in-session behavior to identify leverage points, which can be thought of as sources of motivation for engaging in radical change. Next, we introduce a set of in-session experiential assessments designed to engage the client in a discussion about choosing a new life direction. Finally, we discuss tools and methods that can help you rapidly assess sources of psychological flexibility and rigidity, identify the client's workable and unworkable responses, develop an intervention, and track the client's progress from session to session.

Finding the Leverage Point

In chapter 4, we outlined a sequence of questions designed to help clients make contact with the results of unworkable emotional control strategies and to activate sources of motivation that might propel clients in the direction of radical change. These questions are both provocative and evocative. They create a lot of affect in clients and tend to get to the nitty-gritty of their dilemma. During the conversation, it is important to observe clients' reactions, both verbal and nonverbal, for signs that sensitive issues are being touched upon. In FACT, we refer to this as digging for pain. There are two types of clues that signal proximity to a leverage point: in-session avoidance behavior and "rule speak."

Clue 1: In-Session Avoidance Behavior

Clients will avoid painful stuff in session just as automatically as they do in real life. They will, in effect, display the problem in the course of their interactions with you. Avoidance behavior is so pervasive and automatic that even if clients are trying to make a positive impression on you, they will still engage in avoidance. When you are gently and persistently digging for pain, it is almost inevitable that you will find a sore spot and that clients will react with their characteristic strategies. Look for nonverbal signs of avoidance in clients, such as suddenly breaking eye contact, uncharacteristic pauses in speech, tearing up, lip pressing or biting, looking down or away, putting their head in their hands, crossing their arms over their chest, or hand wringing, to name a few. The nonverbal reactions that occur in direct response to your questions are the most significant signs. In FACT, we call these nonverbal clues "flinching."

Clients will also engage in various forms of verbal avoidance. Changing the topic or flitting from topic to topic, failing to answer a question, pretending not to hear a question, giving a tangential answer to a question, or giving an overly general answer to specific questions might indicate verbal avoidance. Sometimes clients will directly communicate their unwillingness to experience feelings, thoughts, or memories. Comments like "I don't let myself think about it," "I just want to put this behind me," or "I wish I didn't have to deal with this" are clear indications that clients are engaging in emotional avoidance.

Clue 2: Rule Speak

People generally don't realize that they are following rules and, even if they did, they probably wouldn't see the rule as the problem. Indeed, they frequently express their rules with extreme confidence and certainty. Comments like "I can't be intimate with men when I keep having flashbacks of my rape" or "You just don't let people who have hurt you get off scot-free" are examples of rules that are regulating the person's behavior. Content-wise, rules tend to be overly general and are often couched in plural terms (for example, referring to "people," "they," or "them"). They have the quality of being declarations about the "Way Things Are." Another common sign of rule following is statements that are black-and-white in nature, such as "There's no way I can go to work when I feel this bad," or that refer heavily to social norms, such as "You just don't talk about your personal stuff with friends, or they'll get tired of being around you."

Certain qualities of speech may also signal rule following. Often, people's rate of speech speeds up or seems pressured. You might notice that clients' posture is stiffening or that their tone of voice becomes more strident and assertive. Often, colloquialisms are used to emphasize the unquestioned truth of the statement; for example, "You know what they say: Do unto others before they do unto you." When clients are heavily into their stories, which are usually packed with rules, you might even have the impression that they aren't really there. Their lips are moving, but you aren't hearing from the human being; you're listening to a well-worn and often-told story that serves to explain or justify their ineffective actions.

A Clinical Example of Finding the Leverage Point

The following clinical exchange between Julie and Sylvia demonstrates how emotional avoidance and rule following lock them into rigid, unproductive communication patterns.

Sylvia: You don't know how I feel, so don't tell me what I need to do to get back to school. You hardly know how to run your own life, so don't tell me how to run mine.

Julie: (Looks at clinician.) You know, I wouldn't have dared to speak to my parents the way she just spoke to me. (Glares at Sylvia.) You don't speak to your parents that way. It's rude, crude, and disrespectful. Josh never treats me this way, never!

(Comment: Julie deflects the emotional impact of Sylvia's challenging statement and falls into a rule about how children should act toward their parents.)

Sylvia: There you go again. You just can't help yourself. It's always about what Josh would do. I don't give a rat's ass what he would do. It's like if I have a different opinion than you, then I'm being disrespectful. I guess I'm not allowed to speak my mind.

(Comment: Sylvia is more hurt than mad; anger is how she deflects hurt feelings. Her rule is that she has no independent value to Julie and to be loved by Julie she has to be more like Josh than like herself.)

Clinician: Julie, it sounds like you two have this type of head butting a lot. What does this bring up in you? What does her behavior bring up inside you?

Julie: She will just go off and do what she wants, I guess.

(Comment: Julie just avoided answering the question because doing so would require her to contact her emotions.)

Clinician: Can you tell me what you're feeling right now?

Julie: *(Remains silent and looks down for a while.)* I don't feel anything right now. I'm not going to let her hurt me again.

(Comment: Julie won't make contact with what she's feeling. Her avoidance is prompted by a rule that making contact with feelings will re-inflict damage from earlier similar events.)

Clinician: If you were allowing yourself to just feel what you feel right now, what stuff would show up?

Julie: I had to raise her by myself. Her father blew her off when he left. He paid child support, but he didn't care about her. I was the one who worked two jobs and was there for her while he did nothing, and I'm the one who gets blamed. I'm the Wicked Witch of the West.

(Comment: Julie avoids getting present with painful feelings by drifting off into her story of giving everything to others and getting nothing in return. She avoids using any feeling words.)

Clinician: And the fact that, at least at this moment, she does not seem thankful, what does that bring up?

Julie: *(Sniffles.)* I feel alone. I feel rejected by Sylvia. I felt that way after my husband walked out on me. I guess I must have done something wrong to get beaten up like this by life.

(Comment: Julie actually shows up for her painful feelings, then moves away from them by following an old rule that if she is being punished, it must be due to her shortcomings.)

As this dialogue demonstrates, the processes promoting avoidance and rule following often appear and reappear within the clinical conversation. As discussed in chapter 2, the self-stories that clients carry around can function both as high-level rules and as safe havens from painful stuff. In Julie's case, when she is confronted with feelings that remind her of her failed marriage, she tends to drift out of the present moment and into her story. At the same time, she is confusing her history with her ex-husband (and other similar rejections or "failures" in her earlier life) with the quite different demands of interacting with her daughter. As she loses this fundamental distinction (*You are not married to your daughter; you are her mother*), she loses her ability to flexibly respond to Sylvia's desire for more independence. She isn't able to function effectively as a parent because she's so busy trying to avoid feeling rejected by Sylvia. This is her leverage point: In order to be an effective parent, she must be willing to experience her feelings directly and to discriminate between her role as a mother and her status as an abandoned ex-wife.

Helping Clients Choose Life Directions

In FACT, we view the client's dilemma a little differently than in most therapeutic approaches. We see clients as falling prey to an avoidance-based lifestyle, whereas the path to vitality is to engage in values-driven actions. The main barriers to changing direction are being out of contact with the natural emotional signals that would inform them of the need to change, and following rules that promote and justify avoidance strategies. It is often useful to "physicalize" this dilemma using experiential exercises and metaphors, which allow the clinician to sidestep the client's language system and the inflexibility of the problem-solving mind.

Journey and directional metaphors are great tools for creating a big-picture awareness of clients' life direction as embodied in their current behaviors. After all, everyone is headed in a life direction, whether they think they are or not. Two especially effective approaches are the Life Path and Turnaround Exercise and the True North Exercise.

The Life Path and Turnaround Exercise

The Life Path and Turnaround Exercise is designed to create a visual metaphor of the client's life direction that allows the results of values-based behavior to be contrasted with the costs of current avoidance strategies. This helps clients see the consequences of unworkable strategies in terms of the energy they consume and how they impact expressed values. This simple but powerful procedure is demonstrated in the following dialogue with Hank.

Clinician: So, it sounds like before your mood went downhill a couple of years ago, you were very involved in your life. You went camping with your wife and family friends, you were a Little League coach for your two boys, you were in a bowling league, and you had a circle of friends that you and your wife hung out with. I'd like to do something with you that might help crystallize where you are in life at this point. Let's call this your life path. (Draws a straight line on a piece of paper.) We all have a life path. It's basically organized around our strategies for living as best we can. On this end (pointing) is the life you say you'd like to be living. You'd like to be more intimate with your wife, spend quality time with your kids, go bowling and camping, and do your thing at work. On the other end, here (pointing), this is living life by trying to control how you feel and keeping your depression in check. You do this by staying home, sleeping a lot, avoiding friends and fun activities, and missing work. Draw an arrow above this line somewhere to indicate where you think you are right now on your life path and which direction you're moving in. Are you over on the side of vitality (pointing), or are you more over here, on the side of controlling your depression (pointing)?

Hank: Well, I'd have to put it way over on this side, over here. (Draws an arrow pointing in the direction of more control.) Read it and weep, I guess.

Clinician: What do you make of this?

Hank: I'm not living the way I want to. I need to do something about this because it's getting out of control.

Figure 2. Hank's Life Path and Turnaround Worksheet

More Control
What do you want to control, avoid, or get rid of and how are you trying to do that?

More Meaning
What type of life would you choose if you could choose?

Depression and sadness: staying in my room; avoiding my wife and kids; not seeing friends; not working to keep from feeling embarrassed or making a mistake

Spending quality time with my wife and kids; being involved with my friends; coaching Little League; bowling; getting back into work

1. Draw an arrow above the line to indicate where you are on your life path these days and which direction you're moving in.

2. What, if any, are the costs and benefits of pursuing control?
   Benefits are that I can stay out of situations that I may fail at, that I don't have to embarrass myself, and that I avoid conflict. Costs are missing out on relationships with my family and friends and not feeling a sense of accomplishment at work.

3. What behaviors would tell you that you're moving toward more meaning in life?
   Spending more time with my wife and trying to participate more in activities with my kids.

4. When you get stuck, how can you help yourself keep moving toward more meaning?
   Remembering that doing this is something I believe in and that these are things that are important to me.

5. Who or what helps you move in the direction of more meaning?
   My wife can help me. She will call me out if I start to backslide.

Once the Life Path and Turnaround Exercise has been completed (see Figure 2), the therapist can begin to think about how to engineer a turnaround in the client's life. This requires some analysis of the client's predicament and what it will take to move the client in the direction of a more meaningful life. Often, this involves engaging the client in a discussion of what it would take for the first steps of a course correction to occur. Here's an example of this process, continuing the dialogue with Hank.

Clinician: Okay, we have to think strategically here because you're heading in one direction and you have quite a bit of momentum. Let me show you what I mean. I want you to get up and start walking, and when I say, "Now," I want you to turn all the way around in one step and walk in the opposite direction. *(Hank starts walking.)* Okay, now!

Hank: *(Awkwardly tries to pivot 180 degrees in one step and almost falls down.)* Wow, I almost lost it there.

Clinician: Right. I almost sprained my ankle doing that one time. Can you start walking again and show me a safer way to reverse direction?

Hank: Well, first I'm going to stop walking, and then I'm going to pivot about halfway on this foot, then pivot the rest of the way on the other foot.

Clinician: Okay, that's three moves to turn around, and you're very unlikely to fall if you do it that way. Cool. So maybe we have to think about your life path the same way. The first move might be to find a way to stop moving in the direction you don't want to move in. Maybe part of that is figuring out what would tempt you to keep moving in the same direction. What would keep you moving toward controlling your feelings?

Hank: Probably just inertia. It's what I've been doing. It's familiar. If I hide out, then I don't have to be embarrassed or fail at anything.

Clinician: Okay, and what would pull you in the other direction? What would give you the motivation to stop moving in your current direction?

Hank: What I believe in. There's intimacy over there in the other direction. Being a dad is over there. There are all sorts of things associated with going to work and enjoying life again.

Clinician: Is there anything in the way of skills you might need to learn to make that turnaround and keep moving?

Hank: I guess I have to learn to accept the fact that I might make mistakes. And I have to learn how to keep myself motivated even when I don't feel like doing anything.

Clinician: Is there anyone in your life who can support you in making a turnaround—someone you can rely on to call you out if you start heading in the wrong direction?

Hank: I think my wife would be a big ally.

As this interaction demonstrates, generating a turnaround plan is almost like a strategy session. Barriers to life-enhancing actions are identified, and an action plan is developed to address those barriers should they arise.

The True North Exercise

Compass heading metaphors can also be a rich source of information and strategies for change. The metaphor of being on course or off course implicitly conveys the idea that course corrections are not just possible but actually are an ongoing part of any life journey. The following dialogue with Julie and Sylvia demonstrates the True North Exercise. As with the Life Path and Turnaround Exercise, the objective is to get clients to recognize that they are off course and identify factors that are contributing to this problem.

Clinician: Have either of you ever seen or used a compass, either just to play with or to use during hikes to keep track of where you are?

Sylvia: I have a compass app on my smart phone as part of my GPS. It's pretty cool.

Julie: My god! (*Looks at Sylvia's phone.*) I can't believe what kids are into these days. I think the last time I saw a compass was when my dad and I went camping when I was about sixteen.

Clinician: Good. So you both know the reason you have a compass is to make sure you're headed in the right direction and you don't get lost. Because you usually can't see your destination, you have to rely on the compass to tell you whether you're headed in the right direction. Living life is full of challenges. We all have life goals, but it's easy to get blown off course. The fact that both of you are here tells me that you are concerned about the course you're on. Remember earlier how I asked each of you to tell me what your relationship would be like if you could have it any way you wanted it to be?

Julie: We actually have some of the same beliefs is what you said.

Clinician: Right, you both mentioned wanting to be treated with respect, wanting to be able to share fun activities, wanting to trust each other, and wanting to be there for each other in times of need. I took the liberty of writing these things down on this worksheet, which is kind of like my version of a compass. Notice that right above true north it says, "Living the Life I Choose." And over here to the right (*points*), I've written in shorthand what we just talked about under your values. Now, if true north is "I'm living this relationship exactly in line with what I believe in," I'd like each of you to mark where you think you're headed. (*Both mark the compass.*)

Clinician: So, you each went in your own direction here: One headed kind of west and the other southeast. As usual, you are both being independent! (*Julie and Sylvia laugh.*)

Sylvia: But we're going in different directions. Just like I thought, we are way out of touch.

Clinician: So, one way we could read this is "Hey, you're heading west and I'm going southeast. What's wrong with you?" While it's true that you're headed in different directions, is that the most important thing this compass reveals?

Julie: No. It shows that both of us are off track. Neither one of us is going in the right direction.

Clinician: That would be another way to read this—that neither of you is going in the direction you want in this relationship. If you'll indulge me for a bit, I'd like to investigate what's pulling each of you off course.

Sylvia: Well, I get really pissed off when she tells me I'm making mistakes and doing bad things. Usually, the next thing I'll hear is how Josh would be handling this better. Then I tell her to shut her mouth and get the hell out of my way because I'm going to do what I want. I've thrown things at her, and then I ignore her phone calls.

Julie: When she yells at me, I yell back because I'm not going to be spoken to that way. I threaten to cut her off and tell her that she'll have to get a job and pay me rent. I tell her that she's a disrespectful you-know-what.

Clinician: So, it sounds like both of you get drawn into your stuff, like not wanting to be told what to do or not wanting to be talked to in a disrespectful tone. I'm going to write these things down—giving unrequested advice and being disrespect-ful—as strategies that you use. I assume both of you would agree that these strategies aren't working very well. Then, you both mentioned that you yell, threaten, and perhaps punish each other afterward. It sounds to me like the two of you don't have an agreed-upon method for dealing with dis-agreements. *(Both nod.)* I'll put that here in the skills section. You want to learn better skills for resolving conflicts and disagreements.

Figure 3. Julie and Sylvia's True North Worksheet

What are your values?
- *Treating each other with respect*
- *Having fun together*
- *Fostering trust*
- *Being supportive but not controlling*

What are your current strategies, and are they working?
- *Giving unrequested advice (not working)*
- *Being disrespectful (not working)*
- *Yelling at each other (not working)*
- *Threatening or punishing (not working)*

What skills will you need to make the journey?
- *How to negotiate conflicts*
- *How to stay connected with each other even when we disagree and get mad*

Clinical Issues

1. **Awareness** (Able to be present? Aware of private experiences? Able to take perspective? Shows compassion for self and others?)
   Julie—Needs to step back from life story and discriminate past pain and rejection from present emotions.

2. **Openness** (Accepts private events without struggle? Notices and lets go of unworkable rules?)
   Julie—Needs to learn to accept Sylvia's independence as something other than rejection and loss of self-worth.
   Sylvia—Needs to separate from the rule that her mother's evaluations are attempts at control.

3. **Engagement** (Clear values? Can organize for effective action? Can obtain reinforcement? Sufficient interpersonal skills?)
   Both need to get back to positive shared activities like shopping, going to movies, and going out for coffee.

As the preceding dialogue shows, the debriefing aspect of the True North Exercise allows the clinician to engage clients in assessing how well their current behaviors are promoting their desired life directions. The conversation can also include an evaluation of the skills clients need to develop, which can then be converted into a turnaround plan along the lines of that generated with the Life Path and Turnaround Exercise. The worksheet also provides a way for the clinician to create a quick recap of clinical issues and potentially useful intervention targets, as shown in Figure 3.

Case Formulation: Deciphering What You Observe

While a sizable percentage of clients respond very quickly to FACT, some clients need more help, in which case a more detailed case analysis is helpful. Properly evaluating a client's strengths and weaknesses and using this information to create interventions on the spot is essential for promoting radical change in these more difficult clients. After all, if the clinician is confused or unclear about which skills clients need to improve and how to develop them, the resulting intervention is likely to be less precise and effective. In FACT, there are two main components of the case formulation process: assessing flexibility (using the Flexibility Profile Worksheet) and completing a detailed analysis of clients' workable and unworkable behaviors (using the Four Square Tool). Ultimately, a well-thought-out case formulation allows the clinician to select brief interventions that are more likely to lead to radical change.

Assessing Flexibility with the Flexibility Profile Worksheet

In assessing flexibility, we first create a picture of the client's strength in each core process area—the pillars of awareness, openness, and engagement. A general rule in selecting an intervention target is that it's best to use the stronger core processes to shore up and improve the weaker one(s). Therefore, assessing both strengths and weaknesses is an important part of case formulation. The clinician's observations of the client during the interview are critical here. For example, how open does the client appear to be? Does the client talk about being willing to accept painful experiences? Does the client seem open to experimenting with different strategies? Is the client lost in rule following? Is the client able

Figure 4. Hank's Flexibility Profile Worksheet

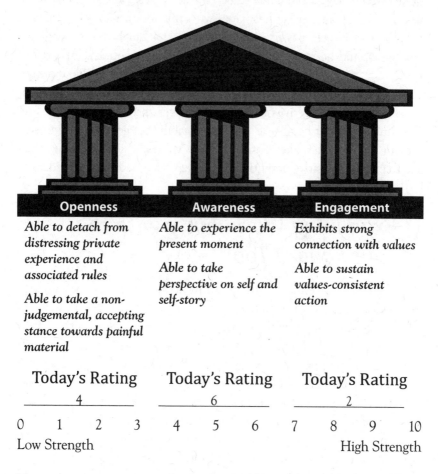

Openness	Awareness	Engagement
Able to detach from distressing private experience and associated rules	Able to experience the present moment	Exhibits strong connection with values
Able to take a non-judgemental, accepting stance towards painful material	Able to take perspective on self and self-story	Able to sustain values-consistent action

Today's Rating — 4

Today's Rating — 6

Today's Rating — 2

0   1   2   3   4   5   6   7   8   9   10

Low Strength   High Strength

Notes (core areas to target in the next visit): *Focus on helping Hank stay present when he begins to disappear into his rumination. He needs to learn to step back from his self-critical story. Help him reconnect with his values about parenting, being a husband, and having friends.*

to stay present and process emotional experience as it unfolds during the interview? Does the client often slip into storytelling mode, or does he or she seem to easily take perspective on current and past life events? Does the client seem connected with his or her personal values? Does the client seem engaged in effective problem-solving actions?

Figure 4 shows an example of a Flexibility Profile Worksheet the clinician filled out for Hank based on the initial session. Note that what stands out for Hank is his weakness in the area of engagement. He is quite disconnected from many valued life activities. He is also a bit weak in regard to openness. He has issues with rule following (believing that the way to feel better is to avoid situations that might trigger negative emotions), and he struggles to accept distressing emotions. His area of relative strength is awareness. While he sometimes does check out during conversations about painful stuff, by and large he is able to stay present and take some perspective on his life challenges and self-story. Therefore, the clinician might be able to use Hank's ability to get present and stay present to help him make contact with his values, which Hank can then use to promote positive activities even when his mood is depressed.

Examining Workability with the Four Square Tool

Clinical interventions with more difficult clients can be complex and confusing, not to mention a moving target. It's easy to get lost when clients' problems shift or their responses to specific interventions vary from contact to contact. Therefore, it's critical to have a simple, accurate way of describing both behaviors that are working well and those that aren't working well. The Four Square Tool can help identify clients' responses that might be targeted for intervention. While it may be useful to conduct this as a formal written assessment after meeting with a client, seasoned FACT therapists often go through this analysis mentally while in session with clients. As illustrated in the example in Figure 5, the two axes of the square are unworkable versus workable strategies and the realms of public and private behavior. We've discussed the concept of workability extensively, so this axis should be fairly easy to understand; it helps you catalog current client behaviors in terms of their workability and whether they should be increased or decreased.

We haven't devoted as much discussion to the continuum of public and private behavior. In FACT (as in all behaviorally oriented therapies), all client responses are considered to be behavior, even responses that occur inside the skin. Private behaviors aren't observable. In general, they involve internal processes like emotions, thoughts, memories, and physical sensations. Public behaviors are responses that can be observed by others. These are often the things clients do or don't do in the process of daily living. For example, Hank is staying home instead of going to work. This behavior is observable to others, so it's public. While staying at home, Hank ruminates about how to get on top of his depression and why he can't be happy like others. Rumination isn't directly observable by others, so it's a private behavior. As the name Four Square Tool suggests, each of the four quadrants may point to potential targets for a brief intervention. Let's examine how that works.

Not working in the public realm. These are behaviors that detract from the client's daily functioning. We normally think of these as either failures of commission (in Hank's case, being irritable toward his kids and saying no to social invitations) or failures of omission (missing work and avoiding friends). When a client has a high rate of unworkable public behaviors, the goal might be to decrease their frequency. For example, the clinician might suggest that Hank spend less time isolating himself in his room and more time in a common area of his house. This would reduce some of the negative impacts of his chronic isolation.

More workable in the public realm. These are behaviors that are generally more consistent with the client's values and create positive life outcomes. In this case, the intervention might be to have them schedule these activities more often (for example, Hank might call his friends and get together to watch some football). These may be old behaviors that have fallen by the wayside, as in Hank's example, or they might be entirely new behaviors. Note that clients may sometimes lack the skills necessary to engage in more effective behaviors. For example, Julie and Sylvia lack conflict resolution skills, so they currently cannot successfully negotiate solutions when they have disagreements. In this case, the target of the intervention might be helping them acquire those skills.

Not working in the private realm. These are behaviors that interfere with the client's ability to remain flexible in situations where that would

Figure 5. Hank's Four Square Tool

		Workability	
		Not working (do less)	**More workable (do more)**
Behavior	**Public**	• Isolating himself at home • Not going to work • Avoiding getting together with friends • Being short with his kids	• Trying to spend time with his wife • Seeking help • Checking in with his supervisor at work
	Private	• Trying to control depression by ruminating and analyzing • Being disconnected from values about family, marriage, friends, and parenting • Following rules about avoiding making mistakes or being embarrassed	• Being able to stay present • Being able to take some perspective on self-story

be helpful. For example, Hank's behavior is being driven by rules that discourage him from entering into situations in which he might make a mistake or risk embarrassment. Hank spends a lot of time analyzing his depression, what is causing it, and what it has cost him, but this mental activity doesn't improve his mood or functioning and actually leads to more confusion about what he should do to address his problems. Often, FACT interventions in this quadrant are designed to help clients learn to simply notice their negative mental activities and not let them excessively regulate their public behavior.

More workable in the private realm. These are behaviors that tend to facilitate the occurrence of more workable public behaviors. For example, clients might be taught to stay present and actively accept the appearance of unpleasant thoughts or feelings while remaining in the observer role, or they might learn to direct attention to what matters in the situation. For example, Hank might learn to make choices about social opportunities based on his values about wanting to be connected with friends.

Clinical experience suggests that just thinking in the terms laid out in the Four Square Tool often allows clinicians to come up with a fairly well-focused intervention, and it only takes a fraction of the time that would be required to write out a formal treatment plan. A final point is that it isn't essential to have information about every quadrant at the start of an intervention. However, if you notice that one quadrant is completely empty, that might have a significant influence on your treatment plan. For example, a client who isn't exhibiting any workable public behaviors might be a candidate for skills training, might be completely out of contact with personal values, or both. As this example suggests, working in one quadrant often involves changing a behavior in another quadrant, just as working with one of the three core strength areas often stimulates development or strengthening of skills in another core area.

Summary: Tracking Progress Is Important

In order to achieve maximum clinical impact, the FACT clinician is devoted to making every minute of every session count—and is also willing to be proven wrong. As discussed throughout this chapter, a principal goal of assessments, case formulation, and treatment planning is to generate the best possible intervention. However, the client might not benefit from the intervention you select, and if that happens, you need to be able to detect this outcome. One way to help ensure effectiveness is to get into the habit of assessing clients' progress during each and every session. This need not be an onerous process; we recommend that you simply have clients rate the severity of their presenting problem, their level of confidence in following through with the behavior changes discussed during the session, and the helpfulness of the session. You'll find details on these simple questions and recommended rating methods in the appendix.

All of the interview and assessment tools described in this chapter and chapter 4 are reproduced in the appendix for your reference. For larger, more usable versions, visit the book's website (nhpubs.com/23451), where you can download full-size versions.

Chapter 6

Promoting Radical Change

In the depths of winter, I finally learned that
there lay within me an invincible summer.

— *Albert Camus*

I n this chapter, we examine some core FACT interventions for promoting the psychological flexibility clients need to pursue a chosen
path in the face of the inevitable challenges life has to offer. By this
point in the change process, the strategies in chapters 4 and 5 have
helped the client make direct contact with the fact that emotional avoidance strategies don't work, that the mental rules that drive emotional
avoidance originate in a rigid and indiscriminate mode of problem
solving, and that the results have been costly in terms of a sense of vitality, meaning, and purpose in life. At this point, the clinician has a pretty
good idea of the client's areas of strength and weakness and has made a
decision about intervention targets. And all of this might have trans-
pired in the first thirty minutes of an initial meeting! Now it's time to
promote radical change.

Strengthening the Pillars of Flexibility

Strengthening the core processes of psychological flexibility is what FACT is all about. At heart, FACT is a behavior therapy because it is based in the belief that, equipped with the right skills, most humans have the ability to withstand what Shakespeare's Hamlet referred to as the "slings and arrows of outrageous fortune." The clinician's task is to help clients develop the needed skills and then apply them in real-life situations. As we have emphasized, this is an iterative process involving instigating new behaviors, assimilating their results, and then refining strategies. Few people manage challenging life situations perfectly, and it isn't really about being perfect anyway. It's about being effective, not capturing a lot of "style points." In the sections that follow, we describe the pillars of flexibility—awareness, openness, and engagement—in more detail and use example dialogues to illustrate how the clinician can increase the client's ability to be in the present moment, be open to private experiences, and engage in actions that promote movement in valued life directions. In part 3 of the book, Case Examples, we'll demonstrate how FACT is applied in actual treatment, demonstrating some core FACT interventions in the process. Table 2 outlines those interventions and which core processes they target.

Table 2. FACT Interventions Demonstrated in Chapters 7 through 10

Pillar	Intervention	Chapter
Awareness	Little Self, Big Self	7
	Present-Moment Breathing	7
	Body Scan	8
	Magnetism	9
	Just Noticing	10
	Mindful Shopping (or other mindful activities)	10
	Being a Witness	10
Openness	Clouds in the Sky	7
	Courageous Steps	7
	Box of Stuff	8
	Facing the Bully	9
	Say It Slowly	9
	Name It and Play with It	10
Engagement	Badge of Courage	7
	To Love and Protect (for parents)	7
	Scales of Choice	8
	Palm Up, Palm Down	9
	Good Start to a Good Day	10
	Words of Wisdom	10

Promoting Awareness

Awareness involves the ability to focus attention in the present moment and take an observing, detached perspective on challenging life situations and the narratives they tend to stimulate. One consequence of being unable to stay present is that clients end up living in the past or the future and therefore can't benefit from immediate experience. This penchant for past- and future-directed mental activity isn't just a benign feature of the human mind; it is a core process that promotes both avoidance and rule following. If we are "off in the clouds," the pain of the present is greatly reduced. If we are living in a self-fulfilling prophecy shaped by the past or seen as inevitable for the future, we are far less intentional in making choices and tend to come under the influence of arcane, ineffective rules about how to live a vital life.

Part of the problem as far as the mind is concerned is that there isn't much for it to do in the present moment. Mental activities tend to be focused on evaluating what has just happened in the external world, and this is a poor substitute for present-moment experience. What is a bored mind to do but to try to get the human to attach to mental machinations (stories about self, others, or both, or renditions of personal history), rather than engage the simple vitality of the moment? This is the evolutionary challenge of having a big brain, and it is often the first thing a person must confront in order to make a radical change in life direction. There are several FACT interventions designed to promote awareness; we will describe some of them in this chapter and demonstrate others in chapters to come.

Creating Present-Moment Attentiveness

Immediate in-session interventions often have the best chance of promoting contact with the present so that the client can become more aware. Comments like "Can you sit with what just showed up for you right now?" "Can you describe how you're feeling as you say that to me?" or "How does your body feel right now as we talk about this?" help anchor the client in the present moment. As discussed earlier, there are usually plentiful signs that a client is struggling with staying in the moment: sighing, looking away or down, an abrupt change of body posture, changing the topic, providing vague answers to specific questions, words, and so forth. The clinician must be able to detect these processes as they happen and freeze them in time. This often involves naming the process as it occurs, asking the client to return to the room, or immediately identifying the private experiences that prompted the client to check out. Having the client practice staying present when these triggers arise teaches important awareness skills. We want to teach clients to look at the present moment with soft eyes, meaning that attention is focused on present-moment experiences in a nonjudgmental, observing way. Simply being aware of what is going on inside gives clients access to the perspective of wise mind.

It is important to avoid making an issue over the client's inability to stay in the present moment. Directive or intellectualized statements like "Why can't you just stay present? It isn't dangerous to be here right now" can actually make being in the present more dangerous for the client through the suggestion that the cost of failure is high. This isn't about how well the client does the present moment; it's about helping the client learn to pay attention, on purpose, and in a particular way. We all drift in and out of the present moment repeatedly during a typical day, and most of us have natural triggers that tend to stimulate present-moment experience. Instead of giving directives and intellectualizing about the value of being present, it is far more effective to gently note that it is difficult to stay present, that few individuals are capable of being present at all times, and that the main goal is to become more aware of opportunities for engaging the present moment. For example, a typical FACT homework assignment might be to have the client use an "awareness thermometer" at the end of each day, assigning a rating on a scale of 0 (completely unaware all day long) to 10 (on par with the Buddha today). The client might be further instructed to make notes about daily events that seemed to trigger more awareness (for example, listening to music, dancing, doing yoga, or working out). The goal might then be to schedule these natural awareness triggers more often on a daily basis.

Developing Skill in Taking Perspective

Learning to take perspective often goes hand in hand with learning to stay present. The biggest barrier to taking perspective is the near-constant drone of the self-narrative—an ongoing process of sense making that is a principal product of the problem-solving mind. The FACT clinician focuses on how clients relate to this built-in process of sense making, not the content of their stories per se. This is true even when those stories contain factually accurate and even compelling aspects of the client's life history. In FACT, we believe that stories are socially constructed entities that explain and often justify a person's current life situation—and frequently past and future life directions. The true measure of a story is not whether it contains factually accurate elements; it is whether the story functions to promote the client's best interests in life. There are stories that promote flexibility and a sense of participation in a vital life, and there are stories that do exactly the opposite. From a contextual perspective, the first kind of story is *functionally true* because it promotes the client's welfare and best interests. The second kind of story is *functionally false* because it distracts the client from actions that create more vitality. The goal, therefore, is to get the conversation to focus on stories as *entities*, or creations of the mind, in order to drive a wedge between the person and the mind. It is then possible to begin evaluating stories using a different yardstick: *Does living according to this story get you what you want in life?*

The problem with stories is that they can be socially reinforced over time in such a way that we come to believe they are true. When clients are immersed in their stories, defending the story is often more important than being effective and living a vital, values-driven life. The goal of FACT is not to create a healthier story to replace an unhealthy one, because all stories are arbitrary creations of the problem-solving mode of mind. Instead, the FACT therapist tries to assist clients in recognizing stories as stories and being mindful of their presence. Again, it is the ability to shift attention away from provocative but less useful mental activity (stories of the past or predictions about the future) to highly relevant mental processes (present-moment experience) that promotes awareness.

Often, tactics that bring the client into the present moment also work to promote perspective on self-defeating stories. To help clients see their stories as less automatic, you can use questions like "As you tell me about your early years as a child and teenager and the things you went through, what shows up inside you? What shows up right in this moment? How does this story make you feel as you tell it?" Another tactic is to have the client project what the impact of the story will be if it is strictly followed. You can help clients see that their stories are actually guiding their current behavior with questions like "If you follow what your story tells you to do here, what's likely to happen next?" or "How will you feel about that outcome if it does happen the way your story says it will? Is this the kind of life outcome you were hoping to get?"

Another FACT strategy is designed to reveal how automatic and arbitrary the mental capacity for storytelling is. One easy way to demonstrate this is to have clients outline how they would respond to the request "Tell me a little bit about yourself" in a range of hypothetical social situations. One situation might be going to a party and meeting someone the client is interested in getting to know better; another might be a job interview; and yet another might be meeting a distant relative for the first time. After inquiring about several scenarios, ask the client, "Which of these stories is the true you?" This highlights how stories are designed to fit specific social purposes, including the purposes of the therapist-client relationship. The therapist should both acknowledge the ever-present nature of stories and stress the importance of holding the content of stories lightly.

It is important not to talk about storytelling in an overly intellectualized or dismissive way. Saying things like "That's just your story" or "Can't you see that you're engaging in storytelling right now?" miss the point and can also strain the therapeutic relationship. The point is to help clients see that stories are seductive because they help us make sense of personal history in relation to current life events and challenges. They give us a sense of coherence and predictability, even if it comes at the cost of personal flexibility. For these reasons, it's important to be able to hold these stories at arm's length, particularly in highly charged life situations.

A Clinical Example of Promoting Awareness

The following clinical dialogue occurs in the second session with Hank. The therapist notices that Hank is having trouble staying present during an interaction that touches on his loss of social connectedness.

Clinician: I'd like to call a time-out for just a bit here. It feels like I've lost contact with you. You seem to be somewhere else. What's going on?

Hank: Well, nothing really, just… I was remembering the last time I felt accepted by people in my life. It's been a long time, man. I just seem to keep going downhill. My wife is angry with me for not getting a paycheck. My kids stay away from me because I'm not in the mood for their roughhousing. It seems like I've been fighting a losing battle to be normal, whatever that means.

Clinician: And as your mind gives you this picture of how your life is going downhill, what images, thoughts, or feelings show up?

Hank: Probably some kind of sadness, but to be honest, I don't feel anything really, just numb.

Clinician: So, if we peeled away that numbness, kind of like peeling away the outer layers of an onion, what would show up for you? If you can, try to just sit with me for a few minutes and imagine that you're peeling away the numbness of this onion to see what's inside. I'll just sit here with you, and we'll take our time together.

Hank: (Looks down for a long time.) I'm sad and lonely and angry at myself for letting this happen to me. I've lost so many years to this depression, and here I am, in exactly the same spot.

Clinician: I can see in your eyes that getting into contact with this stuff hurts.

Hank: Yeah, it hurts a lot, and the problem is, I don't see it getting better in the future. I feel like I'm disabled and can't even provide for my family like a man should. It seems like every event in my life is just more of the same—going more downhill.

Clinician: It sounds like your mind hops right in behind these painful feelings and begins to predict that you'll have more of this, almost like this is the story of your future too. Is that where you were a few minutes ago when I called time-out? Listening to that story of the past and future in your mind?

Hank: Yeah, I spend a lot of time doing that—what did you call it? Living in the past?

Clinician: Better yet, think of your life as a journey where you've reached an important crossroads. To the left is a road called "Live in the past and worry about the future" and to the right is a road called "Be present and do what matters to you." You are absolutely free to pick the road that you want to travel on. No one can stop you from making whatever choice you make. Which road would you pick if you could freely choose either one?

Hank: I'd pick the right-hand fork, for sure.

Clinician: And to do that you would have to be present with sadness, be present with loneliness, be present with anger, right? Your mind's story that you are a hopeless case—that you're going to go downhill—would probably also be along for the ride. Would you still pick the right-hand fork if you knew that stuff was waiting for you?

Hank: I would rather go through that than live the way I'm living now.

In this brief exchange, the therapist brings Hank back into the moment and simply helps him stay present with what is there. The therapist reframes Hank's ruminations about the past and worry about the future as part of the self-narrative process. Hank is then allowed to choose between having his current and future behavior controlled by the narrative or picking a different life direction focused on building present-moment awareness and a sense of vitality. Notice that in order to choose the latter fork in the road, he must be willing to make room for what shows up, such as sadness, guilt, and self-blaming thoughts. In other words, he will have to be open to and accepting of his own stuff, which brings us to the next pillar of flexibility.

Promoting Openness

To be open, people must be able to step back from the evaluative, judgmental, and categorizing activities of the problem-solving mind and accept what is present. This perspective is characterized by a willingness to stand in the presence of uncomfortable material without attempting to struggle with it, change it, or suppress it. One of the biggest barriers to getting into the present moment is that painful stuff can be waiting for us there. If we can't put down the harsh lens of self-evaluation or separate ourselves from our social programming, it's terribly difficult to stand in the presence of painful emotions, intrusive memories, negative thoughts, or unpleasant physical sensations. Thus, clinical discussions about openness often trigger issues about awareness, or being in the present, and vice versa. These two pillars of flexibility often resonate off of one another during FACT interventions. Therefore, if you aren't seeing results from present-moment interventions, you can turn your attention to openness. The reverse is also true: If you're struggling to get a client to be more open to experience, you might turn your attention to present-moment interventions so the client actually shows up and can practice being open to whatever is there.

Developing a Defused, Detached Perspective on the Mind

A major precondition for openness is to see the self as distinct from the mind. This is one of the core messages of FACT: *You are not your mind. You have a mind, but you are not the same as your mind.* This is news for many people; they tend to associate their identity with the activities of the problem-solving mind. When they get lost in thought, they literally lose the distinction between their bigger self and the problem-solving mind. In FACT, the term we use for this type of disappearing act is *fusion.* The word "fusion" literally means "to pour together." In the mental process of fusion, the bigger self is lost when it is poured together with the activities of the problem-solving mind. In FACT, we call the triggers for these mental disappearing acts "sticky thoughts," a generic term for distressing or unwanted thoughts, feelings, memories, or physical sensations. Often, sticky thoughts also evoke rules about what the person is supposed to do now that painful stuff has shown up. This is revealed in statements like "I just don't let myself think about it" or "Let's talk about something else; this isn't something I want to deal with right now," signaling that clients are following rules about how to deal with their painful stuff.

As you'll see when we describe the strategies in Table 2, a basic goal of FACT is to create a rift between the client and the client's mind. Many interventions and associated metaphors are used to both develop and strengthen this rift. One is creating a speaker-listener relationship between the mind (the speaker) and the client (the listener). Speaker-listener relationships are common in every culture and are easily understood at the physical level. The purpose of the root metaphor is to help clients develop the same relationship with the mind as they would with an actual speaker. FACT emphasizes this point with certain language conventions, such as "What is your mind saying to you about this?" and "How does your mind react to what I just said to you?"

Another root metaphor portrays the mind as having its own agenda that might or might not be the same as the best interests of the client. The FACT therapist literally and figuratively pits the client's best interests against the interests of the mind. This shows up in the therapeutic dialogue in FACT language conventions like "Who are you going to listen to, your mind or your own experience?" or "Your mind is going to be very upset if you stop doing what it says. It will probably make even more noise to see if it can get you to go along."

A third language convention attempts to undermine the automaticity and speed of the problem-solving mode of mind. For example, we ask clients to replace the word "but" with "and." "But" is an exclusionary word that often pits a desired and effective life action (for example, "sit down and talk with my spouse about an issue we haven't resolved") with an unacceptable emotional consequence of doing so (for example, "It will be painful if I discover that my spouse doesn't care about me"). Because the emotional consequence is unacceptable, the effective action cannot be undertaken. Most clinicians are familiar with clients who use "Yes, but" as a default response to clinical advice. Gently yet firmly requiring the client to use the word "and" instead of "but" undermines the problem-solving mind's message that effective actions cannot occur while negative emotions, thoughts, or memories are present.

Another common convention is to ask the client to rephrase communications about thoughts, feelings, memories, or sensations in a way that labels the actual psychological process the client is responding to. For example, the statement "I am angry" would be revised to "I just noticed a feeling called anger." This is an example of detaching the self from a private experience by simply naming that experience. In general, naming private experiences makes them seem less overwhelming and dominating.

The clinician must be careful not to intellectualize the concept of defusion, despite the repeated opportunities and perhaps a strong temptation to do so. The processes of detachment from and attachment to private events are always present and continually influence what happens in the therapeutic interaction. Particularly when clients struggle with attachment, it's very tempting to say things like "That's just a thought your mind is giving you," "That's just a memory; it's in the past and there isn't anything you can do but get some distance from it," or "There it goes again! Can't you see your mind is doing it to you again?" Unfortunately, these intellectual truths will be relatively meaningless for clients who have limited ability to get any distance from their thoughts, emotions, memories, or physical sensations.

It is far more effective for the clinician to simply comment on the process that's unfolding for the client, rather than the solution the client should be using. You can implicitly create a distance between the client and the client's mind without the need for any lecturing, pleading, or cajoling by simply saying something like "It looks as though your mind just showed up with some messages. What other messages is it giving you right now?" or "Did you notice that your mind just inserted itself into our conversation? Let's welcome it to the party!" Detachment as a skill is not acquired intellectually; it is learned through experiential practice.

Building an Accepting Stance

A second feature of being open is the ability to take an observer role when distressing, unwanted feelings, thoughts, or memories are present. As the famous serenity prayer suggests, there is important life wisdom in knowing when to accept things and when to try to change them. By way of contrast, avoidance and control strategies are ways people attempt to change their direct experience of distressing, unwanted private events. However, because these events can't really be controlled, eliminated, or suppressed, the energy and attention put into avoidance strategies are wasted.

In this light, acceptance is a stance that saves energy because it involves no effort at all. The energy thus saved can then be devoted to meaningful change. There are several types of human experience that can only be accepted and are not amenable to first-order change:

- Personal history or its manifestations in the moment

- Spontaneous thoughts, feelings, memories, and sensations triggered in the moment

- The attitudes, behaviors, and feelings of others

- The future

Practicing acceptance doesn't make distressing content disappear from the mental landscape, but it does prevent it from being amplified due to the paradoxical effects of suppression or avoidance. Therefore, acceptance talk involves metaphorical communications about adopting a welcoming, compassionate stance when painful stuff shows up. The clinician may say things like "Can you turn around and embrace what is here, instead of trying to push it away?" or "Can you make room for what just showed up right now?" or "Can you take this along with you when you do something you care about?" or "Can you tuck this is in your purse or back pocket and carry it around with you?" Each of these questions suggests hat simply holding painful stuff lightly, without defense, is an alternative to trying to control or suppress it.

It is important to avoid framing acceptance as though adopting this stance is a rational decision clients should embrace, because most clients will already be tempted to see acceptance as another form of emotional control. The client might be thinking, *I see. You're saying that if I just accept my sadness, then I won't be as sad.* It is therefore extremely important for the clinician to remain circumspect about what will or won't happen if the client takes an accepting stance toward painful experiences that have previously been avoided. There are no promises as to what will happen around a particular painful emotion or memory if the client accepts it. It will be what it is, nothing more and nothing less. If the clinician implies that acceptance will help the client suffer less, this sets the stage for the client to use acceptance as yet another emotional control strategy. The clinician instead should say something like "I don't know what will happen if you choose to just make room for this stuff. It could get worse; you never know. I guess we could say that we know for sure what will happen if you keep fighting with this stuff. You'll probably keep getting the results you've been getting. Would you be willing to experiment with a different move and just see what happens?"

A Clinical Example of Promoting Openness

The following dialogue with Julie and Sylvia demonstrates how to rapidly promote an open stance in the clinical conversation. In this session, Sylvia and Julie have been exchanging hostile remarks, and Julie is becoming more and more frustrated and impatient.

Clinician: It sounds like your mind gives you lots of powerful messages about what's on the table when you and Sylvia butt heads. It tells you that if she continues to misbehave, it proves you've failed as a mother. It says that if she doesn't love you in a particular way, you are alone in the world. It portrays you as a good-hearted person who is being taken advantage of and says that you deserve better than the world is giving you. Your mind seems to be pouring gasoline on this fire.

Julie: Yeah, it gets me so upset that I just lose my cool, even though I swear to myself that I'm not going to blow up—that I'm going to stay calm.

Clinician: It would be pretty hard to stay calm while this stuff is on the table. I wouldn't be able to stay calm if that was in front of me. Is there another place to stand with all of this material when it shows up?

Julie: I'm not sure what you mean.

Clinician: Would it be possible to let all those thoughts and images show up, and just leave them alone? Not that leaving them alone will make them go away; they will probably hang out and try to get your attention. But getting tangled up in them seems to draw you away from relating to Sylvia the way you want to. Have you ever considered that being the mother you want to be may require you to be willing to have this stuff show up without getting sidetracked by it?

Julie: I've never thought about it that way before. You mean just let all these anxieties appear and not do anything—don't try to make them go away? That's scary, because I've always thought that I couldn't stay calm if I allowed those thoughts to enter into my mind. If I let them in, I'll get too angry to be civil with Sylvia.

Clinician: Exactly! Notice that another thought just showed up that says, *I can't stay calm if these other thoughts are present.* Could you also welcome that thought and just carry it in your purse along with the others?

In this brief segment, the clinician is systematically separating Julie from her mind, pitting the interests of her mind (to scare her, to make her lose her cool, to make her feel like a failure as a mother) with her best interests (to reconnect with her daughter, to give up on being right about her story of giving everything and getting nothing in return). The goal of this brief intervention is to help Julie accept her sticky thoughts so she can focus her attention on what is really important in the moment.

Developing Life Engagement

Engagement involves the ability to identify closely held personal values and create ever-larger patterns of action that are consistent with those values. As the previous dialogue with Julie suggests, skills like being able to stay present and accept what shows up in the moment are only a means to an end. The end is being able to act in a way that is consistent with personal values. In FACT, we call this "voting with your feet." We are remembered for our actions, not for what was going on between our ears while we were acting. Successful living requires that people engage in valued actions, even when those actions might trigger painful stuff. This in turn requires that people be connected with what matters most to them in life, rather than being lost in the clouds of emotional avoidance and rule following. When we ask clients to imagine what type of life they would choose if they could choose, we are opening a discussion about personal values. When we engage clients in discussion of specific behaviors that might embody those values, we are helping them engage the world on their terms, rather than under the influence of unworkable, socially transmitted rules.

Contacting Personal Values

A unique feature of FACT (and ACT) is its specific focus on helping clients both uncover and reconnect with their personal values. The power of values lies in their ability to organize and motivate complex patterns of behavior over long periods of time. Think of a value as a life principle or life direction rather than a specific life outcome. Various life events or achievements might embody the value, but there will always be more life situations where the value can be applied. A value like "I want to be a loving, thoughtful, attentive life partner" has no end to it. There is always more loving, thoughtful, and attentive behavior possible, up to the point of death. When people lose contact with their values, behavior is instead controlled by social or cultural norms, pressure from significant others, avoid the desire to criticism or humiliation, and so forth. People lose ownership of their daily life directions and experience an associated loss of meaning in life.

In FACT, we use several root metaphors and experiential exercises to help clients initiate contact with deeply held values. One core intervention is the funeral exercise, in which clients visualize attending their own funeral and imagining what they would like to hear in the eulogies offered by their friends, family, children, or spouse or life partner. A similar exercise is visualizing attending their own retirement party and imagining what they would like coworkers, friends, and colleagues to say in their speeches. Clients can then be asked to write down the essence of these eulogies or speeches and consider whether their current life direction seems consistent with what they hope people would say in remembrance of them. This type of exercise is quite evocative and establishes that living according to personal values isn't something to take lightly; you can't push the rewind button and start over. To make the point that we humans are voting with our feet at all times, the clinician can use comments or questions like "So, what would the epitaph read on your tombstone, if you had to write it now?" or "Is there something that you would particularly like to make sure people remember you for?"

As mentioned in the previous chapter, directional metaphors, such as following one's true north or moving in a chosen direction on a life path, can be used to assess how consistent current actions are with personal values. In FACT, we sometimes refer to these exercises as reorienting interventions because they tend to overwhelm the rule-governed responses generated by the problem-solving mind. One sure way to get clients' attention is to begin talking about the big picture of life and what really matters to them. To emphasize the importance of using values to show up even amidst life challenges, you can use questions like "What matters to you in this situation?" or "What do you want to stand for here?" or "What would make this situation honorable, purposeful, and legitimate for you?"

Similarly, discussion centered on values can be used to increase clients' motivation to try new, alternative behaviors that might initially provoke anxiety. To help create readiness for radical change, it can be very powerful to ask questions like "Do you want to do something about where you're headed right now versus where you want to be headed?" or "Would you feel better about the direction your life is taking if you addressed this issue?" or "If you engaged in this behavior, would it tell you that you were living closer to your values?"

The discussion of values shouldn't be used to bludgeon the client. It's painful to contact one's personal values and realize that months, if not years, have been spent living in ways that are contrary to those values. Because of this, some clients become extremely avoidant when they get in proximity to their values. They may profess not to have any values, or they may immediately begin to disavow their importance. It will actually slow down the clinical work if the clinician counters such statements with comments like "Everyone has values, and so do you" or "This is something you must be avoiding because it's painful for you." Instead, the clinician can compassionately note that we all fall out of contact with or fail to act on our values, and that society encourages people to remain unaware of what matters to them because of the potential social ramifications of everyone living according to their individual values. In doing so, the clinician's goal is to make it acceptable to be out of contact with values. After all, we can only start where we are, not where we would like to be.

Choice, Willingness, and Committed Action

FACT interventions designed to increase life engagement not only target the guidance system of personal values, they also emphasize the importance of showing up and making the choice to confront something that clients might previously have avoided. *Choice* is sometimes referred to as a free operant; it is behavior that isn't controlled or regulated by social rules. The act of choosing is utterly incompatible with rule following because choice means doing something because the person wants to, as opposed to doing something because he or she has to. Choice enters into the FACT intervention lexicon in two main ways. First, we use the term *willingness* to describe making the choice to enter life situations that will trigger unwanted, distressing experiences. For example, the clinician might ask, "Would you be willing to go to this gathering of your friends even while your mind is telling you that they look down on you and think you're weak?"

Second, choice is presented as a key ingredient in producing effective life action, or committed action. *Committed action* is choosing to stand in the presence of distressing or unwanted thoughts, feelings, memories, or sensations that arise while engaging in actions that embody personal values. For example, a client caught in a dysfunctional marriage would engage in committed action by choosing to engage in healthy relationship behaviors (such as talking with his or her spouse, making specific behavior change requests, or setting limits on abusive talk) even though these behaviors could produce significant personal pain (such as being criticized, rejected, or divorced). These behaviors are done in the service of being an attentive, responsive, loving partner. Committed action and personal values are like two sides of the same coin, and discussions about committed action often arise as a natural consequence of talking about personal values, through questions like "What specifically could you do that would tell you that you're living in accordance with your values?" or "If you could choose, what would you like to do differently in this situation?"

There are several versatile root metaphors that the FACT clinician can use to motivate willingness and committed action. Journey metaphors communicate the idea that many small, purposeful actions are needed in the course of a long journey. Another use of this metaphor is to make the point that immediate results aren't always pleasant and that it may be tempting to stop traveling in an effort to prevent more negative results; this can be used to communicate the importance of staying connected with the bigger mission of moving in the direction of personal values and continuing to plug away (being willing) on the journey. Yet another use of the metaphor is to highlight that the journey itself is what creates personal meaning. While on the path toward a value, clients might discover that other values have emerged that render the guiding one less important. A FACT saying communicates this important truth: Goals are the process by which the process becomes the goal.

While committed action functions as the doorway to radical change, it can also backfire if clinicians pursue their own agenda with clients. This typically occurs when the clinician is convinced that the client needs to engage in some type of behavior change, such as stopping drinking or taking drugs or curtailing promiscuous sex. Clues that the clinician is inappropriately imposing his or her own values on the client come in the form of comments like "If you choose to continue binge drinking, despite all the bad things that have happened because of it, then I suppose it's your choice to make." While on the surface this seems to imply that it's the client's choice, it actually represents a subtle attempt to pressure the client to select a behavior that may not be intrinsically meaningful to the client. It is important to remember that the therapeutic interaction isn't about what the clinician values; it's about what matters to the client. One good way to prevent this distortion is to ask a question like "If no one knew you were engaging in this action, no one at all, not even your closest friend, would this still be a behavior you would choose?"

A Clinical Example of Promoting Engagement

In the following clinical dialogue with Julie and Sylvia, the clinician uses the information about their values obtained during the True North Exercise to help them interact in a way that's closer to their shared desire to improve their way of relating to each other.

Clinician: It sounds like both of you are pretty strong willed. (Looks at Julie.) I'm sure that Sylvia didn't get any of this from you and that we can place all the blame for her stubbornness on your ex-husband.

Julie: (Laughs with Sylvia.) My parents were both bullheaded, so I probably picked that up from them…and passed it on to my children.

Clinician: Well, being bullheaded isn't necessarily all that bad. Basically, stubborn people are just very persistent. Sometimes that means sticking with something just because you want to be right. But not giving up can be a virtue in the right situation.

Sylvia: That's what my boyfriend says about me. That I'm like a pit bull once I get started. Sometimes, he just leaves when I get cranked because he knows there's no talking to me.

Clinician: So I guess the two of you could keep butting heads like this until the cows come home. And I'm quite sure neither one of you is going to let the other one win. You could continue to just go round and round. Is that what matters to both of you? Is this what you want your relationship to be about—who is right and who is being treated wrongly?

Julie: Not me. I don't like what's happening to our relationship. We used to be close, and now it's like we can't even be in the same room together.

Sylvia: Yeah, it sucks.

Clinician: Is there another way to go about this? I mean, you both tell me you care about what's happening here. You both agree that this relationship is off course. You both get caught up in your own stuff and act in ways you don't believe in. I don't mean you always have to agree on things; that's not the goal. Maybe the goal is just to show up, remember that you both want to be headed toward your true north, and then do the best you can. No one stays on course perfectly anyway; there are bound to be some bad times. The trick is to keep talking and problem solving as you move forward.

Julie: I'm willing to try anything at this point. I can't tell her what to do because she just does the opposite. I guess I can just tell her about my concerns and back off. She has to do the rest.

Sylvia: Maybe we should spend less time talking about my tattoos, piercings, and who I'm hanging with and just go out and do some fun things like shopping or going to the movies like we used to. Also, let's talk about what I'm doing and not how it compares to Josh.

As this dialogue demonstrates, it takes a conscious, intentional choice to transcend personal stories about oneself and others. When storytelling processes become dominant and overly extensive, interpersonal behavior is shaped by such themes as being right, being a victim, or making sure the other person doesn't succeed in life. Fortunately, changing the focus of the conversation to connecting with values, making choices, and engaging in committed actions can have a transformational impact.

Summary: Walking Through a Door

FACT is based on the premise that, if the right door is opened, any person, regardless of how long he or she has been struggling, can walk through it into a completely different life. There are many different potential pathways to radical change, and FACT attempts to create fertile ground for any one of these mechanisms to transform the client. For example, previously feared private events, such as distressing emotions, thoughts, and memories, might come to be seen as signs of personal health and wholeness. Being in the present moment might be experienced as preferable to ruminating about the past or worrying about the future. Oppressive, self-defeating narratives might be seen as stories rather than functioning as self-fulfilling prophecies. Aimless or avoidant living might be supplanted by a values-based approach that produces an overall sense of life purpose and meaning. The beauty of FACT is that any of these processes, singly or in combination, can have a potentially life-altering impact. If one intervention tactic doesn't seem fruitful, the clinician can simply shift the focus to another mechanism for promoting radical change.

Next, in part 3 of this book, we will present detailed case examples showing how to apply FACT with children and families, with people who have substance use issues, with people who have trauma-based mood problems, and with elderly people struggling with depression or demoralization. The goal is to give you an inside look at FACT assessment and intervention principles and practices as they play out in real cases.

Part 3

Case Examples

Chapter 7

Big Like Swallow: FACT with a Sexually Abused Child

Christopher Robin to Pooh: Promise me you'll always remember: You're braver than you believe, and stronger than you seem, and smarter than you think.

— *A. A. Milne*

Childhood abuse and neglect are common, and numerous studies document the negative impact of these experiences on mental and physical health. Results from the Fourth National Incidence Study of Child Abuse and Neglect (NIS-4) suggest that nearly three million children and youth experienced maltreatment during the most recent NIS-4 study year (2005-2006). This translates to one child in every twenty-five in the United States (Sedlak et al., 2010).

A variety of protective factors may ameliorate or reduce the impact of trauma, and some may reduce the likelihood that future traumatizing events will occur. Protective factors include both native and learned abilities that reside within the individual child or youth, such as intelligence, the ability to experience emotion and regulate behavior, the ability to distance oneself, perseverance in applying problem-solving skills, and the strong motivation to achieve. Other protective factors exist within the family context, such as a strong relationship with a caregiver, the presence of a nurturing grandparent, structure and rules for male children, and encouragement of autonomy in female children. A final set of protective factors involves community support, such as supportive teachers, availability of mentors, and access to medical and mental health care (Werner & Smith, 1992).

Unfortunately, there are few well-designed studies evaluating treatments for post-traumatic stress symptoms in children and adolescents (Caffo, Forresi, & Lievers, 2005). The studies available suggest that time-intensive treatments, such as parent-child interaction therapy, may reduce the rates of future child abuse (Chaffin et al., 2004). However, these treatments are not readily available in many areas of the United States and can be prohibitively expensive for lower-income families. In addition, many cases of abuse and neglect are never identified or are identified only after the child has experienced multiple traumas, including physical abuse, emotional neglect, and witnessing domestic violence. Many children and families can benefit from brief interventions at the time when the trauma is first identified. While brief interventions may not entirely eliminate the impact of trauma, they can enhance the child's ability to pursue appropriate developmental tasks and improve the child's relationships with parents and teachers.

Most treatment approaches for childhood trauma involve three stages, and these largely correspond to the three core processes, or pillars of flexibility, we've been discussing: awareness, openness, and engagement. The first stage involves helping children become aware of present-moment experience, both inside the skin (for example, painful emotions) and outside the skin (for example, triggers for distressing emotional experiences, such as being alone in a dark room). The second stage involves supporting them in becoming more open to their reactions to the traumatic experience. This usually consists of both developing and telling a story about their trauma to a nurturing adult. This fosters the ability to view the trauma from a larger perspective, where it is only one part of their life, rather than something that determines their overall identity (for example, a bad boy or damaged goods). The third stage involves supporting their reentry into age-appropriate social, learning, and creative activities. In this stage, they must learn new skills that support stepping back from painful memories and thoughts and engaging in valued directions in life, such as success in schoolwork, development of healthy relationships, and participation in restorative recreational activities. For victims of child abuse, awareness is often a gateway to helping both child and caregivers move beyond unrecognized patterns of avoidance to build a platform for healthy development.

Case Example: Freddy

As is the case for most children who receive mental health services, it was Freddy's pediatrician, Dr. James, who referred Freddy and his family to a primary care psychologist. When Freddy's mother asked Dr. James for a refill of medication for attention deficit disorder (ADD), she explained that Freddy was having "a lot of trouble in his new school" and had been expelled after exposing himself to another child on the school bus. Although Freddy denied it, Dr. James worried that the incident might indicate that Freddy had been a victim of sexual molestation. The primary care psychologist Dr. James referred the case to works in the primary care behavioral health model (see Robinson & Reiter, 2006, for a detailed description of this approach) and provides consultation and brief interventions for clients referred by pediatricians. Her sessions are typically thirty minutes in length and often occur as warm handoff referrals from primary care colleagues, in which the primary care provider introduces clients to her in real time.

Freddy, a ten-year-old Caucasian boy, lives in a small town with Caitlin, his biological mother, his stepfather, and a younger sister. They moved from New Mexico about five months previously so Freddy's stepfather could start a new job. Caitlin is a stay-at-home mom, caring for Freddy, his sister, and her elderly mother, who lives with them and has health problems. Freddy has a seventeen-year-old stepbrother, Shawn, who lives with Freddy's dad and stepmom back in New Mexico, but hasn't had contact with him for the past year. Shawn was jailed six months ago for selling drugs. When Freddy was younger, he had a close relationship with Shawn, and they frequently spent time alone together at his dad's house.

Freddy is a small child. He wears thick glasses and appears younger than his actual age. He's in fifth grade and is currently being home-schooled by Caitlin. He was expelled from school two months ago after a series of incidents involving inappropriate sexual behavior. Caitlin is put off by the school principal and has decided not to appeal Freddy's expulsion, preferring to homeschool Freddy for the rest of the year. Freddy likes to play video games and collect cards related to video game characters. Caitlin says that he hasn't had much contact with his peers since being expelled. He occasionally plays with a younger boy in his neighborhood and with his younger sister. His family doesn't attend church or participate in other community activities. In fact, Caitlin doesn't like the new neighborhood and has some regrets about the family's move. She says that Freddy's stepfather might be losing his job, and that if that happens, they're considering moving to live with a relative in a town two hours away.

For three years, Freddy has taken medication for ADD. Historically, he's had problems with social immaturity, not completing assignments at school, and not doing chores at home. However, he performs well on tests, so his teachers believe that he's capable of being a good student. Freddy believes the medicine helps him, and Caitlin agrees. However, both report that it's difficult to make sure he takes it every day.

Focusing Questions

The clinician's first goal was to get more information about the incidents that led to Freddy's expulsion and to explore Freddy's experience with these incidents. The clinician also wanted to identify how Freddy was trying to work with the problem, as well as his values. One incident involved a conversation about underwear with a younger boy. He asked the boy to bring some underpants with cartoon characters to school to loan to Freddy. On another occasion, Freddy lay down on the floor of his classroom and looked under a girl's dress. When she tried to move, he held her leg and wouldn't let go when she asked him to. The third incident occurred after school on the bus. Freddy reported that he pulled down his pants and showed his penis to a boy sitting beside him.

During the initial interview, Freddy was continuously involved in his handheld video game and occasionally verbalized excitement about his progress in the game. His favorite character, Swallow, was small and wanted to grow up to be big and strong. While Freddy appeared absorbed in his game, he was simultaneously vigilant to the conversation and made several interjections to correct Caitlin or further explain her answers.

Caitlin seemed visibly distressed and quite distractible. She often spoke tangentially and was unsure of dates and other details. She explained that she was stressed-out by getting the family settled and trying to figure out how to homeschool Freddy. She was angry with the school staff and said she wouldn't put Freddy in that school again even if they asked her to. Freddy clarified that the school might want him to come back but couldn't tell the family because their phone was disconnected.

1. What Are You Seeking?

After gathering a bit of background information, the clinician's first move is to try to identify the solution Freddy might be seeking:

Clinician: So, Freddy, can you tell me why you're here today? What are you hoping to get out of this visit?

Freddy: My mom brought me. I gotta get more of my medicine.

Clinician: Does it help you?

Freddy: Yep, I think so.

Clinician: Can you tell me about your game? It looks interesting.

Freddy: Well, it's a game with characters that start out small, and when you play the game right, they grow up.

Clinician: Who's your favorite character?

Freddy: Swallow. Wait, I can show you. (*Shows the screen to the clinician.*) He's little now and he's kind of puny, but he gets brave and strong when he gets big. I'll keep playing; maybe I can show you how he looks at the end of the game.

Clinician: I'd like that, Freddy. While you play, can we talk about what happened on the school bus a little? Dr. James and I want to understand what happened.

Freddy: (*Nods.*)

Clinician: Was it on the way home from school?

Freddy: (*Nods.*)

Clinician: Who was sitting by you?

Freddy: Jose; he's a guy I know. I like him, but he can be annoying.

Clinician: Did he do anything that made you want to take your pants down, or did anyone else? Like daring you to or anything like that?

Freddy: No.

Clinician: How were you feeling just before you did it?

Freddy: My head was all full, and then it just kept building up. It gets like that sometimes. I'm mad and feel like it could explode.

Clinician: So if I had been a fly on the bus window that day, what would I have seen?

Freddy: (*Pauses for a long time.*) Splat!

Clinician: Sounds like you were pretty mad.

Freddy: Yep.

Clinician: And so you unzipped your pants, and then what happened? Did Jose say anything?

Freddy: He just said, "yuck."

Clinician: What did you do then?

Freddy: I put it away, just zipped up my pants.

Clinician: How did you feel at that moment?

Freddy: Uh, I don't remember.

Clinician: Do you have any other ideas about why you took your pants down that day?

Freddy: Maybe I forgot to take my medicine. I don't know.

Clinician: So then you went back to school the next day. What happened then?

Freddy: The other kids laughed at me. They teased me.

Clinician: Oh dear. How did that make you feel?

Freddy: *(Pauses for a long time.)* Hurt.

Clinician: Of course.

Through this dialogue, the clinician figured out that one of Freddy's problems involves how he responds to negative emotional states ("head all full"). Now she can move on to exploring his ways of coping with this problem.

2. What Have You Tried?

Using the second focus question, the clinician can explore not only how Freddy deals with difficult private experiences, but also how he responds to painful interactions, like being teased by his peers after the incident with Jose on the school bus. She anticipates that Freddy was trying to avoid feelings of anger and hurt and that he will need to learn new skills in order to engage in more effective behaviors. She also wonders if he might have been sexually molested and felt afraid to ask for help.

She briefly discusses private body parts and finds that Freddy has a good understanding of them. Further, he indicates that he thinks it's wrong to show his private body parts to others or to touch other people's private body parts. The clinician frames the incident with Jose as a mistake Freddy had made and suggests that she might be able to help him learn how to help himself when he gets the feeling that his head is full. He says that would be helpful because he usually gets into trouble when he has that problem. This leads her to the second focusing question: What have you tried?

Clinician: Freddy, you're smart, and I suspect that you're a good problem solver sometimes. What have you tried to help with the problem of your head being full and having things build up inside of you?

Freddy: I don't know. I guess I just try not to think about it.

Clinician: How does that work?

Freddy: I play my game and then I don't think about it.

Clinician: When you stop playing video games do you think about it?

Freddy: Nah. I watch TV or something. I try not to think about it.

Clinician: How about the problem of being teased at school after you made that mistake on the bus?

Freddy: I don't think about it. I play my game… And, well, if I don't go to school, they can't tease me.

The clinician can see that Freddy is stuck in an avoidance pattern and that it will be emotionally challenging for him to reverse the pattern.

3. How Has It Worked?

To explore the third question, the clinician begins by providing Freddy with information about problem solving. This is often necessary with younger children who might not have learned much about problem solving yet.

Clinician: Freddy, most of the time I can solve problems that come up in my life, but sometimes I get stuck. I try to solve a problem and it doesn't work, and then I don't know what else to do. It's easy to keep trying the same old solution, even when it doesn't work. And sometimes the way I try to solve a problem causes me more problems. Do you know what I mean?

Freddy: I don't know... I think so.

Clinician: One way to decide if we're solving a problem well is to look at whether the solution helps us be who we want to be in the world. For example, I want to help people, help plants grow, and be kind to animals. Who do you want to be, Freddy?

Freddy: I want to have friends.

Clinician: What else?

Freddy: Be good at numbers.

Clinician: Like math and computer stuff?

Freddy: Exactly.

Clinician: So, let's look at the problem of feeling upset, like your head's all full. That's a problem because it can make it hard for you to do what you think is best. It might also cause you to make mistakes because you do things without thinking. You said you try to solve this problem by not thinking about it. Does that work?

Freddy: (Pauses for a long time.) I don't know.

Clinician: Does it help you have friends or learn math?

Freddy: I don't think so.

Clinician: You know, I don't think I can make myself not think about something. In fact, if I try to not think about something, I think about it more. Let's try an experiment. I want you to not think about Swallow, just for a minute.

Freddy: (Closes his eyes.) I'm thinking about Swallow anyway, even though I'm trying not to.

Clinician:	So not thinking about something doesn't work very well, and it doesn't seem to help you have friends or learn math.
Freddy:	Yep.

4. What Has It Cost You?

Next, the clinician wants to help Freddy understand and assess the costs of his avoidance-based strategies, particularly in terms of his social goals.

Clinician:	How about the solution of not going to school so you won't be teased? Does that help you have friends or learn math?
Freddy:	No, but I don't get teased.
Clinician:	Yeah, that's a hard choice: not being teased *(raises left hand)* or trying to make friends *(raises right hand)*.
Freddy:	Yep.
Clinician:	So, let me see if I have this right. You can stay home and not be teased, but then you can't make friends.
Freddy:	Yeah, that's not so good... Maybe I should try to get into school again.
Clinician:	Well, maybe. Let's also look at what it costs you to try not to think about things when your head feels full. Does that solution cause you any problems?
Freddy:	Maybe... Sometimes I just explode.

Setting the Stage for Radical Change: What Kind of Life Would You Choose?

The previous four focusing questions have set the stage for radical behavior change. Freddy has readily agreed with the idea that some of his efforts to solve his problems aren't helping and are, in fact, limiting his ability to do something he values: make friends. Seeking to elicit an optimistic response, the clinician frames the question about life direction in terms of a world where anything is possible.

Clinician: Freddy, in a world where anything is possible, what would you be doing in life right now?

Freddy: Going to school, playing with friends…being good at math.

Clinician: And?

Freddy: Maybe getting to do stuff with my mom and stepdad.

Clinician: And?

Freddy: Maybe I could make up computer games and draw pictures of creatures for the games.

Clinician: Okay, being good at math would help you develop games, and having friends would help you know what kind of games to invent—what kids would like to play.

Freddy: Yep.

Choosing Direction: Life Path and Turnaround Exercise

The clinician uses the Life Path and Turnaround Exercise to help Freddy reframe his problem and identify more effective ways to deal with his hurt feelings and buildup of negative emotions (see Figure 6). Freddy describes his desired life direction, one with more meaning, as growing like the Swallow character in his video game. It also included making friends, learning math, going to school, and having fun with his parents. He sees himself as traveling mostly in the direction of more control, trying to protect himself from hurt feelings and from having future problems with exploding. The clinician suggests that it might be possible for Freddy to learn skills for working with his head being full and for protecting himself so that he could have these problems and still go to school to learn and make friends. Freddy doesn't know how he can motivate himself to move toward more meaning, but he wants to hear the clinician's ideas about this. He sees his parents and his grandmother as potentially helpful to him.

Figure 6. Freddy's Life Path and Turnaround Worksheet

More Control	**More Meaning**
What do you want to control, avoid, or get rid of and how are you trying to do that?	What type of life would you choose if you could choose?

Feeling hurt	*Growing like Swallow—being strong*
Exploding	*Making friends; learning math; going to school; having fun with my parents*

1. Draw an arrow above the line to indicate where you are on your life path these days and which direction you're moving in.

2. What, if any, are the costs and benefits of pursuing control?
    Benefit of not going to school is not getting hurt. Benefit of not being around people is not exploding and getting in trouble. Costs of not going to school and being around people is not having friends and getting to play with them.

3. What behaviors would tell you that you're moving toward more meaning in life?
    Learning math; spending time with other kids; going out with my parents to do fun things.

4. When you get stuck, how can you help yourself keep moving toward more meaning?
    I don't know.

5. Who or what helps you move in the direction of more meaning?
    I don't know...my parents and maybe my grandmother when she's feeling better.

Case Formulation: Four Square Tool

The clinician completes a Four Square Tool (see Figure 7) to help her better understand which private and public behaviors are working for Freddy and which are not. He needs help addressing his unworkable social behaviors of a sexual nature. His private instruction to himself (*Just don't think about it*) is costly and perhaps related to his impulsive social behaviors that lead to problems. His behavior of playing video games possibly works in some ways but not in others. When it is excessive it may lower the probability of engaging in public behaviors that are more purposeful and supportive of his values, such as asking adults for help in working with painful private behaviors.

Based on the content of the Four Square Tool, the clinician decides to focus on Freddy's problematic private behaviors, with a secondary goal of supporting ongoing values clarification and creative daydreaming and enlisting his parents' support in reinforcing his more workable public behaviors (studying, playing cooperatively with his sister, and spending time with a neighborhood friend). She also plans to encourage Freddy's parents to actively supervise playtime with his neighborhood friend and to identify social skills that Freddy needs help with. She hopes to teach his parents more about engendering social skills so that they can actively coach Freddy before and after supervised playdates with friends.

Figure 7. Freddy's Four Square Tool

		Workability	
		Not working (do less)	**More workable (do more)**
Behavior	**Public**	• *Engaging in aggressive play with sexual content* • *Staying home (and avoiding school)* • *Playing video games too much*	• *Actively studying homeschooling assignments* • *Playing cooperatively with his younger sister* • *Asking to play with a friend in his neighborhood* • *Playing video games well*

	Private	• *Suppressing the feeling that his head is all full*
		• *Avoiding feelings of hurt and other private experiences by following rules that limit his growth and skill development*
		  o *Just don't think about it.*
		  o *Don't make trouble.*
		  o *Play your game and everything will be all right.*
		  o *Take your pill and everything will be okay.*
			• *Dreaming about a future where he is successful (has friends, is stronger and brave, has meaningful work)*
			• *Imagining better times with his parents and grandmother*

Treatment Summary

The clinician saw Freddy three times over the course of one month. His first follow-up visit occurred one week after the initial visit, and the other took place one week later. Treatment goals included creating a safe environment where Freddy might develop more openness and awareness with troubling feelings, thoughts, and perhaps memories of frightening experiences. She also hoped to assist Freddy in developing a perspective on his sense of self that included past problems, awareness of current private and public experiences, and a sense of hope and confidence about pursuing friendships, succeeding in school, and relating to adults in his life. Figure 8 shows a graph of his problem severity ratings for the problem "head gets all full."

Figure 9 shows a graph of flexibility marker ratings made by the clinician at the end of each session. Initially, Freddy's awareness and openness scores were particularly low, whereas his engagement score was higher. As he made gains in the first two areas, his engagement score also improved. While treatment ended earlier than hoped for, Freddy was making definite gains in psychological flexibility.

Figure 8. Freddy's Problem Severity Ratings

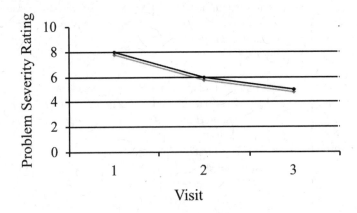

Figure 9. Freddy's Flexibility Profile

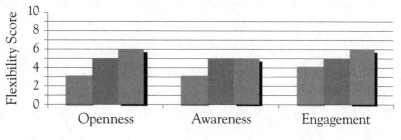

Flexibility Markers for Visits 1-3

Promoting Awareness

During the time remaining, the clinician focused on interventions to strengthen Freddy's awareness. These included helping him see a difference between his little self (a child who is a student, son, and brother, and who has school and peer problems and was hurt by his brother) and big self (a child who is able to evolve in difficult situations, show kindness to himself and others, be brave, and be aware and accepting of feeling hurt). The clinician also taught Freddy how to use his breath to anchor himself in the present moment. (Caitlin left the clinic to take her husband to work during the last twenty minutes of the initial visit.) During these interventions, Freddy continued to play his video game but remained attentive to the clinician, and soon, without prompting, he stopped playing in order to participate in experiential exercises.

Intervention: Little Self, Big Self

Little Self, Big Self is an intervention that helps school-age children develop a perspective of self that includes the past, the present, and a desired future. It is particularly useful with children who, like Freddy, are receiving negative feedback from others and who may have experienced some form of trauma. It can strengthen both openness and engagement and is useful in a single session but can also be easily built upon in a series of visits. (See Figure 10 for the clinician's Little Self, Big Self diagram for Freddy.)

Clinician: Freddy, I want to draw a picture and use it to help you learn something about who you are. Here, in the middle, I'll write a few things about you: You're ten, a fifth-grader, a big brother, and a son.

Freddy: Yeah.

Clinician: We're going to call that your "little self." Now I'm drawing a really big circle around it, and we'll call this your "big self." It includes lots of things about you—even your ideals or principles, or what I call your values. Your big self can do things that your little self can't. The little self can tell stories about you, and the big self can hear them, just listen. The big self can understand a lot more than the little self.

Freddy: Like when Swallow grows; then he can do a lot of things.

Clinician: Yes, that's what I mean. I'm going to write some things in this large circle that the big self can do. Will you help me add some more things?

Figure 10. Freddy's Little Self, Big Self Diagram

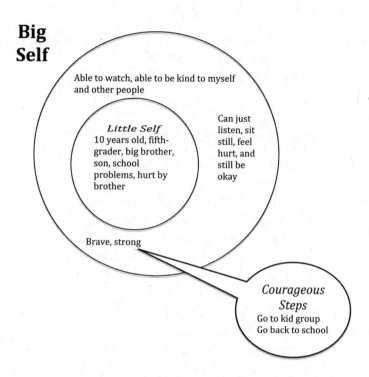

Freddy and the clinician continued to work together on this, and then the clinician brought a male doll into the interaction.

Clinician: This is Bob. He has some problems with his head getting all full. Sometimes he explodes. Other times he's able to use his big self to help him watch his head and see what's happening in there—just looking at all of the thoughts and feelings. The big self is kind of like the sky; it can hold a lot of clouds— pretty clouds and scary storm clouds too.

The clinician held the doll and used her other hand to indicate a circle around its head. Then she indicated a larger circle that encompassed its head and body.

Clinician: See, his big self is out here. There's lots of room there and his big self can just watch.

Freddy: (*Watches and nods.*) Okay.

Clinician: I want to teach you one more thing today. It's a technique to help you move from your little self to your big self, to grow stronger, like Swallow.

Intervention: Present-Moment Breathing

Next, the clinician taught Freddy Present-Moment Breathing, a versatile technique that can be combined with interventions designed to help both adults and children focus attention on the present moment and continue engaging in committed action, even while experiencing distressing feelings, memories, thoughts, or physical sensations. To use this technique, first teach clients diaphragmatic breathing. Then, as they engage in diaphragmatic breathing, have them use the phrases "breathe in" and "breathe out," saying the phrases to themselves slowly to help focus attention. Then have them shift to the words "here" and "now" to promote present-moment awareness.

After instructing Freddy in this sequence, the clinician asked Freddy to imagine that every time he said "here" and "now" he moved a little more into his bigger self. Freddy indicated that this was helping him get more of a sense of his bigger self.

When Freddy and Caitlin returned for a visit the following week, Freddy asked Caitlin if he could talk to the clinician alone. He told the clinician that he'd practiced the breathing and getting in touch with his big self and then said he wanted to tell her a secret that he'd kept for a long time. He then told her that when he was eight years old, his stepbrother, Shawn, had come into his bed at night three times and put his mouth on Freddy's penis. Then he tried to get Freddy to put his mouth on Shawn's penis, which scared Freddy and made him cry. Each time, Shawn got mad and left Freddy's bed. The last time Shawn touched Freddy's genital area was on a city bus. He grabbed his crotch briefly and said, "I don't need you anymore. I have somebody better now, and you'd better not ever tell anybody, or I'll get you." The clinician took out

Freddy's Little Self, Big Self diagram from the first visit and wrote "hurt by brother" in tiny letters in the middle circle.

Promoting Engagement

During the second visit, the clinician used interventions with both Caitlin and Freddy to strengthen their engagement. With Freddy, she used the Badge of Courage intervention, and with Caitlin, she used the intervention To Love and Protect.

Intervention: Badge of Courage

The Badge of Courage is a great intervention for helping children connect with personal values and planning small behavior changes to enhance consistency between values and behavior. In this case, because of the need to devote time to intervening with Caitlin and working with a Child Protective Services case worker, the clinician used the Badge of Courage intervention only very briefly. However, this short dialogue provides sufficient information to serve as a basis for a more extensive intervention.

Clinician: Freddy, you are so brave to tell me about what happened to you. I'm going to make you a badge of courage. (Draws the badge on a piece of paper and then cuts it out and gives it to Freddy.) I think your stepbrother made a big mistake, and now you're growing like Swallow, getting strong enough to help yourself and your stepbrother. This is your badge of courage.

Freddy: Thanks. But I'm worried about what my parents will say. I don't want them to get mad at me or Shawn.

Clinician: You're very kind, Freddy. I want to help you with your parents. Is it okay for me to talk with your mom for a few minutes, just to ask for her help?

Freddy: Sure.

Clinician: While I talk with her, would you make me a list of any other values or qualities you'd like to see in the big self part of you? *(Hands Freddy the worksheet and a marker.)*

Freddy: Okay.

Intervention with Parents: To Love and Protect

The clinician then met with Caitlin and summarized Freddy's report of being sexually abused. She asked Caitlin to help Freddy by pledging her love and support to him. The Love and Protect intervention is designed to help parents whose ability to provide critical support to a child is challenged by the difficulty of accepting their own distress. The clinician asked Caitlin to indicate which feelings were most difficult and then to state, "I feel this, and I pledge to love and support Freddy here and now." Her most difficult feelings surrounded the idea that she had failed Freddy by not being more vigilant about what happened when he was at his dad's house. Caitlin agreed to talk with Freddy's stepfather that evening and go through the same exercise with him. The clinician also worked with Caitlin to devise the following homework plan:

1. Mom and Dad will take turns going for daily walks with Freddy, just to hang out and talk.

2. Every other day, Freddy gets to choose a fun activity with one or both of his parents, such as going to the park. He can invite his sister or his neighborhood friend.

3. Freddy's badge of courage is to be displayed on the refrigerator.

4. The family will start having ten-minute family meetings each week. The meetings will begin with each person talking briefly about something of personal importance (for example, being honest, saying thank you, offering to help, or drawing pretty pictures).

Caitlin also agreed to bring Freddy back to the clinic for another visit in one week.

Promoting Openness

Both Caitlin and Freddy's stepfather accompanied him to the third visit. At the beginning of the session, Freddy's stepfather said that he'd been laid off and the family was going to move in with a relative in another town. The clinician made calls to Child Protective Services and Community Mental Health Services in that town. She learned about a social skills group that Freddy could attend at a family and child services agency. During this final visit, the clinician worked to promote Freddy's openness during this vulnerable time. She used the Clouds in the Sky intervention to help promote his ability to tolerate his negative memories, feelings, and thoughts, and the Courageous Steps intervention to help him practice openness in addressing barriers to taking steps toward greater meaning on his life path.

Intervention: Clouds in the Sky

Clouds in the Sky is a useful intervention for any population and a good choice for children because they can readily relate to it. In essence, it involves guiding clients through a visualization in which they identify troubling thoughts, memories, and feelings and then place them on cloud shapes, with jagged storm clouds for distressing content, and pretty, puffy clouds for pleasant thoughts and feelings. It is essentially a metaphor, and it includes the idea that the sky is big and can hold a lot of clouds and the idea that the client can simply let the distressing thoughts, memories, and feelings float onto a cloud.

Intervention: Courageous Steps

Courageous Steps is, in a sense, an extension of the Badge of Courage intervention. It is used to help clients identify steps that would take them in chosen directions on their life path and therefore promotes engagement. Successful engagement relies on strong openness, and the clinician used this intervention with Freddy to promote openness as well as engagement. She created a variety of contexts for Freddy to explore private events that could be barriers to taking action in real life. She started by using Freddy's Big Self, Little Self diagram, drawing a line from the word "Brave" (inside the circle representing Freddy's big self) to a bubble in the margin of the paper. Then she asked Freddy to think of two courageous steps he could take that would help him travel in his chosen direction on his life path. Freddy responded readily: "Go to that kid group—the one you said would help me—and go back to school." The clinician asked Freddy to imagine that he was at the kids group and started to feel uncomfortable and uncertain about what to say or do. She asked him to use his big self to care for his little self. Together, the clinician and Freddy developed additional practice situations to help him learn to open to his private experience and continue to act in skillful, meaningful ways, including asking his parents to support his return to school. As his skills for taking an open stance improved, he was more confident about taking courageous steps. He and the clinician then asked his parents to support him in taking these steps.

On a Final Note

When working with children who have experienced abuse or trauma, all too often mental health clinicians are limited to only brief contacts with the child and family. In these time-limited situations, it is essential to make the most of every minute. This is the spirit of FACT: focus and take action. Fortunately, as this case example demonstrates, much can be done to begin healing and to strengthen families in as few as three visits. Strengthening the relationship between children and their parents is always critical, particularly when children have endured traumatic experiences.

General Pointers about Using FACT with Traumatized Children and Their Families

Address the needs of parents as soon as possible when working with traumatized children. Dance around the pillars of flexibility—openness, awareness, and engagement—and teach parents to support the interventions you introduce. For example, a parent can help the child make a drawing of a sky with clouds and then write both pleasing and painful thoughts on the clouds and, in the process, model acceptance.

It's helpful to use toys with children. Even with middle school children, toys can be useful prompts. They bring a real-life quality to therapeutic interactions and may deepen the child's understanding of metaphors. A great resource for toys is The Creative Therapy Store (www .creativetherapystore.com).

Be aware that a child may have had positive responses during traumatic sexual experiences. Ask about this, accept whatever response you get, and affirm the complexity of human responses. Many sexual abuse victims eventually struggle with guilt over the fact that certain aspects of the trauma were physically or emotionally enjoyable. The clinician should normalize this type of reaction and remind the child that, despite such responses, abuse still involves being exploited by someone older who should know better.

Consider the possibility that the abused child might benefit from social skills training. Traumatized children often engage in social avoidance strategies that restrict their opportunities to learn from direct experience in social interactions with parents, siblings, peers, teachers, and others. The clinician should be willing to both model and coach appropriate social skills during a session, particularly when the topic of conversation turns to problematic interactions with peers, teachers, or siblings. Once equipped with better social skills, traumatized children can usually catch up quickly and develop age-appropriate social relationships.

Chapter 8

Lost in Space: FACT with a Poly-Substance-Abusing Adult

Just 'cause you got the monkey off your back
doesn't mean the circus has left town.

— *George Carlin*

Recent studies suggest that in any given year about 8.6 percent of the U.S. population will develop a substance use disorder. There has been a steady upward trend in the prevalence of such disorders over the last decade (Grant et al., 2004). Outcome research suggests that there's plenty of room for improvement in existing treatments (see Nathan & Gorman, 2002). For example sobriety rates from the evidence-based treatment known as the community reinforcement approach hover around 50 percent, with clients experiencing a high rate of relapse after treatment is discontinued (Roozen et al., 2004). On top of this, clients with drug and alcohol problems are notoriously difficult to keep in treatment; more than 50 percent drop out of treatment (Nathan & Gorman, 2002).

What makes the use of drugs and alcohol so attractive is that they are extremely effective numbing agents. They take the edge off of painful emotions, intrusive memories, and unpleasant physical symptoms of stress. Because of the rapid onset of their effects, using drugs or alcohol is quickly reinforced and becomes a dominant form of emotional avoidance. At the same time, it is important to note that abuse of drugs and alcohol tends to co-occur with other forms of emotional avoidance—binge eating, self-mutilation, and suicide attempt, to name a few.

For most people, the main result of long-term patterns of alcohol or drug abuse is losing contact with any sense of life direction. Getting the next high becomes the new life mission, and after many years of living this way, most people are completely lost. Because there is no intrinsic motivation to do anything other than get high (and avoid the ever-growing list of painful stuff in the client's life), the likelihood of getting and staying sober becomes increasingly lower. The decision to get help typically isn't made by clients; rather, it's triggered by external events such as spending time in jail, having their children taken by Child Protective Services, or hitting rock bottom in terms of social costs (for example, losing a marriage, a job, close friends, or a house). Thus, a central clinical concern is how to help these clients develop internal motivation to get sober and live a valued life.

Case Example: Ben

Ben, a thirty-four-year-old man, is homeless and unemployed. He is on parole after being convicted of assault and drug possession and is required to receive counseling as a condition of his parole. Ben recently moved to a new town and has no family or relatives nearby. He's currently couch surfing at the homes of various friends and acquaintances. After being an addict for fifteen years and landing in jail three different times, all for drug-related offenses, he's been clean from drugs and mostly sober for the past twelve months.

Ben is the youngest of three brothers who all have or have had substance abuse problems. Their father was an alcoholic who was violent toward his wife and children. Ben's mother died in a car accident when he was twelve years old. His father was driving the car and was drunk at the time, but he was never prosecuted. Ben started drinking when he was thirteen and started using amphetamines when was sixteen. He was very involved in school sports, but he didn't study and his failing grades eventually made him ineligible for team sports. He dropped out of high school when he was sixteen, and by age nineteen he was injecting speed, using various other drugs, and often drank to come down from the drugs. After that, Ben's only periods of sobriety occurred when he was in jail.

After being released from jail the first time, he met a recovering drug addict, Christina, and they briefly lived together. She became pregnant by accident and told Ben she would have the baby if he stayed clean. After only four months, Ben started to use again and even secretly pawned some of her expensive jewelry. One day Christina found him injecting amphetamines. She kicked him out of the house and had a restraining order placed on him. She swore he would never see his child.

After this incident, Ben went into the most destructive phase of his addiction. He nearly died in a car accident and was hospitalized on several occasions for drug overdoses. He constantly thought about killing himself and frequently engaged in high-risk behaviors like picking fights at bars and driving while intoxicated. He was jailed after he assaulted a drug dealer with a baseball bat, breaking the man's jaw and collarbone. Ben went through withdrawal while he was in jail and it nearly broke his spirit. While he was in jail, he wrote to Christina, but she never replied.

Focusing Questions

In the initial session, the therapist quickly discovers that Ben is coming only because the court has ordered him to. He seems irritated and his demeanor is very evasive. He avoids making eye contact and frequently makes snide comments about having to see a counselor.

1. What Are You Seeking?

After gathering a bit of background information, the clinician's first task is to try to identify what Ben is seeking by coming in for therapy, given that he is being required to receive counseling and may have little or no intrinsic motivation to use counseling for positive purposes.

Clinician: Okay, Ben. If I understand it correctly, we will be meeting for a while whether you like it or not. I have to inform your probation officer if you don't show up for a session. Just to let you know, I've never done this type of work before, so I don't want to fail with my first referral from the probation department. (Smiles.)

Ben: (Grins, then speaks with a snide tone.) Nah, I'm going to be a good boy and do exactly what you tell me to do.

Clinician: What do you want to use this time for? Do you have any idea what could be valuable for you to focus on?

Ben: I don't know. What do you think?

Clinician: I don't know either. Maybe this is one of the first hurdles to face. What could you get out of this that would make a difference for you?

Ben: Oh boy, I hope you don't want me to go over my childhood and all that stuff again.

Clinician: Only if you think it's important that I know about it. I'm more interested in knowing what would tell you that things were getting better for you.

Ben: You're not like other counselors I've worked with. You're a little crazy, right?

Clinician: Please don't tell anyone. (Smiles.) It's a trade secret.

Ben: (Laughs out loud.) Gee, just what I need: a wacky psychologist. Okay, so I suppose you want me to say that I would stop using drugs if this treatment worked. But I'm an addict, and as soon as I'm out from under the man, I'm probably going to go back on the streets and start using again. That's the only time I really feel good and not screwed up inside.

2. What Have You Tried?

Ben's responses haven't been terribly revealing, to say the least. This suggests that he has very little confidence in his ability to live a different kind of life. The fact that he links drug use with feeling good and not feeling screwed up inside is worth exploring more. The second focusing question is helpful in examining this link a little more closely.

Clinician: It sounds like you use drugs because they make you feel better, "not screwed up inside," as you put it. When you don't use drugs for any period of time, like now, what do you end up feeling like inside?

Ben: Terrible. I feel terrible. I can't stop thinking about how I screwed up my one chance to have a normal life. I've stolen from people I care about, I've lied to people, I've used people, and I've hurt people. The biggest thing I feel is that I'm going to be a worthless addict until the end.

Clinician: So, besides using drugs and booze, have you tried anything else to deal with these thoughts and feelings?

Ben: I can remember that sports helped me take my mind off things. But to be truthful, I've been out of it since I can remember. I've always used booze or drugs. It's my life. That's all that I know how to do.

3. How Has It Worked?

While drugs and alcohol help numb distressing private experiences, they don't change the negative, oppressive quality of those experiences. Chemicals simply help people escape from those experiences, but only temporarily. When the high is gone, the negative stuff returns, often with a vengeance. This reality is what the therapist wants to help Ben get into direct contact with in the next part of the interaction.

Clinician: So, the drugs and alcohol help you feel better and less screwed up. Do they actually create positive thoughts and feelings inside you, or how does it work in your case?

Ben: Oh no. No, no. No way do I have anything positive. When I'm high, I just don't give a shit about what's going on in my brainpan. I can just take a vacation from all that garbage.

Clinician: Interesting. So being high allows you to be around all your stuff without getting dragged into it. How long do you get to be on vacation?

Ben: It just depends on what I'm high on. When I start to flame out, that's when the vacation is over.

Clinician: So the party is over when the drug wears off. What do you do then?

Ben: I take more drugs. You don't have to be a genius to figure that out.

Clinician: And over time, have you noticed that you have to use more drugs or use them more frequently to stay on vacation?

Ben: That's what being an addict is all about, man. The drugs own me.

4. What Has It Cost You?

The "garbage" that Ben is running from can only be avoided; it cannot be eliminated, and there are huge costs accruing from the avoidance strategies he has been using. The clinician wants to bring Ben into contact with those costs.

Ben: Getting high on speed isn't the right answer, huh?

Clinician: Well, what does your experience tell you?

Ben: That it sucks big-time! *And*, that I love it.

Clinician: Tell me, why does it suck to do drugs?

Ben: It starts to rule your world, and then nothing else matters. As long as you have your next fix, you're okay, but when you run out, you get freaked out. But at the same time, nothing beats taking a boatload of speed—until you have to come down.

Clinician: Come down?

Ben: Yes. You can't take amphetamines all the time because you get burned out and don't get high anymore. You can only tweak for a week or so, and then you have to sleep for a few days and catch up on meals, things like that. Then you go at it again.

Clinician: It seems like it doesn't leave much energy for things other than finding more drugs or coming up with money for drugs.

Ben: No, exactly. But you don't care about anything, even stuff that should be more important.

Clinician: So, over time, do you feel that staying high has basically helped you deal with your garbage? Has being high worked to keep your life moving in the direction you would like it to?

Ben: Are you kidding? What are you trying to get at? I'm hooked on drugs and alcohol, man. I'm an addict, for Christ's sake. I just about croaked in jail when I had to kick the stuff. Stop with the head games, man.

Clinician: I guess I just wanted to know if being high has helped you come to grips with what you think and feel inside. Has it helped with that?

Ben: No freaking way! Same old crap. Same old head.

Setting the Stage for Radical Change: What Kind of Life Would You Choose?

While Ben feels trapped in his addictive behaviors, he also recognizes on some level that this strategy isn't working. As with most people struggling with addiction, his values and meaningful life directions have been compressed by the ever-present urge to get high. The clinician needs to help him reconnect with a vision of how he'd like his life to be, however absurd this might seem to a person who basically has given up all hope.

Clinician: I'm curious, what would you like to see happen in your life? In a world where anything was possible, what kind of life would you choose to live?

Ben: You're crazy! What do you mean, "anything"? Nothing can happen here!

Clinician: Exactly! If that's so, then we can take the liberty to talk about anything, because nothing different will ever happen.

Ben: Well, you go to work so you can pay your bills so you don't have to steal from people. You eat meals and do laundry. Maybe you hang with friends or people you care about. Gotta make sure they aren't tweakers, though.

Clinician: So staying sober gives you the chance to make these other changes in your life?

Ben: Yeah. But it's just too damn hard to stay clean when you have so much worthless time to kill. I have nothing to do during the day when I'm not using. That is the worst. It really eats me alive.

Clinician: So, what eats you alive? What's eating at you?

Ben: (Goes silent, looks down, and crosses his arms.)

162

Clinician: (Remains silent for two minutes.)

Ben: (Twists in his chair.) That I don't get to see... (Cries quietly.) That I don't get to see my child.

Clinician: Wow. I didn't know you have a child. Is it a boy or girl?

Ben: Must be around three now. I don't know if it's a boy or girl.

Clinician: I guess you and the mother don't have any contact?

Ben: No, Christina hates me more than the plague, and she has every right to.

Clinician: What happened?

Ben: I was an idiot. I had everything I could wish for, and I blew it to take speed. She found out, and since then I haven't heard a word from her. I send a child support payment to probation each month, so I don't even know where they live.

Clinician: Judging by your tears, it seems like this is something that means a lot to you—being a father and seeing your child.

Ben: But it will never happen. Forget it. End of conversation.

Choosing Direction: True North Exercise

The clinician needs to help Ben get in touch with his current life direction, particularly since it appears he is just barely able to stay sober because he lacks a sense of larger life purpose. The clinician uses the True North Exercise (see Figure 11) to accomplish this and begin a discussion about what Ben could do differently in his daily life.

Clinician: Let's say your direction in life, the direction you're telling me you'd like to be headed in, is true north on this compass. (Shows Ben the worksheet and points to the true north arrow.)

I've written down some of the things you just said were important to you: Being a father, having a family, holding down a job so you can pay bills and support yourself and your family. So, if true north on this compass means you're headed exactly in the right direction, that you're living according to your values, where would you put your compass heading right now?

Ben: *(Marks a spot on the compass almost 180 degrees due south.)*

Clinician: So you're telling me that, right now, you're headed in the opposite direction of your values?

Ben: Yeah, I'm just existing—trying not to use so I don't go back to prison. If I'd known this is what being sober would feel like, I would never have stopped using. I feel worse now than when I was an out-of-control addict. The time I spend sober just seems so worthless.

Clinician: Honestly, I don't know what's possible in terms of you becoming the father you want to be. It's clear that this is something that is both important and painful for you. I guess I could say this: I don't know what will happen with Christina and your child if you stay sober and start to live according to your beliefs. But I think I do know what will happen if you get back into drugs, and I think you know too. The challenge is learning how to live with your garbage without resorting to solutions that make it worse.

Ben: That's true, but I don't know what else there is.

Clinician: Exactly. That's exactly what I mean: You don't know. You've never been there, so how could you? Are you willing to not know *and* stop doing what you know doesn't work?

Ben: This is going to be very scary.

Figure 11. Ben's True North Worksheet

LIVING THE LIFE I CHOOSE

N
W—E
S
X

What are your values?
- Being a father
- Having a family
- Being able to support myself and my family

What are your current strategies, and are they working?
- Staying sober just to stay out of jail
- Thinking about past mistakes and blown opportunities
- Thinking about using to relieve stress
- Staying disengaged to prevent failure

What skills will you need to make the journey?
- Learning to cope with daily mental garbage
- Learning to deal with cravings to use
- Finding life goals that create interest
- Learning to live in the present, rather than getting stuck in thoughts about the past

Clinical Issues

1. **Openness** (Accepts private events without struggle? Notices and lets go of unworkable rules?)
   Enmeshed with emotional avoidance rules; seems emotionally distant and disengaged. Doesn't like getting close to his own negative stuff.

2. **Awareness** (Able to be present? Aware of private experiences? Able to take perspective? Shows compassion for self and others?)
   Gets into story of being an addict automatically; has trouble just being with himself.

3. **Engagement** (Clear values? Can organize for effective action? Can obtain reinforcement? Sufficient interpersonal skills?)
   Very disengaged; his principal problem is not having a connection to anything that matters.

Case Formulation: Four Square Tool

As the Four Square Tool reveals (see Figure 12), Ben, like most addicts, is an emotional avoidance machine. His instinctive response to any psychologically painful event is to run away from it. Because of his pervasive avoidance, he not only is out of contact with his values, but also views valued living as a pipe dream. He's overidentified with his story of being an addict, and this story doesn't have a happy ending. Helpful interventions must promote his ability to stay present when negative thoughts, emotions, or memories show up. Rather than just hanging on to his sobriety by a thread, he needs to develop a set of valued actions that make being alive interesting for him. The only apparent leverage point is cultivating his value of being a father to his child, as this would require that he stay sober and develop a wider range of life pursuits.

Figure 12. Ben's Four Square Tool

		Workability	
		Not working (do less)	**More workable (do more)**
Behavior	**Public**	• *Isolating himself from others* • *Lacking an organized, purposeful daily routine* • *Couch surfing rather than having a stable residence*	• *Coming to treatment* • *Complying with requirements of probation* • *Being sober for 12 months*
	Private	• *Losing himself in his story of being an addict* • *Ruminating about past mistakes* • *Following rules that say his emotions are toxic and must be controlled or he will use again* • *Being out of contact with his values* • *Following the rule that the reason to stay sober is to stay out of jail*	• *Has strong values about being a father* • *Has ability to withstand urges to use*

Treatment Summary

The clinician saw Ben a total of six times over a twelve-month period, until Ben was given permission to move to another city to take a new job. As illustrated in Figure 13, his problem severity ratings dropped 50 percent over the course of treatment. Regarding his flexibility profile (Figure 14), his levels of openness and engagement were initially very low, but within three sessions he made significant gains in both areas. These changes, particularly increased engagement, had profound impacts on his life. He made contact with Christina through his probation officer and had several supervised visits with his child—a son named Phillip. Ben also became a sponsor for two members of his Narcotics Anonymous group. Except for one four-day relapse into drinking, Ben remained sober throughout treatment.

Figure 13. Ben's Problem Severity Ratings

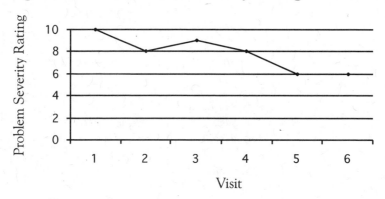

Figure 14. Ben's Flexibility Profile

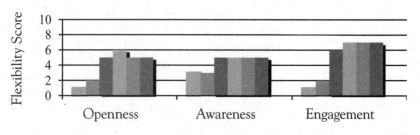

Flexibility Markers for Visits 1-6

Promoting Awareness

One of the clinician's immediate objectives was to teach Ben how to stay present and nonjudgmental when his self-lacerating thoughts, painful emotions, and intrusive memories showed up. Without this important skill, which strengthens the pillar of awareness, the chances were extremely high that he would start using again in an attempt to control these very uncomfortable experiences. To help Ben in this area, the clinician taught him the Body Scan.

Intervention: Body Scan

The Body Scan is a highly flexible intervention that can be used not only to teach present-moment awareness skills, but also to promote the client's ability to adopt a nonjudgmental stance toward painful private experiences. As such, it helps strengthen the pillars of both openness and awareness.

Clinician: So how do you want to experience being sober? I mean so it doesn't seem as worthless as it does now.

Ben: Making the worthless time seem more worthwhile? I never thought about it that way. Right now I'm just struggling to make it to the end of each day because I feel so awful.

Clinician: Awful? So what shows up when you aren't doing anything, when the time feels worthless?

Ben: Shows up? Nothing shows up. It's just so boring and dull that I want to scream and hit the walls... Is that what you mean?

Clinician: I just wonder what you experience when everything slows down and there's nothing to distract you. What shows up inside your skin?

Ben: I don't know. I never hang around that long.

Clinician: Okay, then let's look for it right now.

Ben: What do you mean look for it? Here? Now?

Clinician: Yeah, would you be willing to try that?

Ben: I guess so.

Clinician: Just close your eyes and lean back for a while. See if you can hang on to whatever shows up and just sit back and watch, like it's a 3-D movie with sensations… Now I want you to just notice your breathing for a while… Notice how your body moves when it breathes… Notice your chest rising and falling, your stomach moving in and out… You can feel the air passing in and out. Perhaps you'll notice that the air you inhale is slightly cooler than the air you exhale. Cold air in; warm air out. *(Pauses for a moment.)*

   Now I want you to shift your attention to what's going on between your ears, what your brain is doing right now… See if you can watch it flow, just like you just did with your breathing… Just observe what's going on inside your mind, any thoughts you are having, perhaps memories that are showing up or emotions that present themselves. See if you can just be an observer of whatever shows up *(Pauses for a moment.)*

   While doing this, see if you can pay attention to what you experience in your body…maybe in your stomach, chest, arms, or legs. *(Pauses for a moment.)*

   Now I want you to shift your attention to the sounds outside your body. See if you can remember what you'll see in front of you when you open your eyes. When you have a picture of it, you can open your eyes whenever you're ready. *(Pauses.)*

   So, how was that?

Ben: Weird, weird crap.

Clinician: Weird? Was what you experienced weird, or was it just that doing the exercise seemed weird?

Ben: Seriously weird stuff bubbling in my body.

Clinician: Okay, were you able to take a look at the bubbling stuff?

Ben: I was able to watch it, but it wasn't easy. Why should I?

Clinician:	What's bubbling inside of you?

Ben: *(Pauses and looks down.)* Everything that hurts, man—where I am in life, how I'm doing right now, the fact that I've lost a family and will never get to see my child, how people look at me and judge me. I'm a loser, a junkie, and a drunk. I want to get high and stop feeling this.

Clinician: Wow, those are harsh words. Sounds like this stuff has been around for a while—the bubbling crap and the craving to escape, I mean.

Ben: Yeah… But usually I only experience it briefly. I've always turned it off with speed or booze. Now it's parked inside my skull. It's really bad at night. I can't sleep because the horror show never shuts down. I was so close to getting hammered last week, just so I could get some sleep!

Clinician: Okay, I see. And even though your brain told you to get hammered, you were still able to make a choice that came from your values, right? Just like a few minutes ago, when you did something completely different than what your brain was telling you to do.

Ben: The weird crap and my brain are a nasty team.

Clinician: And then there's you, the person who's there to see the weird crap and the brain that are working together and conspiring to make you run.

Promoting Openness

Being able to stay present when painful internal material showed up would be extremely helpful for Ben. But he also needed help learning what to do with his stuff, how to carry it, so to speak. To help promote openness, the therapist used the Box of Stuff intervention.

Intervention: Box of Stuff

The Box of Stuff intervention is a powerful physical metaphor that helps clients make direct experiential contact with an important FACT paradox: that choosing to make direct contact with unwanted and distressing private experiences can actually make those experiences feel less toxic and easier to carry.

Clinician: What if there were ways of carrying your bubbling crap so it wouldn't push you around as much?

Ben: How? What do you mean, carrying it?

Clinician: What if the biggest problem isn't the bubbling crap itself but how you carry it? Let me show you. (*Picks up a box full of papers.*) Think about this box as something unwanted that I have to carry around. It has all kinds of ugly stuff in it, like the thought *I'm an addict and always will be*, the shame you feel about all the people you've ripped off, and the thought that you blew it and will never see your child. There is some really bad stuff in here—some really hurtful stuff. How would I carry this box if I wanted to hold on for more than just a couple of minutes? Would I hold it out at arm's length because I don't want to see what's in it?

Ben: Okay, I see what you mean. No way would that work—not in the long run.

Clinician: (*Brings the box close to his body.*) If I hold it in close, I can carry it a lot longer, *and* I have to be willing to be in contact with what's in the box because I can see every little piece of paper that's in there.

Ben: So keep your enemies close, is that what you're saying?

Clinician: If the goal is to avoid your bubbling crap and that's the only thing that matters, then you don't care how long you can last and you hold this box as far from yourself as you can. As you told me before, you put up with your stuff for only so long, then you go out and use. If your goal is to be able to last a lifetime, then how you carry that box of bad stuff is all-important. Have you had a lot of chances to make a choice like this?

Ben: Well, kind of. In jail, I noticed that when I sat down and let the tsunami of pain wash over me, which I did when hope failed me, it sometimes kind of relieved the pain. Is that what you mean?

Clinician: If you can bring up the box of stuff on purpose and practice holding it close, maybe you can see something about it you haven't seen yet. Instead of having it show up randomly on its own, you can invite it to show up so you can practice carrying it. I'm guessing there will be no shortage of opportunities to practice carrying this in a different way.

Ben: Yep, it's around all the time. I can easily pick it up, but I'd hesitate to do so.

Clinician: "And"—You can easily pick it up, *and* you hesitate to do so. Would you be willing to try this on your own, say three times a day for ten to fifteen minutes? Just let your crap be there in your head and carry it around? Would that be possible?

Ben: I can't make any promises. Can I call you or come in if I get cravings to use that I can't control?

Clinician: Sure. And here's another strategy: you could put cravings to get high in that box and carry them around too.

Promoting Engagement

Prior to the fifth session, Ben started binge drinking after he made a mistake at his new job in a machine shop. He was sharply criticized by his supervisor, and that elicited some strong cravings to get drunk. He started drinking after work and continued to drink for four days. He arrived at the counseling session looking dirty, disheveled, and hungover. Ben's commitment to his valued life direction was clearly suffering, so the clinician opted to work on strengthening the pillar of engagement to help Ben solidify his commitment to staying sober in service of his larger life values.

Intervention: Scales of Choice

Scales of Choice is an intervention that promotes engagement by focusing on clients' ability to choose between radically diverging life directions. Regardless of the choice made, there will always be "reasons" for choosing the other life course, even if it involves the use of old, ineffective strategies.

Ben: Oh, shit… I screwed up; I knew it would end like this.

Clinician: What happened? You look like something the cat dragged in.

Ben: Damn. I'm just not a person you can count on. People hate me, and I don't blame them. But this was not my fault.

Clinician: What wasn't your fault?

Ben: The machine—the drill got stuck and the shaft was crooked. I didn't know what to do. I got really scared. Then the machine punched the holes wrong and the foreman shouted at me. I felt like I was seven years old again and my dad was coming after me. I just wanted to disappear.

Clinician: So, since this happened, what have you been up to?

Ben: I got some vodka, went home, and started drinking. I don't remember much, but it was awesome to get rid of everything I was feeling. Time flies when you drink like that. On Saturday I ran out of booze, but I called a friend who brought more. I'm really sick because I'm hungover and my stomach is killing me from drinking so much. When I woke up this morning, I decided it was time to stop and come in for help.

Clinician: What strategies did you use when you felt like a seven-year-old and the foreman was yelling at you?

Ben: What's with this strategy thing? I couldn't take it. I've been counting the days knowing that something like this would eventually happen.

Clinician: Okay, so your bubbling crap showed up and your mind said, *This is too hard; you have to run and hide from this bad stuff. Go get drunk and you'll feel better.*

Ben: What do you mean? I'm a drunk, a junkie, a loser. This is what I always do.

Clinician: Sitting there feeling like a bad little boy, you had a choice to make, and you were weighing your options. Imagine that I have one of those old-fashioned balance scales here in my hand. On one side is *I'm a drunk, a junkie, a loser. This won't work. You can't trust anybody. It was not my fault. It was only a matter of time.* Is there more?

Ben: What do you mean more?

Clinician: More reasons to go get drunk.

Ben: Yes, I craved getting drunk like I used to, when I could just say screw it, get loaded with friends, and pass out.

Clinician: So, your mind came up with a lot of good reasons for choosing to get drunk. Let's call my left hand "checking out." Then, let's call my right hand "checking in." Can you come up with anything to put on this side of the scale?

Ben: Come on, stop playing head games!

Clinician: How about being a father for your child and having a family? How about having a job and being able to support yourself? Would it be okay if I put those reasons on this side of the scale?

Ben: Whatever.

Clinician: So, which of these two sides carries more weight for you, Ben? I'm not saying you should do one or the other. You get to choose.

Ben: *(Points to the checking in side of the scale.)* What have I done? What should I do now? My life is chaos again.

Clinician: Maybe the first step is to go to work tomorrow and talk to the foreman. See if you still have a job.

Ben: Okay, that's what I'll do. And you won't report me to my probation officer?

Clinician: Well, you aren't drunk right now and you're choosing to go back to work. I'd say that works for me.

Ben: Yes. Damn right it works.

Clinician: What about the choice to use or not use alcohol again? Has the bubbling crap been showing up and trying to tell you what to do?

Ben: Boy, has it ever. I've been a mess all weekend. I've barely slept an hour at a time. My mind is going crazy about all this. I keep going over and over the mistakes I've made and now I'm making them again. I just feel like somehow I'm going to blow it again and go back in the hole.

Clinician: So your mind is taking you off into the future again, and it isn't a pretty sight. What's the worst thing that can happen to you in the here and now?

Ben: The worst thing? Not being allowed to see my kid and being rejected and judged by Christina again. She doesn't know about any of this, but if she did, that would be the end.

Clinician: Okay, and how would that go down?

Ben: That would be hell on earth. I would probably relapse and start doing drugs again and end up in jail.

Clinician: That tells me that you're solidly on the side of the checking in side of the scale—that it's really important to you to be a father and maybe even a life partner.

Ben: I don't understand. What do you mean? I've been drinking nonstop for days.

Clinician: Yes, and your drinking is designed to protect you from the pain of failing. Getting high isn't what you stand for here. The more you drink, the more it tells me how badly you want to be a father and life partner.

Ben: I guess I should clean up my act and make contact with Christina so I can see Phillip again.

On a Final Note

Working effectively with clients who have substance use issues can be a daunting task. In general, FACT views addictive behaviors as a form of emotional avoidance. Long-term patterns of substance abuse almost invariably create a disconnection from personal values, so in most cases the FACT approach with such clients is to first focus on and help them get in contact with their values. This usually creates a healthy anxiety and increases the client's motivation to do something different. As Ben's case shows, there's no guarantee that simply being sober will automatically put the person back in contact with valued life directions. Often, clients in recovery develop mood problems just like Ben did. These mood problems, such as depression (numbing) or anxiety (distraction), may function as subtle and more socially acceptable forms of emotional avoidance.

General Pointers about Using FACT with Clients with Substance Use Issues

Disease and illness models or interpretations of addictive behaviors not only are scientifically questionable, but also allow few avenues for radical change. After all, if you have a disease, then you're sick, and it usually takes quite a while to heal a chronic illness.

It is important to look beyond various forms of substance abuse and instead focus on their function. Refocusing the conversation on what clients are trying to accomplish mentally or emotionally by using substances creates many more pathways to radical change. It is also important to empower clients with the right to choose to use or not use, based on their personal values. When clients have a long history of addictive behavior, it is often a good idea to start therapy with a discussion of their values and then look at the costs of addictive behaviors in terms of the ability to move in the direction of those values.

Looking at substance abuse and addiction as forms of emotional avoidance also tends to decrease stigma, from both therapist and client. As Ben's case demonstrates, undermining self-stigmatizing behavior is a crucial target of treatment. Like Ben, most addicted clients have a story that explains their continued problems with substances. These stories can seem quite plausible and may help take some stigma off the client (for example, "my dad and brothers are alcoholics," "I was abused as a child," or "I hate myself"). Don't get caught up in the content of the story. Instead, respond to the client's self-narrative in a nonjudgmental, compassionate, curious way, implicitly modeling an accepting stance for the client.

Another difficulty arises when therapists use the idea of choice in a coercive way. Either blaming the client for making bad choices or implying that you know what the better choice is for the client is likely to make discussions about choice feel aversive, rather than empowering. In FACT, choice is centered on personal integrity, and is not used as a form of social control.

Chapter 9

Playing It Safe: FACT with an Adult Survivor of Sexual Abuse

It is madness to try to be who you were.

— *A trauma survivor*

Studies suggest that about 20 percent of all women in the United States are victims of either childhood sexual abuse or incest. Although men are also victimized, the overwhelming majority of abuse victims are female (Tjaden & Thoennes, 1998). Approximately 40 percent of women surveyed in a primary care clinic reported some form of childhood sexual contact, and among that 40 percent, approximately one in six reported being raped (Walker, Torkelson, Katon, & Koss, 1993). Sexual abuse survivors exhibit a wide range of physical, emotional, and social impairments, including chronic pelvic and abdominal pain, mixed depression and anxiety, post-traumatic stress symptoms, addiction, obesity, headaches, insomnia, and sexual dysfunction. It is safe to say that no single life event has a more profound impact on the long-term welfare of a child than being the victim of sexual abuse. Survivors of abuse often seek help from physicians, social service workers, or mental health clinicians for their long-standing and complex health and mental health problems.

FACT is an excellent approach for adult survivors of abuse because it doesn't take the position that a "bad" history inevitably means clients are fated to live dysfunctional lives. However, among clients with a history of trauma, the residual elements of traumatic events (memories, thoughts, emotions, and physical sensations) are understandably part of their present-moment experience. These experiences can be painful and provocative, as violations of trust, lack of safety, and misuse of power are almost impossible for an abused child to integrate or understand. Abused children quickly learn that emotional and behavioral avoidance strategies can reduce fear, anxiety, and possibly the potential for more victimization. In early adolescence, many abused children convert to more adult avoidance strategies, such as drug and alcohol use and sexual promiscuity. These numbing strategies help control trauma-related anxiety but come with the cost of behavioral problems, such as addiction or unplanned pregnancies.

This detour into early adulthood is costly in another important way: Abuse survivors never get the opportunity to learn how to effectively relate to their own history or the emotions it provokes. Instead, they live in a story that explains both the necessity of avoidance and the consequences that will ensue if they engage in life activities; for example, "People can see I'm damaged and look down at me, "To avoid humiliation, I need to avoid people," "I don't deserve to get good things in life," or "No matter what I do, I will lose out." This pattern of widespread avoidance creates a world that is, in some ways, just as traumatic as the childhood events that set it into motion.

Case Example: Gloria

Gloria, a thirty-four-year-old married mother of two boys, ages eight and ten, was referred by her doctor because of increasing problems with headaches and chronic GI problems. She had seen a variety of medical specialists and undergone many tests without any physiological causes for her problems being uncovered. Her doctor was concerned that anxiety and stress might be triggering her physical symptoms. Gloria had been experiencing headaches almost daily and reported that they were extremely painful: 7 to 8 on a 10-point pain scale. She was also suffering from what she described as gut-wrenching pain in her stomach and abdomen and described herself as being tied up in knots physically, with lots of general aches and pains on a daily basis.

She also reported that she had been experiencing problems with anxiety that had worsened significantly over the previous six months. Gloria's husband had worked the night shift at his job for many years and was responsible for taking their children to various school and after-school events. Gloria avoided as many of these out-of-home activities as possible, leaving that part of parenting to her husband. Gloria also avoided driving unless someone was with her due to concern that she could have an anxiety attack and get into an accident. She also experienced extreme fearfulness around people and tried to avoid going out of her house.

Recently, her husband's work schedule changed and he had to work days, putting Gloria in the position of having to manage her children's transportation needs. She had been asking friends and family members to do the driving for her but worried that they were getting tired of her requests. Gloria stated that her husband was very supportive of her and that they had remained close. Although she'd kept in touch with friends dating back to her high school days, she seldom saw them because she feared they would see how messed up she was.

Gloria reported that she had been sexually abused as a child by several different perpetrators. Her mother was addicted to drugs, was physically abusive of Gloria, and frequently brought strange men home with her. Several of these strangers had sexual contact with Gloria, often after her mother had passed out. Gloria became dependent on alcohol as a young teenager and left home when she was sixteen. She stopped drinking when she became pregnant with her oldest child and has been sober since then. Through much of her adult life, she has slept poorly because she didn't feel safe in the dark and because of nightmares. She received trauma counseling on several occasions and had also been treated with a variety of antidepressant and mood stabilizing medicines but didn't feel that she had benefited much from those treatments.

Focusing Questions

Given Gloria's long history of isolation and avoidance behavior, the clinician wants to quickly engage her in determining what "better" would look like. This will help clarify her change agenda and highlight the tension between what she's seeking (emotional control) and a better alternative (acceptance).

1. What Are You Seeking?

The clinician allows Gloria to describe her current situation briefly, then shifts the focus to what Gloria hopes to achieve via her current strategy of avoidance.

Clinician: I'm really glad that you took the step of coming in to seeing me. Dr. Yeager is very concerned about your physical health and the effects stress might be having on your body. Can you tell me a little more about what's going on?

Gloria: I'm a mess. My stomach hurts all the time, and it's hard to even eat. I have headaches almost daily. I'm very concerned that there's something wrong with my health. My doctor keeps telling me that my health is fine and that stress is what's causing all these symptoms. Plus, my anxiety attacks are getting so bad that I'm beginning to have them in my bedroom, where I used to feel safe.

Clinician: So, not only do you have a lot of physical discomfort, but now your anxiety has started to show up in places where it promised it wouldn't bother you?

Gloria: Yes, and I'm getting scared because if my anxiety attacks start happening anywhere at random, I don't know what I'm going to do. I need help.

Clinician: Gloria, if you can, try to complete this sentence for me: "I will know that I'm better when…."

Gloria: When I can feel safe in my house again and not have anxiety there. I don't want to have to deal with anxiety everywhere I go. I already can hardly go anywhere unless someone is with me. I just freak out.

Clinician: So you would be pretty satisfied with our work if you could go back to your earlier arrangement with your anxiety. It owns the world outside your home, and you own the world inside. Is that correct?

Gloria: Yes. That sounds pretty pathetic, but that's where my life is at. I've been through a lot of bad things, and I've been anxious since I was a kid. With everything that's happened to me, this is just the way my life is. I don't see myself ever not being anxious; there's just too much stuff I have to deal with every day.

Gloria's responses quickly establish that her overarching goal is to create safety: safety from flashbacks, safety from the evaluations of other people, and safety from feeling vulnerable. She's linking her problems with anxiety to childhood events in a story that makes it inevitable that she will always be messed up. Given that, her fallback position is to try to manage the damaging impacts of her anxiety.

2. What Have You Tried?

Next, the clinician wants to explore the different tactics Gloria has used to try to feel safe.

Clinician: It sounds like one of the strategies you've used is to avoid situations that might trigger anxiety. What kinds of situations can set you off?

Gloria: Basically, any time I leave my house I feel anxious, and some situations make it worse. I can't go into a grocery store during busy times of the day. I would freak out. I can't drive by myself; I have to have my husband with me. My two boys are on soccer teams, but I almost never go to their games or watch them practice. There are too many people, and if I started to get anxious, I would be too far away from home. I can't go into a movie theater, and even restaurants freak me out, so I almost never go out to eat with my husband.

Clinician: Are there other strategies besides avoiding situations that you've tried to help make your situation better?

Gloria: I used to drink a lot when I was younger. That was really the only way I could get away from the anxiety. I still had anxiety and flashbacks about things that happened to me as a child, but for some reason they weren't as bad. But I was headed down the wrong path—going in the direction my mother went—and I decided to stop when I got pregnant with Peter, my oldest boy. Now I just try not to think about the bad stuff that happened when I was a kid. It just makes my anxiety worse. I've been in therapy several times, trying to get over this stuff, but I don't think it has really helped.

3. How Has It Worked?

Gloria's strategies are nearly all predicated on the necessity of avoiding contact with her intrusive memories and painful feelings, yet she doesn't seem to be in contact with the real-world results of these strategies. They don't seem to quell her anxiety, so the clinician's next task is to draw Gloria's attention to this paradox.

Clinician: It sounds as though, despite your best efforts to control your anxiety, things aren't improving. Whereas before you felt safe in your home, now you're starting to have anxiety attacks there. Would you say that over the last five years your anxiety has gotten better, stayed about the same, or gotten worse?

Gloria: It's getting out of control. That's why I came in to see you. I didn't want to. I feel anxious just being here talking with you. I feel embarrassed talking about this with someone who's almost a complete stranger.

Clinician: I'm really, really glad that you came in to see me today. That was a very courageous step on your part. I know that you're in a lot of pain, and I'll try my very best to help you figure out how to make your life work better. It seems like you're in some kind of strange loop here.

Gloria: What do you mean by "strange loop"?

Clinician: Well, on the one hand, you're determined not to have anxiety, and you've been very good about avoiding situations that produce anxiety. You've followed this strategy for a long time, and if it was going to work, you'd think that you would have less anxiety now. But you're telling me that you feel more anxious than ever and that things are getting out of control. Is it possible that this strategy of avoiding your anxiety is actually, strangely, creating anxiety?

Gloria: You mean I'm making my anxiety worse by trying to avoid it?

Clinician: You're not trying to make your anxiety worse. You're trying to make it better. No one wants to be anxious. But what does your experience tell you here? Has your anxiety actually gotten better over time, or is it getting worse?

Gloria: I guess it's getting worse. Are you saying I should ignore my anxiety? Because that would be really hard to do. I think my anxiety would just take off, and I worry that I might go insane.

Clinician: That's a very alarming thought your mind just gave you: *Let your anxiety show up, and you'll go insane.* Who will you trust here? Your mind says that you can control anxiety and fear by staying out of situations that trigger them, by not thinking certain kinds of thoughts or dwelling on memories, but your experience says that the more you avoid situations, the more anxious and fearful you get. So what are you going to trust here: what your mind is telling you, or your actual experience?

Gloria: I need to do something different because this isn't working. But what should I do instead?

Clinician: I don't know. But I think we can agree on this: If you keep using the same strategies you've been using, you'll probably keep getting the same results you've been getting.

Gloria: You mean this is hopeless?

Clinician: I don't mean that you're hopeless as a person; it's just the strategy you're using that's hopeless. It's bound to fail, no matter how long you use it.

4. What Has It Cost You?

Gloria's chronic problems with stress, sadness, and anxiety are the direct result of following her avoidance strategies, and her pervasive reliance on avoidance has produced other significant real-world consequences that Gloria is minimizing. This is Gloria's leverage point and can help create the motivation needed if she is to change tactics.

Clinician: Gloria, you looked a little sad when you were talking about your kids and how your anxiety has affected them. What was going on for you as you talked about them?

Gloria: I feel like I've failed as a mother, that I'm teaching them all the wrong things. They plead with me to come watch them play. Sometimes I promise them that I'll go to a game. But when it gets close to time to go, I get so anxious and jittery that I just can't do it. I have to make an excuse. But they know I'm making something up, and I can see the disappointment in their faces.

Clinician: I'm wondering: Are there similar impacts with your friends or your husband?

Gloria: My husband and I have been married for ten years, and we've never seen a movie together. I can't handle being in a dark place like a theater. Over the years, we've pretty much stopped being social with his friends unless they come over to our place. If he wants to go out to eat, I usually find an excuse not to go.

Clinician: It sounds like a hidden cost of this whole battle with your anxiety and fear is that your key family relationships aren't what you'd like them to be. That must make you very sad.

Gloria: *(Tears up, looks down, and pauses.)* Yeah, very sad indeed.

Setting the Stage for Radical Change: What Kind of Life Would You Choose?

It is clear at this point that her deteriorating relationships with her husband and children are a sore spot for Gloria. This suggests that she has some deeply held values about family that could be used to create an alternative way of approaching her need for safety.

Clinician: Gloria, let's imagine that you have a magic wand and you can just wave it at this situation and live the kind of life you want to live, with no impediments. What would your life look like if that magic happened?

Gloria: Well, for sure I'd go to my boys' soccer practices and games. I actually like soccer and maybe would help out at the practices or games. I would go out to dinner with my husband and might even try to go to a movie with him. I know that he's very frustrated about how this has messed up our alone time. It would be good to get that back.

Clinician: Very cool! I can see in your eyes that these are life goals that matter to you. These are the things that would create a sense of vitality and life meaning for you.

Gloria: The problem is, I can't do any of this because of my anxiety.

Clinician: Exactly. Well said.

Choosing Direction: The True North Exercise

At this point, the clinician wants to clarify the main leverage point in this interaction: that Gloria isn't behaving in a way that's consistent with her values in regard to her children, her husband, or her friends. It has already been established that her anxiety isn't being controlled and that she isn't feeling safer in any sense. Her health is compromised, and she's more anxious than ever. The question is whether Gloria wants to keep traveling in the same unworkable direction. The clinician uses the True North Exercise (see Figure 15) to explore this and begin a discussion about what Gloria could do differently.

Clinician: (Holds out a True North Worksheet.) Let's imagine that life is kind of like taking a long journey. You set your sights on some life destination, and the goal is to keep traveling in that direction. You have a life compass heading, so to speak. Let's say that when you're on track and headed in the right life direction, that's true north. So, here I've written what your true north is. It includes all of the things you've told me you'd like your life to be about: being involved with your kids, spending more quality time with your husband, and reconnecting with friends. Now, let's check your actual heading. On this compass, mark the direction that you're currently traveling.

Gloria: (Marks the compass at 160 degrees.) Well, this is hard to do. This is kind of pathetic, actually.

Clinician: So you aren't heading in the direction of your values. I know it can be painful to see that. The goal for me here is just to help you identify where you're starting from, because you can only start to change direction from where you are, not where you'd like to be. What would it take for you to change this heading, even if just a couple of degrees back in the direction of true north?

Gloria: I guess I have to learn to deal with my anxiety and fear and not feeling safe.

Clinician: And your experience says you can't deal with this stuff by avoiding it, right?

Gloria: I guess not, but the very idea of not trying to feel safe is already making me anxious right now!

Figure 15. Gloria's True North Worksheet

What are your values?

- *Being a positive role model for my kids*
- *Being more involved with my kids and their activities*
- *Spend quality time with my husband*
- *Connecting with friends*

What are your current strategies, and are they working?

- *Avoiding going out to dinner and movies*
- *Backing out on promises to my kids*
- *Staying at home to be safe and hiding out in my room*
- *Not seeing friends in order to avoid being seen as a mess*

What skills will you need to make the journey?

- *Finding better ways to cope with anxiety and fear*
- *Learning how to safely feel not feeling safe*

Clinical Issues

1. **Openness** (Accepts private events without struggle? Notices and lets go of unworkable rules?)
   Following rules that being safe means anxiety must be absent; that anxiety will run away with her and make her crumble.

2. **Awareness** (Able to be present? Aware of private experiences? Able to take perspective? Shows compassion for self and others?)
   Seems quite self-aware and has some perspective but is overidentified with her self-narrative of being broken and fated to live a marginal life.

3. **Engagement** (Clear values? Can organize for effective action? Can obtain reinforcement? Sufficient interpersonal skills?)
   Has powerful values about being a wife, mother, and friend, but these are being overwhelmed by rules.

Case Formulation: Four Square Tool

As shown in Figure 16, Gloria's Four Square Tool, her responses suggest that her behavior is organized around two main rules. One is that to preserve her "sanity," she must avoid any situation, interaction, or activity that might trigger anxiety. The second rule is that leaving her anxiety unchecked or uncontrolled will be toxic, having a negative impact on her ability to function and leading to further social humiliation and rejection. Most of her public behaviors are organized around this rule, so a key target for the clinician is to get Gloria to use more approach behaviors. To do so, Gloria must learn detachment and acceptance skills that will enable her to simply stand in the presence of her anxiety, fear, and ideas about safety and accept them for what they are (activities of the mind), not what they advertise themselves to be (life mandates).

Figure 16. Gloria's Four Square Tool

		Workability	
		Not working **(do less)**	**More workable** **(do more)**
Behavior	**Public**	• *Asking friends and family to drive kids to school and activities* • *Not going out with husband* • *Lack of participation in social activities* • *Staying at home and hiding out in her bedroom*	• *Making sure her children get to school and get to participate in after-school sports* • *Trying to spend quality time with kids and husband at home* • *Going to therapy and following up on health care needs*

	Private	• *Following rules*
		  1. *Anxiety is toxic and must be controlled.*
		  2. *She can't do important life activities if anxiety is present.*
		• *Habitually criticizing herself for not performing up to her standards*
		• *Habitually identifying with a self-story of being broken*
			• *Being very connected with values about being a good mother*
			• *Valuing intimacy with her husband*
			• *Having some ability to take perspective on her difficulties*

Treatment Summary

The clinician saw Gloria three times over a span of six weeks, and Gloria made remarkable progress. By the end of this brief treatment, she was regularly taking her sons to soccer practice and had attended a couple of games. She surprised her husband by scheduling a movie and dinner out for their tenth anniversary. She also engaged in other "unsafe" out-of-home activities without fleeing anxiety-producing situations. She reported that her anxiety gradually diminished in intensity during these activities. As Figure 17 shows, her severity ratings for her problem (defined as not functioning as a parent, wife, and friend) decreased dramatically. As Figure 18 shows, she made significant improvements in psychological flexibility, most notably in her ability to be aware and engaged. Not surprisingly, Gloria's physical symptoms also improved markedly over the course of therapy. The frequency of her headaches decreased, as did her abdominal pain.

Figure 17. Gloria's Problem Severity Ratings

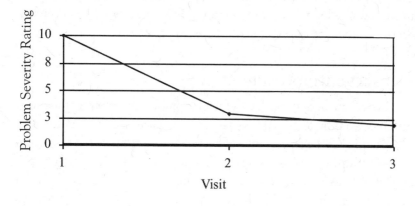

Figure 18. Gloria's Flexibility Profile

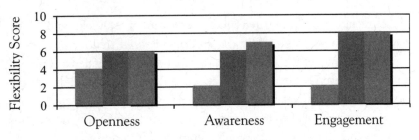

Flexibility Markers for Visits 1-3

Promoting Awareness

Gloria's main problem was that she was unable to use her attention flexibly when her anxiety, negative thoughts, and memories showed up. Consequently, she would get "lost" in her struggle to control these experiences, resulting in them becoming more dominant and intrusive. The clinician wanted to use an intervention that would help Gloria keep perspective in the face of these provocative experiences.

Intervention: Magnetism

Physical metaphors can be useful for promoting both present-moment awareness and the ability to take perspective, particularly when the metaphor highlights the importance of keeping some distance from provocative or distressing private experiences when they show up. In this case, the clinician used the metaphor of magnetism because of Gloria's tendency to become absorbed in her anxiety and her associated self-narratives.

Clinician: Gloria, did you ever get a chance to play with magnets when you were in school, or even just goofing around as a kid?

Gloria: Yeah, I remember an experiment with magnets in science class in high school.

Clinician: Yeah, me too. Apparently one of the best ways to understand a magnetic field is to use a magnet with a tray of metal shavings. Probably 90 percent of us poor high school students had to do that experiment. Do you remember how it works? If you hold the magnet too close to the shavings, they just jump through the air onto it. But here's the really cool thing: If you hold the magnet at exactly the right distance from the tray, the shavings will move and become organized in a way that mirrors the invisible magnetic field that the magnet is generating. The magnet actually organizes the shavings in its own pattern.

Gloria: So if you get too close, the shavings cover the magnet, but if you find the right distance, the magnet organizes the shavings. That's pretty neat.

Clinician: I like to think of our attention as a kind of magnetic field. If we're too close to whatever is showing up inside, those thoughts and feelings can get so close that they seem to be part of us. But if we keep some distance, our attention can help us maintain control over our awareness and give us more perspective. When we don't get covered with all of those shavings, we can see other aspects of our experience. In a sense, coping with anxiety is really a war over who will control your attention. If your awareness gets too up close and personal with anxiety, it sticks to you like those metal shavings. The metal shavings might even have names on them, like "I'm damaged goods," "I'm letting my kids and husband down," or "I can't cope with anxiety if it shows up." What happens if you let your awareness get too close to those shavings?

Gloria: They stick to me and I can't get them off. That's what it feels like when I'm really anxious and spiraling out of control.

Clinician: Got it. So what do you think would happen if you were able to pull back and put your attention where you want to put it?

Gloria: I guess it would seem less urgent to do something to get rid of the anxiety or whatever is causing it.

Clinician: Right, you wouldn't feel defined or dominated by the anxiety, so the impulse to avoid or run away from it wouldn't take over. So let's take this one step further. What would happen if you held your attention at exactly the right distance from what you're most afraid of, like those thoughts or memories that you don't want or emotions that are painful?

Gloria: Hmm. Well, they wouldn't go away. I know you're going to tell me I can't get rid of them, so I'm not going to go there. But maybe it would change their pattern and how I relate to them. Is that it?

Clinician: Well, what does your experience tell you? How do you relate to those difficult thoughts, memories, and feelings now?

Gloria: I get totally caught up in them, and even when they aren't there, I'm always on guard against them. It's like I can't see anything except my anxiety.

Clinician: So you get covered up by your anxiety and all those other ugly experiences. In a way, it's like they define you, rather than the other way around. What if you held your ground and determined where you were going to put your attention?

Gloria: I've never really thought about it that way. I just assumed that those thoughts and feelings came at me and I had no choice but to fight and try to control them. But you're saying I do have a choice.

Clinician: Your attention and ability to step back and take perspective are yours to use as you like. You can let anxiety take over and get so close that you can't see anything else, or you can hold your ground and exert your magnetic field. You can't change the shavings, but you can change the location of your attention magnet.

Promoting Openness

Gloria had a very dense self-narrative that incorporated her extensive trauma history in a way that portrayed her present and future as dark, foreboding, and full of failure and rejection. She saw herself as, in effect, damaged goods and lucky to have any kind of life at all. The clinician wanted to get inside this narrative and figuratively pit it against Gloria's declared values. The clinician used two interventions to help accomplish this: Facing the Bully and Say It Slowly.

Intervention: Facing the Bully

Facing the Bully is a straightforward intervention for helping promote defusion from beliefs, mental rules, and self-stories. Basically, it involves recasting them as something like a playground bully who is forcing the client to behave in ways that are unworkable and self-defeating.

Clinician: When we were looking at your true north values, what messages appeared on the message board in your mind?

Gloria: That I will never be able to live that way because of my anxiety and emotional problems. I've lived with abuse all my life, and I can't expect much. People view me as an emotional cripple. Even my husband seems tired of me always struggling and making excuses, and my kids treat me like I'm damaged goods.

Clinician: So your anxiety is pushing you around, almost like a bully. Let's call your anxiety a "she bully." What is she threatening you with?

Gloria: She's telling me to not even bother, that I'll never be free of fear and anxiety.

Clinician: So she isn't just threatening to give you anxiety; she also tells you what to expect in the future.

Intervention: Say It Slowly

Say It Slowly is just one of many FACT interventions designed to promote defusion through the use of stilted or unnatural speech. In this case, defusion is created by having the client say difficult mental content out loud extremely slowly, so that the words lose their original meaning. Other variations on this intervention strategy include singing negative thoughts out loud, saying them in a silly cartoon character voice, or pretending that they are pets that can be taught to do tricks, such as rolling over, shaking paws, and so on.

Clinician: Can you stay in this room with me and your bully and just be aware that you are here, with me, right now, talking about what really matters to you? What shows up?

Gloria: (*Cries.*) That I'll never be normal. That I won't get what I want in life because I don't deserve it. That no matter what I do, in the end I will lose out.

Clinician: Can you just let that story be here right now? See it as a set of words on your mind's message board. I'd like to ask you to read the words out loud. As you read them, pronounce them very slowly, maybe leaving a couple of seconds between the words, like you forgot your glasses and are having trouble making out the words.

Gloria: (*Speaks very slowly.*) I won't get what I want in life. No matter what I do, in the end I will lose out. I'll never be normal.

Clinician: Now, repeat that for me, speaking very slowly, like you just did, five times in a row.

Gloria: (*Complies.*)

Clinician: How was that?

Gloria: That was weird. I've never said those words out loud on purpose. I usually try to put those thoughts out of my mind.

Clinician: So, maybe when you don't think them, then they think you?

Promoting Engagement

Gloria needed to connect with the legitimacy of her anxiety and fearfulness. Once these emotions were no longer being generated by avoidance, they could tell her that something personally meaningful was at stake. The clinician wanted to help Gloria make a connection between her anxiety and her values. This would legitimize her choice to endure anxiety and fearfulness in the service of living a vital life.

Intervention: Palm Up, Palm Down

Palm Up, Palm Down is a useful intervention for helping clients understand that engaging in valued actions requires that they be willing to accept the difficult or painful private experiences that often show up along the way. A similar intervention can be conducted with an index card, writing fears on one side of the card and values on the other.

Clinician: (*Holds hand out, palm down.*) Think about the top of my hand as all the things you're running from, trying to avoid, or scared of. What would you put here?

Gloria: Anxiety, fear, nightmares, sadness, and thoughts that I will lose out, that I don't deserve happiness. A really big one is being seen as weak and broken by others and being pitied.

Clinician: Cool. (*Turns hand palm facing up.*) Now, on this side are all things that you want to be about in your life. What goes here?

Gloria: I would like to be there for my kids, to be able to play with them, to be involved in their school or PTA, to build my relationship with my husband, to be a good friend, and maybe even to start a new career.

Clinician: (*Slowly turns hand over, back and forth.*) So, Gloria, is it possible that the flip side of everything that is important to you is also capable of producing what you are afraid of...and that the flip side of what you're afraid of is what's important to you? Could the situation be that you can't have one without the other—that they are like the front and back sides of a coin? No fear, no importance. No importance, no fear. Could we agree that doing almost anything that matters to you will bring its opposite? Could it be that when you choose to do what matters, you by necessity are inviting your fears to come along with you?

Gloria: Are you saying that when I do something I want to do, my bully is going to be there too?

Clinician: Isn't that your experience? You try to do something, or even think about doing something important, and—voilà!—there she is. Now here's the most important question of all: How are you going to use your attention magnet when she shows up?

Gloria: I'm going to keep enough distance that this stuff doesn't stick to me. At least I can try.

Clinician: Gloria, I'm wondering if you would be willing to do something to practice this. How about taking your sons to soccer practice one time between now and when we meet again. I'd like you to do that and invite your bully along for the ride. I'm guessing that you'll get many chances to practice using your magnet differently, and that's okay. Practice doesn't make perfect, but it does make permanent. If you don't practice using your attention magnet in situations that are important to you, it will be hard to learn how to do this quickly and purposefully.

Gloria: Well, I'm getting anxious just thinking about doing this even once. What if I panic out there and people see that I'm a basket case?

Clinician: This is good. Your bully is all cranked up because you're about to take your life back and disobey the story she's been feeding you. Now, what's important to you here: heading toward your true north, or controlling anxiety and feeling safe? You get to pick.

Gloria: I'll give it a try, but I'm not sure how I'll do.

On a Final Note

As Gloria's case demonstrates, even clients with a long history of dysfunction can experience transformative change in just a few sessions. In FACT, what matters isn't the content of the client's current private experiences or the content of the client's history. What matters is how clients hold their private experiences and personal history. There isn't a personal history so dark that it can't be held softly and accepted for what it is. On the other hand, all humans are capable of generating dysfunctional self-stories and being dominated by them. FACT seeks to remove the psychological dominance of this mental architecture so that clients can redirect their life energy into activities that dignify what it means to be human.

Gloria's case highlights how to address trauma-based mood complaints, including depression, anxiety, anger, and boredom. Emotions, memories, and physical reactions, even painful ones, are not the problem. The problem is trying to avoid making contact with those experiences. The more persistent the client's attempts to control or eliminate unwanted private events are, the more the client will experience those private events. Being willing to be anxious is, paradoxically, what makes anxiety less toxic. Likewise, being willing to be sad is what makes depression less toxic. In FACT, we want to help clients make direct contact with the futility of emotional control as a strategy for promoting personal health and well-being.

FACT employs metaphorical interventions to imbue small positive behaviors with larger-than-life personal meaning. When Gloria went to one of her sons' soccer practice, she wasn't just engaging in an exposure treatment, she was changing direction and starting to head toward her true north. The significance of this behavior was revealed in the domino effect it created. Before long, Gloria decided, on her own, to take her husband out to dinner and a movie, behaviors that may seem small on the human scale but that had huge personal meaning for her.

General Pointers about Using FACT with Adult Survivors of Childhood Trauma

When dealing with individuals with long-standing patterns of trauma-based avoidance, it is extremely important for the clinician to practice compassion and to appreciate the amount of courage it takes for clients to face previously avoided material. Choosing to stand in the presence of painful emotions and memories leaves clients vulnerable to the damage that supposedly was being prevented by following the avoidance agenda presented by the problem-solving mind: *If you keep this stuff from showing up in your life, you will be healthy.* When people overidentify with such rules, avoidance seems like the natural and right thing to do. Discovering that a long-practiced strategy is destined to fail can be very deflating and lead to more self-criticism, guilt, and associated mood problems. The clinician must lessen the emotional impact by clearly stating that it is the strategy that is hopeless, not the client. The clinician should express unbounded optimism in the client's ability to detach from unworkable rules and try something different.

With clients like Gloria, attempting to change long-standing patterns of avoidance using insight into personal history isn't likely to achieve much. Knowing how you got stuck doesn't tell you how to move forward. Responding to the literal content of the client's self-narrative can actually increase, rather than decrease, the client's conviction that the story is true. Our view is that self-stories are the by-products of the sense-making operations of language and that their meaning is socially determined. Therefore, it is more effective to play with the functions of language through interventions like Say It Slowly than it is to try to change the content of the story.

Chapter 10

Disconnected and Demoralized: FACT with a Depressed Elderly Woman

Pray that your loneliness may spur you into finding
something to live for, great enough to die for.

— *Dag Hammarskjöld*

L ife expectancy in many countries has increased consistently in
recent decades. In the United States, the proportion of people
over age sixty-five increased from 4 percent in 1900 to 12 percent
in 2000. Population experts estimate that by 2020 more than fifty million
Americans—about 17 percent of the population—will be at least sixty-
five years old (Meyer, 2001). Serving the health needs of this segment of
the population is already straining and will continue to strain govern-
ment assistance programs, and lack of timely attention to their mental
health needs is likely to only worsen physical health outcomes.

   The fact that aging is often accompanied by the loss of significant
others and friends, changes in social and family roles, and impairments

in physical and mental functioning makes it an emotionally and spiritually challenging process. Developmental psychologist Erik Erikson (1968) described the struggle of our older years as finding integrity versus despair. Older adults naturally reflect on life accomplishments and setbacks in an effort to make sense of life and to prepare for the end of life. The combination of changes in daily roles and reminiscing about and integrating the past can exact a significant emotional toll on the aging individual. However, older adults need not lose their independence and passion for life as they confront increased social, financial, and physical health problems.

Unfortunately, older individuals do not as a rule seek out traditional counseling services; they are far more likely to receive care from a primary care or social service provider. Thus, it is important to give them access to brief intervention services in primary care centers, assisted living facilities, and nursing homes. This population's need for psychological flexibility is no different than that of younger adults, although interventions must be crafted in keeping with the unique challenges associated with aging. To age well requires that people be open to change, be able to enjoy the present moment, and strive to live in accordance with personal values.

Case Example: Lawanda

Lawanda, a seventy-three-year-old Native American widow with three daughters, was referred to the social worker at her assisted living facility by her physician, Dr. Marks, because of concerns about depressed mood, sleep problems, and uncontrolled diabetes. Lawanda had moved to the facility nine months previously, when she had to stop driving due to problems with concentration. Recently, she had a disagreement with one of her daughters—the one who lives closest to her. She felt that her daughter had treated her grandson harshly by sending him to live with his father, about a hundred miles away, after he had been arrested for vandelism. Their disagreement developed into a major argument, and Lawanda walked out of her daughter's house in a huff. Lawanda was worrying about this situation at night and consequently slept poorly and felt tired during the day. To conserve energy, she started taking shorter daily walks.

Lawanda's diet was poor; she typically cooked a pan of canned biscuits on Sunday afternoon, along with a soup of some kind, and lived on these throughout the week. Her main activities were sitting by the window, reading, and watching television. She'd always been an active person, but she just didn't see the point anymore. Between the decline in her physical health, recent family problems, and severe financial stress, she felt life had less meaning for her. She denied having suicidal thoughts, explaining that she didn't believe in violence toward herself or others. However, she did believe in giving up on her health as a way of speeding up the process of ending her life.

Lawanda had dropped out of school at age fifteen and eloped to another state to marry her first husband. Both this marriage and her second marriage were marked by physical and mental abuse. Lawanda was bright and had succeeded at a variety of jobs, including factory work and floristry. She'd been able to support herself and her daughters during and after both of her marriages. She had received help for depression symptoms several times when she was in her thirties and forties and reported that the talking part of those treatments was better than the medications. The episodes of depression were usually triggered by major life stresses, including divorce, domestic violence, the deaths of loved ones, and back surgery. She began working as a hospital volunteer during her second marriage, and she'd maintained this activity until about two years ago, when her health began to decline. Lawanda liked being with people and missed her volunteer work. Lawanda explained that she'd always moved a lot and never really felt at home anywhere except near the ocean, and that she moved to her current location because it was near the ocean and near one of her daughters.

Focusing Questions

In the first interview, the clinician wants to explore Lawanda's view of her current life situation and what would make her feel that things were working better for her.

1. *What Are You Seeking?*

The clinician begins by trying to engage Lawanda in a discussion about her physical health problems, life stressors, and what she would like to gain from their work together.

Clinician: Dr. Marks thinks that stress is affecting your mood and your health. What do you think?

Lawanda: Dr. Marks wanted to change my diabetes medicines again and said she was concerned about me. I've lost my appetite and haven't been walking much, and my blood sugars aren't good. My blood pressure was up today too, and my heart rhythms are kind of off.

Clinician: Lots of things to worry about, sounds like.

Lawanda: I agree. You know, life is just one darn thing after another.

Clinician: What's the darn thing that's hitting you hard right now?

Lawanda: Well, it's my grandson, Eddy. He's sixteen, and he's been hanging out with some losers. He got locked up for breaking into a school when he and his friends were drinking. Kind of funny 'cause he never liked school that much.

Clinician: How did that make you feel?

Lawanda: Worried. His mother is my youngest daughter, and she's raised him and his sisters as a single mother for the past seven years. I don't care much for his father, and I thought my daughter might send Eddy down to live with his dad. I didn't want that and I told her so, but she did it anyway and told me it was none of my business. She was real sharp and hurtful. She has a tongue on her, that one. (*Looks down and starts to cry.*)

Clinician: I'd like to understand how you're feeling right now.

Lawanda: Like there's a big hole in my heart. It don't matter what I think. I'm a has-been in my grandson's life, and in my daughter's life too. If I died, it wouldn't make much difference to anybody... They'd just go on without me. That's the way it is. (*Pauses.*) How long is this going to take? I haven't eaten anything, and I need to get home and eat. Are you going to give me some medicine or what?

2. What Have You Tried?

Given Lawanda's strong avoidance response to the pain of psychological separation from her daughter, the clinician decides to move in the direction of exploring Lawanda's history of coping with conflicts with her daughter and her specific strategies for coping with the current conflict.

Clinician: I hope you can stay a few minutes more. I'd like to know more about how you and your daughter have made it through hard times in the past.

Lawanda: I can stay. (*Takes a plastic bag from her purse with a biscuit in it.*) I guess we have... I guess we just start acting normal over time...but not this time.

Clinician: Okay, I hear that, and I'd like to know what you do when things are normal between you and your daughter.

Lawanda: We talk on the phone when she's on her way home from work or in the evenings when she takes her walk after dinner. She tells me about her day and how the kids are doing. I talk to the kids on the phone when they're around. But it wouldn't seem normal for me to talk to her and not talk about my grandson, and she don't want me to say nothing about it, so it just can't be normal now.

Clinician: Okay, I guess things can't be normal right now, so you aren't trying to do the usual things and the situation is hurting you. I can see it causes you a lot of pain.

Lawanda: Yes, it does.

Clinician: When that pain is there, what do you do?

Lawanda: Well, I'm not a glutton for pain, so I try to do something that makes it better—like have a biscuit or watch a TV show. I never watched TV much until my health got bad.

Clinician: Anything else you do?

Lawanda: I guess I sometimes think about other times in my life when people have treated me badly, and then I feel worse. That happens more at night, so I get up and have a biscuit with jam and a big glass of chocolate milk. This calms me down some, and then I watch TV or listen to the radio or pray.

Clinician: You pray.

Lawanda: Yes, I pray every day…sometimes lots of times during the day, but I guess not so much lately.

3. How Has It Worked?

Lawanda seems to engage in a lot of activities that help her distract herself from how she's feeling. However, her emotions are still percolating beneath the surface and coming up in the form of depression and demoralization. The clinician wants Lawanda to make contact with the workability of her coping strategies.

Clinician: You're trying a lot of different things to try to cope, like watching TV and listening to the radio, having snacks, and praying. I'm not surprised to see that you're experimenting to find out what works, because you seem to be a pretty good problem solver. Let's take a minute to look at what you've tried and how it's working for you. Let's start with your snacking choices. Is that working for you in the sense of helping you feel better?

Lawanda: Only for the moment. Then I feel guilty and worry about what's happening inside my body, because I have diabetes and heart problems. You knew that, didn't you?

Clinician: Yes, that's one of the reasons I asked, and I think I understand what you're saying. The short-term reward for unhealthy snacks is comfort, but then you get the rebound sense of worry really pretty quickly. What about staying home a lot— is that helping you feel better?

Lawanda: Not really, maybe not even in the short term. And it isn't working in the long term because I'm feeling worse.

4. What Has It Cost You?

In short order, the clinician was able to help Lawanda articulate that the snacks she ate to comfort herself weren't helpful to her management of diabetes. This begins to address the question of costs. The clinician then draws out how excessive TV viewing is not only interfering with Lawanda's sleep but also reducing her energy level, which impairs her ability to take walks and socialize with other residents during the day.

Clinician: So, when you stay up late watching TV, does that influence how you feel about the problem with your daughter?

Lawanda: Well, if the show is good, I don't think about her.

Clinician: Okay. And how does staying up late influence you the next day?

Lawanda: Well, not so good I guess. I'm tired and don't want to go out, and I still feel bad about the situation with my daughter.

Setting the Stage for Radical Change: What Kind of Life Would You Choose?

The clinician wants to get a better sense of what Lawanda's values are with respect to her role as a grandmother and mother and how those values might serve as a leverage point for helping her change how she approaches interpersonal conflicts. Along the way, the clinician introduces the concept of workability and also discusses that some pain is inevitable when engaging in valued actions.

Clinician: Let's say my neighbor has a barking dog that wakes me two hours before I have to wake up most every morning. There are a lot of ways I could deal with this problem. I could call the Animal Control office and tell them I think the dog is neglected, or I could write my neighbor a letter threatening to call Animal Control. I could just keep steaming about it but do nothing. I could ask my neighbor to come over for tea to discuss the problem. One way to decide what to do is to focus on the result I want: to keep that dog from barking, right? I don't care what the impact on my neighbor is.

Lawanda: (Nods.)

Clinician: Another way to decide is to look at what my values are in being a neighbor. By values, I mean the principles I want to live by. With regard to the problem of the barking dog, I would ideally like to show respect to the dog, the dog's owner, and myself. Asking my neighbor to come over for tea to discuss the problem would be the most workable option if I was guided by my value of showing respect. While this strategy might be closer to what I believe in, it might be more difficult in the short run than some of the other options. The conversation with my neighbor might get a little tense, or I might still have the problem of the barking dog after we talk. Even so, it would probably work better for me in the long run than the other options because it's the neighborly thing to do. This is the way I like to think about how well something works: whether it's true to my values, not just whether it solves a problem. So I'd like to spend a little time clarifying the ideals or principles that are important to you in interacting with your grandson and daughter.

Lawanda: Well, I would want to be like you with the dog, to show respect, but it's also different, because I want to show my love to my daughter and grandson and show that I believe in them—and that I believe in them being able to show love to each other.

Clinician: Okay. It sounds like showing respect and love and confidence in them is your benchmark for deciding how well the things you are doing are working. *(Writes these values on a piece of paper and shows them to Lawanda for confirmation.)* Let's talk about strategies you could use to cope with this disagreement that also match your values benchmark. Let's start with your prayers. What do you do when you pray?

Lawanda: I think about the people or the problem I'm praying about, and then I think about love and caring being there. When I pray for my daughter, I pray for her to be brave and strong.

Choosing Direction: Life Path and Turnaround Exercise

The clinician wants to help Lawanda reframe her problem, recasting it as how she can behave in accordance with her values even while feeling disrespected and abandoned. This would place the responsibility for finding positive ways to cope more in Lawanda's hands, rather than requiring her daughter to change.

As can be seen in Figure 19, Lawanda describes her desired life direction of greater meaning as showing love, respect, and confidence in her family members and, more broadly, for people in general and ultimately all living things. The direction of exercising greater control but moving away from meaning involves behaviors that help her avoid feeling hurt and disrespected. Lawanda feels pulled in the direction of less meaning by her story of being right and her desire to avoid the pain of rejection. She can also see the costs: being lonely and feeling isolated from her family. Lawanda is able to identify behaviors that would tell her she's moving toward more meaning: talking with her daughter and grandson, but she isn't sure how to keep herself moving toward more meaning if she encounters obstacles. However, she does know that silence (turning off the TV) and spiritual practice would be helpful. She believes that prayer can help her better connect with her values.

Figure 19. Lawanda's Life Path

More Control	**More Meaning**
What do you want to control, avoid, or get rid of and how are you trying to do that?	What type of life would you choose if you could choose?
Feeling hurt, disrespected, and rejected by my daughter; watching TV, eating foods that aren't good for me	*Showing love, respect, and confidence in my daughter and grandson; showing respect for people in general and all living things; protecting my health*

1. Draw an arrow above the line to indicate where you are on your life path these days and which direction you're moving in.

2. What, if any, are the costs and benefits of pursuing control?
    Costs of "being right" is that I'm lonely. Benefit of not talking to my daughter is not getting hurt; cost is feeling isolated and unable to help my grandson. Benefit of watching TV and eating bad snacks is comfort; cost is being more lonely and disconnected and hurting my body.

3. What behaviors would tell you that you're moving toward more meaning in life?
    Talking with my daughter and grandson; talking with my neighbors and walking; taking better care of myself.

4. When you get stuck, how can you help yourself keep moving toward more meaning?
    I don't know. Maybe praying or going to church. Or maybe turning the TV off and listening to music.

5. Who or what helps you move in the direction of more meaning?
    I'm not sure. Maybe going to church—maybe the people there can help.

Case Formulation: Four Square Tool

The clinician completes a Four Square Tool (Figure 20) to create a broader picture of Lawanda's life context that can be used to develop an intervention to improve Lawanda's psychological flexibility. Lawanda's relative strength is in the pillar of awareness. While she is aware of her public behavior, she has more difficulty recognizing her thoughts and feelings. She isn't open to some of the thoughts and feelings that her current life context is provoking, and this is causing her to pull back from daily activities that could give her life meaning. She is paying a heavy price for following a common rule that often leads to unproductive conflict between parents and adult children: *If my children respect me, they will follow my good advice.* This rule is particularly powerful for Lawanda in the context of her grandson being sent to live with his dad, as she feels this will cause him to have more problems, while at the same time her grandson will also have less access to her helping hand. Lawanda is trapped in a invisible blanket of righteousness (*I am right and my daughter is wrong*) that doesn't protect her but instead causes her to become increasingly rigid and disengaged. This only contributes to what she is most afraid of: too much emotional distance from her daughter and grandson. Lawanda's disengagement, or avoidance, has also begun to generalize. Not only is she pulling back from her family, she's also pulling back from her social world, such as her church and friends and social activities at the assisted living facility.

Figure 20. Lawanda's Four Square Tool

		Workability	
		Not working **(do less)**	**More workable** **(do more)**
Behavior	**Public**	• *Staying home and watching television* • *Keeping to herself* • *Criticizing her daughter and telling her what to do* • *Buying unhealthy foods* • *Snacking on unhealthy foods when sad*	• *Calling her daughter and grandson* • *Going for walks* • *Going to church occasionally* • *Talking with neighbors occasionally* • *Praying to help herself feel better*

	Private	• *Criticizing herself for her failing health*
		• *Identifying with her self-story of being old and unwanted*
		• *Following rules:*
		  1. *Adult children should obey the parent and not doing so is disrespectful.*
		  2. *You can't show people how you feel because they don't care.*
			• *Connecting with values about being a grandmother and mother*
			• *Being able to focus on the present moment when asked*
			• *Being quite connected to her spirituality*

Treatment Summary

The clinician saw Lawanda five times during a four-month period. Her first follow-up visit occurred one week after her initial visit. Lawanda's other visits were two to four weeks apart. She attended all scheduled visits. The clinician's treatment goals included helping Lawanda find more workable strategies for addressing the conflict with her daughter and helping her develop greater psychological flexibility for coping with interpersonal conflict in general, as well as the challenges of aging. Figures 21 and 22 summarize Lawanda's changes over the course of the five visits. As Figure 21 indicates, the severity scores for her family problems declined consistently over the course of treatment. Figure 22 documents her improvements in openness, awareness, and engagement over the course of treatment.

Figure 21. Lawanda's Problem Severity Ratings

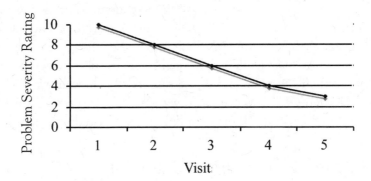

Figure 22. Lawanda's Flexibility Profile

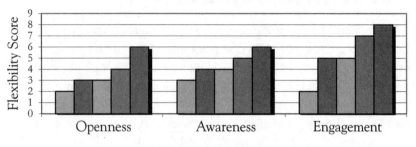

Flexibility Markers for Visits 1-5

Promoting Awareness

In the initial visit, the clinician targeted Lawanda's skills for being aware of her thoughts and feelings in the present moment. To that end, the clinician coached Lawanda in two interventions: Mindful Shopping and Being a Witness. As you'll see, the two interventions are closely interwoven. Although Mindful Shopping is the first topic discussed, Being a Witness must be fully developed before the client can engage in mindful activities. At the end of the session, the clinician also helped Lawanda brainstorm how she could get her day off to a good start, as described in the section "Promoting Engagement," later in this chapter.

Intervention: Mindful Shopping

Mindful Shopping is just one example of the many day-to-day activities that can serve as the basis for informal mindfulness practice. In this case the clinician chose grocery shopping because of Lawanda's health status and poor diet; however, different activities like mindful eating, dressing, or walking can be used depending upon the particular circumstances of the client.

Clinician: What's grocery shopping like for you?

Lawanda: I don't know. I shop for the bargains, particularly on things I like, like canned biscuits. Sounds terrible for a diabetic, but it's the truth.

Clinician:	If you were choosing foods that would promote a good start to your morning, what would you choose?
Lawanda:	Whole-grain bread, peanut butter, apples—I like apples too.
Clinician:	I'm going to make a note of that. (*Writes on a piece of paper.*)
Lawanda:	Good. That will help me remember.
Clinician:	I think it will take more than remembering; it really takes choosing with awareness in the grocery store. There are so many colors and sale signs. They can distract you, and it's easy to walk out with stuff you don't really want to eat rather than the food you wanted to buy to promote your health. I have an exercise that I'd like to teach you. If you can practice it every morning, I think you'll get good enough at it that you can use it at the grocery store to help you choose with awareness.
Lawanda:	Okay, you've got me curious now. What do you have in mind?

Intervention: Being a Witness

Being a Witness is an excellent intervention for helping clients develop mindful, present-moment awareness. To introduce this intervention to Lawanda, the clinician began by discussing the nature of thinking and feeling and how difficult it is to be a witness to one's own internal experience, particularly when those thoughts or feelings are troubling. Then the clinician explained how to do the exercise (see Figure 23 for the handout).

Clinician:	I recommend that you plan to sit for five or ten minutes every morning in a certain place in your home, sitting for the purpose of becoming more aware of your thoughts, your emotions, and sensations in your body.
Lawanda:	I usually sit in the living room in my easy chair. It's comfortable; that's where I watch TV.
Clinician:	Okay, you can sit in your easy chair. I want you to have the room quiet. The point of sitting is to notice what's happening

in your mind and your body…to just witness what's going on inside of you. This might sound easy, but it's actually difficult for most people. I've taught quite a few people about this, so I've developed this little handout to guide you through some of the details. Read through it and tell me what you think.

Lawanda: This sounds like meditation; I'll try it—couldn't hurt me.

Clinician: Good. I look forward to hearing how it goes. Once you've practiced this for a few days, try going to the grocery store and getting in a similar frame of mind before you shop. I'll be curious to see if that makes a difference in your experience at the store.

When she returned the next week, Lawanda said that she had found the witnessing exercise difficult, but she was sticking with it and had discovered that paying attention to her breath and to her hands was helpful. She said her mind was all over the place some mornings but sometimes seemed to slow down. She had gone grocery shopping and had deliberately slowed down the act of selecting food items, and she felt like this had helped her select foods that were better for her diabetes. She was eating toast with peanut butter for breakfast more often, and biscuits with jelly less often. She also reported that she had spent more time talking with friends at her assisted living complex and had started going to church again. In addition, she had called her daughter a couple of times, but had felt tense throughout the conversation and stewed about it afterward. One time she tried using the witnessing exercise after a call to her daughter and had noticed that she felt very sad about not being respected.

Promoting Openness

As noted earlier, Lawanda overidentified with a rule that her daughter should follow her "good advice." In order for Lawanda to develop more flexibility in her response to the conflict with her daughter, she needed to develop a new relationship to this unworkable rule. To that end, the clinician used two related interventions: Just Noticing, and Name It and Play with It.

Being a Witness

1. Try to practice this exercise at the same time each day, if possible. Set aside five to ten minutes. Start with five minutes and work your way up to ten, using a timer, if possible.

2. Turn off the television and radio.

3. Sit down and find a comfortable place for your hands, maybe palms up and in your lap. Try to maintain an awareness of your hands and keep your eyes open.

4. Notice your posture. Try to sit up straight. Imagine that your head is light and floating above your shoulders.

5. Take ten slow, deep breaths. Notice how the air enters your body and how it leaves…over and over again. Go back and check your hands and your spine. Are your hands relaxed? Is your back straight?

6. Continue to notice your breath and start to watch your mind.

7. Notice the quality of your mental activity. Is your mind going fast? Is it very busy? Is it anticipating when you'll stop doing this exercise and what you'll do next? Is your mind sorting through something that happened yesterday or a year ago? Is your mind lost in an emotional experience, like fear? Are you planning for the future or swept up in a fantasy? Does your mind feel dull or slow?

8. As you notice the quality of your mental activity, smile a half smile, like you might smile while watching a child who is busy, trying this and that, and oblivious to you watching.

9. Continue to watch your breath, your hands, your spine, and your mind, and also notice the rest of your body. Maybe you will notice sensations: hunger, pain in your back, heaviness in your chest, the feeling behind your eyes before you cry. Just notice, again with curiosity and acceptance.

10. When you space out and go into a daydream (and you will), go back to your breath, your hands, your spine, and your half smile and start noticing again.

Intervention: Just Noticing

Just Noticing is an intervention that both creates more awareness and promotes a detached, open stance toward distressing private experiences. In Lawanda's case, the clinician elected to use it in combination with another defusion exercise, Name It and Play with It, which will be described in the next section. The clinician wanted to begin by promoting Lawanda's awareness of thoughts and feelings that were pushing her around in interactions with her daughter.

Clinician: You've made some progress, taking steps in the direction you're choosing on your life path. Maybe we could build on that to work on what's going on with your daughter. Are you willing to do an experiment with me?

Lawanda: I guess so.

Clinician: Okay. What I want you to do is start talking about your daughter and how she responded to your advice. I'm going to write down some of what you say, and then we're going to look at it.

Lawanda: Okay. Well, like I told you, I told her not to send Eddy to live with his dad, and she did it anyway. I don't know why she won't listen to me. She didn't want to be married to that man, so I don't see how she could now decide that he could help raise Eddy.

Clinician: And your feelings?

Lawanda: Well, I'm ticked off. She's making a mistake, and she doesn't have to. If only she'd listen to me.

Clinician: Okay. Here's what I have. It's kind of a shorthand version, and I hope I have it right: "You told her; she didn't listen. She's making a mistake and you're mad."

Lawanda: That's pretty much it.

Clinician: Okay, so these thoughts and feelings turn up when you think about the problem with Eddy. Are there other thoughts and feelings that show up?

Lawanda: Well, sometimes I think she should treat me better, with more respect.

Clinician: Okay, I'm writing that thought down here too. And the feeling that goes with that one?

Lawanda: Kind of sad first, then I get mad.

Clinician: So now I've got sad and mad showing up alongside the thought that she should treat you better. Are there other thoughts and feelings that tend to come up when you think of this problem?

Lawanda: The thought that I'm not needed, not important. Of course, that hurts and makes me sad.

Clinician: I've written that down too. By the way, you're doing a great job of just noticing thoughts and feelings. I think practicing being a witness is helping you become more aware of thoughts and feelings. Are there any other memories or feelings coming along for the ride?

Lawanda: I'm remembering the things I used to hear from my first husband, cruel things like I was ugly and fat and didn't deserve to be treated right. Then he would shove me around or throw stuff at me.

Clinician: Wow, that sounds scary. It's interesting how that memory just kind of pops up with the other thoughts. I'll write that down here because it sounds like a powerful one. Next, we're going to come up with some nicknames for your thoughts and memories so you can call each one by name when you notice it.

Intervention: Name It and Play with It

Lawanda needed to learn skills that would allow her to be more mindful during disagreements with her daughter, even when her mind was racing. The clinician introduced the intervention Name It and Play with It to help Lawanda develop a more flexible relationship to her unworkable rules.

Here's the list of thoughts, feelings, and nicknames that the clinician and Lawanda generated:

Thought or Memory	Feeling	Nickname
I told her; she doesn't listen.	Mad	Mother knows best.
She should treat me better.	Sad, mad	Mother deserves better.
I'm not important.	Sad	Poor me.
My second husband saying that I'm ugly and don't deserve respect, shoving me around.	Afraid	Scared me.

Clinician: I'm cutting this list of nicknames up so that each nickname is on a separate small piece of paper. I want you to put them in a bowl and place it on a table near the chair where you practice being a witness. Every day, after you practice, I want you to choose one or two slips of paper and then play with them.

Lawanda: What do you mean, "play with them"?

Clinician: Well, you can use your imagination here. The idea is to read the words and find a way to be silly with them. So you could say them in a silly voice, sing them, or hold them while you do a funny dance.

Lawanda: That sounds pretty funny to me. I can try it.

Clinician: I think it might help you develop a different perspective on them, and that might help you get less upset and be a little more intentional when you're having a disagreement with your daughter.

Promoting Engagement

During the first visit, Lawanda identified protecting her health as a valued life direction, and during that session the clinician helped her brainstorm strategies for making better dietary choices and improving her blood sugar levels. However, she had clearly been aware of what she needed to do for some time already, so following through on these strategies would require developing more strength in the pillar of engagement.

Intervention: Good Start to a Good Day

People who are struggling often get into negative feedback loops in which their daily routines don't affirm their values, but instead focus attention on stressful aspects of life that cannot be controlled. By engaging in some type of values-based activity immediately as their day begins, people can create a snowball effect that helps them connect with their values throughout the day. Good Start to a Good Day is one such intervention; it helps the client engage in a specific behavior right after waking up that is values-consistent and promotes awareness. Other similar interventions might include spending the first five minutes after awakening lying in bed and mentally rehearsing values-based actions in situations anticipated during the day or starting the day with any other activity that brings the client into purposeful contact with core values.

Clinician: Lawanda, I'm wondering what each day might look like if you developed a routine that helped you get it off to a good start. By "good start," I mean that you would do something that reflects your values, like showing the respect you feel for all living things: people, plants, and animals. Do you have any ideas about something you could do to start each day by affirming what matters most to you?

Lawanda: I see what you mean—like maybe I would go out and take a walk and notice my neighbors and the flowers and trees.

Clinician: Good ideas! You could really notice each thing you come into contact with—look right at it and nod, smile, or give some other sign of respectful acknowledgment. In a real simple way, it would be you walking with your values. Would that be something that might be helpful to you?

Lawanda: It would, I think.

Intervention: Words of Wisdom

Even as Lawanda began to restore contact with many aspects of her world, she continued to struggle during interactions with her daughter. The clinician used the Words of Wisdom intervention to help Lawanda connect with hidden thoughts and feelings that might help her engage with her daughter.

Clinician: This exercise involves using your imagination. You can close your eyes if you like. I want you to imagine that you're waiting for a child to show up. It could be your grandson when he was young, maybe just four or five, or it could be another young child. This child will bring you some advice from the perspective of a child. This child may help you see how you can show your love and respect for your daughter and how you can put this into action even when it feels very difficult to do so. *(Pauses.)*

Lawanda: Okay, I'm listening.

Clinician: Wait for the child to speak or show you something. *(A few minutes of silence pass.)*

Lawanda: I see a little boy with a small teddy bear; he has tears on his cheeks. He says the bear made him get in trouble, but he forgives it because it's his bear. He says he always lets the bear be on his bed all day and that it sleeps with him every night.

After discussing this image, Lawanda decided that it meant she could do something loving toward her grandson and daughter every day, even though she might be upset by their actions. She found an old teddy bear and put it on her couch to remind her to see her daughter with the innocence and nonjudgmental perspective of a young child.

On a Final Note

Older adults face many challenges, and they can easily slide into a demoralized state that leads to depression. Financial problems, health problems, and loss of social support naturally trigger a sense of loss. When the response to these kinds of psychosocial stresses is to avoid making contact with distressing thoughts, feelings, or memories, people can quickly lose more ground and end up at risk for unnecessary loss of independence and even premature death. FACT is an ideal approach for older adults, as it emphasizes a commonsense approach to coping with life's ever-changing panoramas that honors the wealth of experience and knowledge that these clients bring to therapy.

General Pointers about Using FACT with Older Adults

The clinician must show compassion and be able to empathize with the unique struggles of aging, a stage of life replete with changes and challenges that can turn the "golden years" into a time of demoralization. Many of the changes associated with aging that have the greatest impact cannot be undone; they can only be accepted as the individual moves on in life. Acknowledge the emotional impact of the various losses and changes these clients are confronting. Focus on helping them connect with their strengths and their values, and support their efforts to continue to pursue a meaningful life, including preserving their independence and cultivating a loving connection with existing friends and family.

As discussed, aging well involves addressing many difficult challenges. Younger therapists may have limited personal experience with these challenges, and both the older client and the therapist may perceive a bit of a gulf between them. It is important in this case to openly acknowledge this gap in experience while communicating a genuine desire to learn more about what the client is dealing with. Don't assume that aging clients are unable to learn new skills or are somehow going to

225

be stuck in a demoralized state because of real-life losses. While some clinicians might see these attitudes as an empathetic stance, older clients may see them as defeatism on the part of the therapist and consequently might be reluctant to engage in the therapeutic relationship.

Another important tip for working successfully with older adults is to speak clearly and directly at the individual, as many older adults have hearing deficits, and to avoid using jargon. While the current generation of younger and middle-aged adults tends to be more psychologically minded, today's older adults were raised in an era when self-awareness and psychological thinking weren't emphasized. Older adults may see a therapist who uses jargon as out of touch, or even as speaking in tongues. It's important to describe psychological concepts in commonsense terms and to check in with older clients frequently to ensure that they are accurately tracking intervention concepts and strategies.

Part 4

FACT with Couples and Groups

Chapter 11

Until Death Do Us Part: Conducting FACT with Couples

To be fully seen by somebody, then, and to
be loved anyhow—this is a human offering
that can border on miraculous.

— *Elizabeth Gilbert*

Most experienced clinicians would probably agree that, of all therapy modalities, working with couples is the most difficult. The root of this difficulty can be traced back to the effects of language itself, which endows humans with the unique capacity to form symbolically meaningful relationships with other humans. To be sure, there are other examples of long-term, close-knit relationships in the animal world, but assuredly none are as far-reaching and socially complicated as the union of two humans. Ultimately, humans are social creatures, and union in a couple represents both the pinnacle of cooperation and the finest hour of our capacity for attachment. The world's greatest poetry, music, and art often arise from the sense of attachment and longing that one human has for another. While a goose and a gander might spend their adult lives together, they don't write love poems to each other, make vows to each other based in their religious convictions, or bring other geese around to celebrate their union.

Any human endeavor so rich in symbolism is going to have a dark side to it, and human relationships are no exception. We are capable of generating expectations of others that are almost a setup for failure (for example, *My partner will help me feel like I'm worthy of being loved*). We create conditional tests of the other person's fidelity to the union and find them wanting (for example, *If he really loved me, he would know what I need emotionally without me having to tell him*). We can imagine a different relationship with another person and find that more desirable than the relationship we are in presently (for example, *If I'd known you were going to be this controlling, I probably would have married Tom, who was much more laid-back*). We can withhold affection and use it as a tool to force the other person to behave differently (for example, *If you won't take the garbage out, don't expect me to be sexually responsive at night*). We have even made it an art form to blame the other person for the way we feel (for example, *When you criticize my weight, you make me feel like I'm not attractive anymore*). In short, the same human abilities that produce attachment make being attached an extraordinarily complicated process. Not surprisingly, about half of all marriages end in divorce, and most marriages end within five years. However, there are marriages that last a lifetime, so it's natural to wonder what distinguishes lasting relationships from those that fail.

The research on why marriages fail or succeed suggests that certain communication practices and patterns are pivotal factors in promoting healthy, long-lasting relationships and that their absence leads to relationship failure (Gottman & Notarius, 2000). However, many of the best-researched communication patterns (such as demand-withdraw, in which one partner makes demands for change and the other tries to withdraw from the discussion) are simply by-products of a more fundamental stance taken by each person in a relationship. If we look for the wellhead of vital relationships, the most basic proposition is that psychologically flexible humans create psychologically flexible relationships. While there might be a handful of relationships characterized by a beatific love at first sight and never having a fight, for the other 99.9 percent of humans, intimate relationships are a testing ground for psychological flexibility.

It should come as no surprise that the same cultural forces that create psychologically rigid approaches to living also tend to produce rigid, maladaptive behaviors in relationships. Being intimate requires that we be open not only to our own distressing, unwanted stuff, but also to the distressing, unwanted stuff that our partner is carrying around. To be intimate requires that each partner be able to stay present with the other, even when their self-stories are being triggered. To be intimate requires that they share a value about intimacy that goes beyond how happy each is with the other today, over the last several days, or even over the last several weeks. We must be willing to behave like loving partners even when we aren't feeling "in love." This is the hallmark of what it means to be in a committed relationship.

Thus, at their core, successful long-term relationships are characterized by a mutual openness and acceptance, based in shared values that are put into action on a daily basis. In short, a successful relationship is FACT in action! New developments in couples therapy support this notion. For example, integrating acceptance and mindfulness strategies into couples therapy has been shown to dramatically increase marriage survival rates (Christensen & Jacobson, 1998).

This chapter provides a case example to illustrate the use of interventions targeting the core strengths of awareness, openness, and engagement over the course of three sessions with a couple. After the case example, we introduce five FACT strategies for couples. Not all couples need all five strategies, but most need at least one or two.

Case Example: Eve and Malcolm

Eve and Malcolm have been married for thirty-seven years. Eve is sixty, and Malcolm is sixty-three. They have struggled off and on during their relationship. Eve is more demonstrative, outgoing, and affectionate. Malcolm is quiet and less receptive to giving or receiving affection but is very focused and intense. Despite their differences, Eve and Malcolm have managed to create a positive, cohesive family. They have three adult children, all of whom are professionals and have their own families. Eve worked as a schoolteacher for thirty years and is now retired. Malcolm recently sold his plumbing business and made a lot of money from the sale. They both enjoy being physically active and traveling, and their retirement dream has always been to engage in outdoor activities like golfing and camping and to travel abroad.

Three months before he sold his business, Malcolm started to experience fatigue and abdominal pain. He was examined by his family physician and referred to a specialist for testing. The testing revealed a large tumor on Malcolm's pancreas that was classified as malignant and inoperable by the oncologist. Malcolm was told that he might live at most for six months, and palliative care was started in the form of large doses of painkillers.

Eve and Malcolm are struggling with each other at this point. Malcolm has more or less retreated into his head and isn't responding to Eve's requests to share his thoughts and feelings. Eve is in a state of shock that her life partner is about to die. She needs Malcolm's support but isn't getting it. She's also concerned about how much he's drinking and how many pain pills he's using.

Focusing Questions

Despite scheduling an appointment for them both, Eve arrives at the first meeting by herself. The clinician therefore faces a familiar challenge in couples therapy: trying to get a picture of what's going on in the relationship as seen through the eyes of only one person in the couple.

1. What Are You Seeking?

When only one member of a couple arrives for the first session, it is often useful to get a sense of the dynamic that led the absent member to make the choice not to show up. The clinician is mainly interested in how this decision is impacting the member of the couple who is present in the session.

Clinician: I see that Malcolm decided not to come today. What's going on? I thought both of you were coming in.

Eve: Yesterday he changed his mind and just said, "I'm not going." I tried to get him to change his mind, but he wouldn't discuss it. That's the problem: He does nothing at all anymore. He barely responds when spoken to. He just sits around or lies in bed most of the day. He has pretty much stopped talking to me. He won't even eat with me and mostly eats directly from the refrigerator when I'm out of the house or asleep. At first he didn't even tell me he had cancer. I found out because I saw a bottle of pain medicine and asked him why he was taking it. That's how I found out. He's just withdrawing into himself. Thankfully, he finally let me to talk to his doctor, so now I know what the situation is.

Clinician: So, how are you dealing with this, Eve?

Eve: Well, there's no hope that he will survive more than six months, maximum. I can cope with that, I think, even though it's horrible. I just can't stand that he's shutting me out. Right now I need him as much as he needs me. Next summer I'll be a widow. I know that, and that's just how life turned out. There's nothing we can do about it. Strangely enough, I can accept that Malcolm will die, but not that he's shutting me out of the final months of his life.

Clinician: It sounds like life has taken a turn that neither of you could have predicted: that your life together will be over very soon. I can only imagine what you and Malcolm must be going through right now. I'm so sorry that you're in this painful situation.

Eve: It is terrible and unfair, and I think he has just given up. If I weren't there, he wouldn't bother to buy any food and probably wouldn't even shower or change clothes.

2. What Have You Tried?

Given the amount of stress on Eve and the fact that Malcolm has been checking out, the clinician wants to get a sense of how Eve is coping.

Clinician: What do you do to cope with this on a day-by-day basis?

Eve: I actually don't know—don't know what I'm doing, or if I'm even coping. I talk to Linda, our daughter. She's the only one who really has grasped the magnitude of the situation. She's always been close to Malcolm; she's a daddy's girl. She isn't handling this well. She's been staying at our house a lot, leaving her husband to take care of their kids. Maybe one way I'm coping is by going for walks with friends now and then. I really enjoy going for walks, but now they make me sad because I think about all the times I went for walks with Malcolm and how he used to be more open with me. Now he doesn't want to walk with me anymore. He's tired and doesn't seem to care if we spend any time together. I just try to take it one day at a time. The truth is, I mostly don't let myself think about him dying.

3. How Has It Worked?

Superficially, Eve's coping strategies look quite reasonable. She's using existing social supports, she's trying to get Malcolm to engage in positive activities, and she's focused on responding to the crisis at hand, rather than the long-term implications. However, each of these strategies also seems to trigger even more sadness. Next the clinician turns to how these strategies are working for Eve.

Clinician: It seems like wherever you turn, there's some kind of memory or connection to Malcolm that you have to come to grips with. You mentioned that you don't let yourself think about this stuff. How do you feel that strategy is working?

Eve: Actually, it isn't working at all. I can't tell you how many
                times I have gone through the day he dies and the funeral,
                how all the children and grandchildren will react, what to do
                when, and how everything will be… (Cries and laughs silently
                at the same time.) I've even thought about what to serve for
                dinner when the kids come home after the funeral.

Clinician: It seems to me that you're doing what anyone would do in
                this painful situation: trying to keep these reactions and feel-
                ings at bay by just not thinking about them. Yet you're telling
                me that you can't help but think about all of it anyway. And
                then other actions you take, like talking with your daughter
                or walking with friends, they tend to trigger the stuff you're
                trying not to think about. So, what do you think—is not
                thinking about it going to work in the long run?

Eve: Probably not.

4. What Has It Cost You?

Eve's main strategy is to avoid thinking about Malcolm's impending
death. And because she wants to protect and support Malcolm, she also
isn't approaching him directly about her struggles with the situation. The
clinician wants to explore this with Eve so that she can reach out to
Malcolm and perhaps get him to come in for a follow-up session with her.

Clinician: It sounds like you're trying to both avoid and approach this
                situation at the same time. You want to avoid having all
                these unpleasant thoughts and emotions about Malcolm
                dying. At the same time, you're trying to approach Malcolm
                for support but feel rebuffed by him. Is it possible that by
                being unwilling to have your own pain here, you are actually
                making it more difficult for Malcolm to have his?

Eve: Yeah, I guess. I haven't thought about it that way. I tiptoe
                around all of this. At the same time, I know how scared and
                sad Malcolm is. I hear him crying in the bathroom at night

when he thinks I'm asleep. I think he's doing all of this to protect the kids and me. He must feel so completely alone.

Clinician: That sounds terrible for both of you. I mean, it sounds like it goes both ways—that this loneliness affects both of you.

Eve: Yes, it does. I haven't felt like I shared a moment with him for two and a half months now. That's scary. I've almost gotten used to the idea that we're never going to share anything again, even though we still have time to do that.

Clinician: That's so sad. Do you think there's anything you could do to get him interested in coming here with you?

Eve: I think I know what I can do to convince him. But if I don't manage to do it, I'll come back by myself, because it's helpful to me to talk about this.

Treatment Summary

Eve managed to get Malcolm's attention and was able to communicate what she'd been feeling about their relationship. She called the next day and told the clinician that Malcolm held her as she expressed her feelings and cried. She didn't feel he was emotionally present during this interaction, but he did allow physical contact, which he had shied away from since the diagnosis. In addition, he agreed to come in for a counseling session with Eve. They met with the clinician twice, the first time a few days after Eve's session, and the second time about two weeks later. In just two sessions, they made huge progress in being more open with each other about the pain they were experiencing. They also decided to engage in several valued activities, including taking a short trip abroad that they had planned prior to Malcolm's diagnosis. In addition, they met with their children to plan a memorial service in keeping with Malcolm's religious beliefs. Malcolm died three months later. Although he was in considerable pain, he was coherent, and Eve was by his side when the end came.

Promoting Openness

After a brief introduction, the second session began with an attempt to get Malcolm to describe what he was going through and how it was affecting his view of the relationship. In addition to promoting openness, the clinician set the stage for radical change by getting at the question of what kind of life Eve and Malcolm would choose for their last few months together.

Clinician: As you know, Malcolm, I met Eve several days ago, and she told me about your cancer, how severe it is, and how it has affected your marriage. I understand that she talked to you about this that night.

Malcolm: Yes, that's right.

Clinician: She didn't tell me on the phone what she said to you. Can you tell me how that conversation went for you?

Eve: I talked about…

Clinician: Wait a second, Eve. Sorry to interrupt you, but I'd like Malcolm to tell me before you describe it, if that's okay.

Eve: Of course.

Clinician: What did Eve say to you?

Malcolm: She…she told me she was sorry.

Clinician: What made you realize that she was sorry?

Malcolm: She cried and said she was sorry.

Clinician: Did she describe what she was sorry about?

Malcolm: (*Looks at the clinician for a long time.*) That I'm sick and will die soon.

Eve: No, Malcolm, that's not what I said.

Malcolm: Well, what else could you be sorry about?

Eve: That you don't talk to me and that you're shutting me out—
             that's what I was trying to tell you. (*Cries.*)

Malcolm: But we did talk, didn't we? And now we are here talking
             again. What else am I supposed to do?

Clinician: Eve, please tell Malcolm and me what you tried to communi-
             cate that night.

Eve: (*Turns to Malcolm.*) I'm sorry that you shut me out. I don't
             know what you're thinking about. I don't know how you feel,
             and I haven't ever felt this lonely in my life. That's what I said
             that night, and it's true, Malcolm. I feel completely lost trying
             to deal with this by myself, and I need for you to share this
             awful situation with me.

Malcolm: (*Speaks harshly.*) You might as well get used to it, because
             soon enough you *will* be alone.

Clinician: Eve, what would you wish for right now? What do you need?

Eve: To have Malcolm hold me and tell me how he's feeling right
             now. I'm longing for my man, my support and life partner.

Clinician: Malcolm, can you understand what Eve wants you to do for
             her?

Malcolm: (*Remains silent for a while.*) Yeah...

Clinician: Because if I've understood Eve correctly, even though you are
             kind of reserved, over the years you two have been able to
             talk about and deal with some challenging life situations.

Malcolm: Yeah, we have.

Eve: Not now.

Malcolm: (*Remains silent, looks down at his hands, and seems tense and
             nervous.*)

Clinician: Malcolm?

Malcolm: (*Makes brief eye contact, then quickly looks down at his hands.*)

Clinician: Malcolm, you said that you could understand what Eve is asking for. Are you willing to give her what she needs right now?

Malcolm: *(Remains silent for about thirty seconds.)* Yes, I think I can.

Clinician: Could you just connect with Eve by looking at her right now? She needs you, and she's willing to share whatever you have to share with her.

Malcolm: *(Quickly glances at Eve and then looks down.)*

Eve: Malcolm? Malcolm, look at me! I'm your wife and I'm here for you, right now.

Malcolm: *(Makes eye contact with Eve.)* I know, and I'm sorry for what I'm putting you through.

Promoting Awareness

At this point, the clinician had succeeded in creating more openness in Malcolm and Eve's interaction. They were struggling with some extraordinarily difficult feelings, but they weren't avoiding each other by changing the subject, and they weren't blaming each other. There was some integrity developing in this exchange, and the clinician wanted to bring the reality of what they were facing together into greater focus.

Clinician: Did you know that when a bull elephant is about to die, he separates himself from the herd and won't let any other elephants near him? No one really knows why bull elephants do this, but I have a theory. I think pulling away eases the pain of loss, both for him and for the herd. Elephants are quite intelligent, and they form lifelong social bonds with every other elephant in the herd. If the dying elephant just disappears into the sunset, the rest of the herd is spared the pain of seeing him die. I think that one of our basic instincts is to try to protect others from the pain of seeing us die. Even animals do this. *(Looks intently at Malcolm and remains silent.)*

Malcolm: (*Speaks in a thick voice.*) Well, I cannot…

Clinician: What is it that you can't do, Malcolm?

Malcolm: I don't know… I don't want to make her feel more pain. It's not fair; she shouldn't have to…

Clinician: Eve says she needs you; she can't do this alone. She wants to live with you until the end, to be your wife and life partner.

Malcolm: (*Remains silent, then tears begin to stream down his face.*) I don't want to die, I don't…

Eve: (*Cries and puts a hand on Malcolm's shoulder.*) Malcolm, Malcolm. (*She hugs him and both cry.*)

Promoting Engagement

This was a very tender moment. It was difficult for all three people to simply be present with the fact that two people who had loved each other every day for almost forty years would soon be separated against their will. Nothing could be said or done to alleviate this sad reality. In such raw moments, knowledge, science, and professionalism have no place; nothing could be added to what was happening in that moment. The best the clinician could hope to do was show up and share the experience with openness. In that moment, tears flowed for everyone, and they all remained silent, other than crying, for five minutes. Malcolm rested his head on Eve's shoulder with his hands to his face and wept uncontrollably. Finally, Eve broke the silence. She looked at the clinician and gave him a warm smile. Then she told Malcolm that she loved him dearly. The clinician decided to try to elicit commitments from Eve and Malcolm concerning how they would spend their last days together.

Clinician: If I could wave a magic wand and you could make a wish, what would you wish for in your last months together?

Eve: I'd like us to spend as much time together as possible and to share everything each of us is going through. I'd like Malcolm to talk to me and tell me how he feels and what he needs, and I'd like to share with him in the same way. I'd like for us to sit down with our children and explain what's happening and prepare them for the loss of their father. We've spent so many years together and have done so many things together as a family.

Clinician: It sounds like what's most important to you is that Malcolm stays present for you and that you have some quality time together with your children. How about you, Malcolm?

Malcolm: I want to be there for Eve. It's going to be hard for both of us. I'll try to let her know when I need to be alone, and I want her to allow me that. I think meeting with the kids is a good idea. We've both been avoiding sitting down and having a heart-to-heart talk with them. I was also hoping… Well, we've already paid for a two-week tour in South Africa. I think we both figured that wasn't going to be much fun, given the bad news. But I want to go anyway, as long as my health doesn't get in the way. We had both planned on this trip.

Eve: I'd like that, Malcolm—one last trip. We've always traveled well together.

The clinician's last meeting with Malcolm and Eve occurred about two weeks later and only lasted about twenty minutes. Malcolm was calm and emotionally present. He and Eve held hands and frequently smiled at each other. Eve said that when they went to bed at night, they usually held each other and talked about all sorts of memories, and this often brought up tears for both of them. They were scheduled to leave for South Africa the next week. Malcolm's doctor had provided a lot of instructions to help him cope with the demands of the trip, and both of them were excited about what they would see and learn—and about spending the time together doing something they enjoyed.

On a Final Note

When working with couples, it's important to keep in mind that their decision to seek therapy is usually a last resort. Most often, couples have tried a lot of different things over a period of months or years to resolve their differences. Many of their strategies are avoidant in nature, being designed to prevent unresolved issues from surfacing or to quell negative emotions that surface when the avoided issues show up.

As was the case with Eve and Malcolm, it is quite common for one member of the couple to be more eager to participate in treatment and the other to be identified as the person with "the problem." Another common situation is for the couple to be caught in a struggle about which person has "the problem," with each pointing at the other. As Eve and Malcolm's case demonstrates, any type of change is costly when the couple is locked in a struggle over who's right and who's wrong.

Five FACT Strategies for Couples

A primary goal of FACT is to teach couples how to negotiate what we call "low-cost change." Low-cost change is change that doesn't require anyone to be right or wrong. In fact, attachment to the idea of right and wrong is what prevents change in relationships. Values-based change is a win-win proposition for each member of the couple because, instead of trying to get each other to change, the couple is making changes based in shared values about the relationship. Several FACT strategies can help clinicians create a context for low-cost change in a relationship. Table 3 summarizes them.

Table 3. Five FACT Strategies for Couples

Strategy	Impact
Find a common valued area and then model and teach cooperative behavior to help the couple move toward that value.	Provides a basis for cooperation and optimism about change.
Focus on short-term changes that produce immediately apparent positive outcomes for the relationship, particularly in less problematic areas of the relationship.	Paves the way for successful work on more problematic areas.
Focus as much on the process of change as on the change itself.	Teaches fundamental steps for the dance of change.
Teach skills to make flexible attempts at behavior change and to alter change tactics based upon direct results.	Encourages individual responsibility for evaluating the impact of requests for change.
Help each person learn to accept changes in the other.	Encourages each to be mindful of change in the other and to allow behavior changes to evolve.

Finding a common valued area. Once an area that is valued by both partners is identified, the clinician can observe the couple's behavior in relation to that value and provide modeling as needed to help the couple learn how to engage in cooperative behavior change efforts in the valued area. Focusing on an area where the couple has shared values will typically increase their motivation to change and to decrease the use of old, unworkable communication styles.

Focusing on short-term changes with immediate effects. Focusing on short-term changes that produce immediately apparent positive outcomes for the relationship can be extremely beneficial, even if the changes occur in less troublesome areas of the relationship. For couples with a long history of unsuccessful struggle, achieving any sort of positive outcome can soften rigid mental views that each person has become overly attached to. This builds some positive momentum that will allow the clinician to help the couple address more substantial problems.

Focusing on the process of change. Change is a complex course of action for most humans and elicits discomfort even in people who are psychologically flexible. To persevere through a lifetime of change, a couple needs to learn the dance of change, and this is facilitated by focusing on the process of change as much as, if not more than, specific changes. Amidst the inevitable changes that occur in the lifetime of a relationship, the one stable point of reference is both partners' values-based commitment to being in the relationship, and this can be a touchstone for reorienting to the process, rather than the content, of change. We once heard some words of wisdom in a Steven Levine workshop: "Marry your partner not for one lifetime, but for a thousand lifetimes."

Learning how to flexibly pursue behavior change in the other. One common and alarming attribute of distressed couples is that they engage in the same unworkable communication strategies over and over again. The FACT approach places the emphasis on helping each person evaluate the workability of change requests on the basis of real-world feedback, or contingency-based learning. This helps partners avoid being tied to a rule about what the other person "should" do. Instead, partners look at the actual results of their requests for change to see whether the behavior in question has shifted in response to the requests. If the requests for change don't work, why continue to make the same requests over and over, as so often occurs in distressed couples? FACT encourages couples to be pragmatic and willing to change tactics.

Helping partners learn to accept change in each other. Finally, and most importantly, the fifth FACT strategy is to help couples learn to accept changes in each other. This is an essential skill for a flexible, long-lasting relationship, as life itself is a process of continuous change, all the way to the grave. Integrative couple therapy (Christensen & Jacobson, 1998) goes so far as to propose that the very attributes that attract members of a couple to each other eventually become a core source of conflict! Unfortunately, many people in relationships overidentify with an idea along the lines of *You were like that, which I liked, and now you are like this, which I don't like, so please go back to the way you were.* The fact that a partner is different is something that, in many circumstances, can only be accepted. Relationship struggle is often the result of partners trying to change attributes or behaviors in the other that aren't amenable to direct change. In fact, the partner who is trying to enforce change often becomes part of the problematic behavior pattern that is deemed unacceptable. Somewhat like the paradox of emotional control, the harder one person tries to control the behavior of the other, the more out of control that person's behavior becomes. When the focus of the conversation is shifted to values and commitment, repeated unworkable attempts at behavior change can be replaced with acceptance strategies. Although the outcome is by no means guaranteed, taking an accepting stance toward a distressing or unwanted new behavior often allows that behavior to evolve naturally based upon direct results within the relationship.

Chapter 12

The More the Merrier: Conducting FACT in Groups and Classes

I have always known that at last I would take this road,
but yesterday I did not know that it would be today.

— *Narihara*

While treatment resources for people with psychological problems are diminishing, more and more people are in need of these resources. Conducting FACT in a group or classroom format is a cost-effective alternative and may actually have clinical advantages compared to more-time intensive individual, couples, and family treatments. People with problems in interpersonal functioning often benefit a great deal from participating in group therapy. In a group, it is possible for members to see other members with similar life problems make remarkable changes in a short time period. Members benefit not only from witnessing these role models but also from seeing the contrast between processes that contribute to psychological flexibility and those that do not. In fact, watching another group member struggle with difficult issues may help clients take a different perspective on their own struggles. Additionally, people are often more receptive to feedback from a fellow group member than from a therapist or group leader.

Since FACT is based on a uniform model of human suffering, a single FACT group can include people with a mixture of clinical problems, such as depression, anxiety, eating problems, or substance abuse issues. In addition, FACT classes can be designed for conditions that would not ordinarily be treated in mental health or substance abuse treatment settings, such as chronic pain, health anxiety, or living with chronic disease. Group formats are also a highly flexible way to help clients develop the skills needed to cope with life's many challenges. A group or classroom intervention can focus on developing general life skills, such as mindfulness or personal problem solving, or be focused on promoting coping strategies for a specific life issue, such as dealing with divorce.

In this chapter, we briefly review the evidence in regard to conducting FACT in a group format and examine some innovative applications. We also present practical guidelines related to conducting FACT in a group format, such as how to prepare clients for groups, how to assess progress during a group, and how to structure work with a group to maximize the impact of each session. In addition, we present a three-session FACT protocol that can be expanded for clients who want or need more skills training, and we demonstrate some core interventions for each session. Finally, we review a case example of a chronically suicidal client being treated in a FACT group setting.

Does FACT Work in a Group Format?

There has been a good deal of research on using acceptance and commitment therapy in a short-term group or classroom format, applied to various populations (children, parents, teenagers, and adults) and a range of problems. An evaluation of the impact of a two-day group ACT workshop offered to twenty parents of children diagnosed with autism indicated that parents reported lower levels of depression and improved levels of general psychological functioning after the intervention (Blackledge & Hayes, 2006). Similar results were found with a short-term class program designed for parents of children with pervasive developmental disorder (Tani, Hyougo, Gakuen, & Kitamura, 2010).

Clinicians in Australia have developed and tested a manual-based ACT group intervention for thirteen- to eighteen-year-old adolescents with both internalizing and externalizing problems. The group format seemed both feasible and acceptable, as 90 percent of participants completed treatment, showed clinical improvement, and rated the group as preferable to individual treatment (Tan & Martin, 2008).

There is growing evidence to support the benefits of time-limited FACT groups for adults with a range of emotional health issues. One study involved forty-seven patients with self-harming behaviors who received twelve group sessions over a fifteen-week period. These patients demonstrated superior outcomes on measures of depression, anxiety, quality of life, and frequency of self-harming behaviors (Osterholm & Johansson, 2009). Clinicians and researchers in Sweden are exploring the use of FACT groups for depression, eating disorders, and prescription drug addiction. Many of these groups use an open access approach, allowing new patients to join the group every three weeks. This allows the group to build cohesion and maintain continuity of treatment while also decreasing wait times for new clients who need access to care.

In the sections that follow, we will examine some important steps in developing and implementing a successful group program. As we go through these steps, keep in mind that some of them might not be needed if you conduct a time-limited, psychoeducational class.

Preparing Clients for Group Therapy

Once a client agrees to participate in a group, the group leader should have a pre-group orientation visit with the client. This visit usually takes thirty to sixty minutes, and the agenda typically includes reviewing a group confidentiality agreement, giving the client information about the experiential nature of ACT group work, and emphasizing the importance of practicing new behaviors between group sessions. In addition, the clinician should explain whether and how new members are added to the group once it starts (for example, that the client will start with a cohort of other group members and that no other members will be added until the fourth week). Finally, the clinician assesses the client for risk factors, such as sensory or cognitive impairments or problems with learning style, that might limit the client's ability to participate in or benefit from group treatment.

Measuring Clinical Progress

Either during or after the pre-group orientation, the client should complete baseline measures of psychological flexibility, health status, and, in some cases, symptom severity. These measures should then be administered periodically over the course of group treatment. We recommend the Acceptance and Action Questionnaire – 2 (AAQ-2; Bond et al., 2011) as a measure of psychological flexibility and the Duke Health Profile (DUKE; Parkerson, Broadhead, & Tse, 1991) as a measure of general health and mental health status. Although FACT isn't focused on treating symptoms per se, some clinicians include measures of symptom severity, such as the Personal Health Questionnaire – 9 (PHQ-9; Lowe, Unutzer, Callahan, Perkins, & Kroenke, 2004), a brief measure of depression.

Creating a Structure for Group Work

During the pre-group orientation visit, the clinician should use a modified version of the FACT focusing questions described in chapter 4 to enhance the client's motivation to attend all group sessions and practice newly acquired skills between group sessions. We recommend using the following series of questions, with adjustments as needed to fit the language and ethnic and cultural context of the client:

1. How long have you had the problem that brings you here?

2. What have you tried? Have you previously been treated for this problem? If so, what was the result?

3. What do you want from life?

4. What are the barriers to doing what you want in life?

5. What do you do when those barriers show up?

6. Are you at war with the barriers?

7. What are the consequences of being at war with the barriers?

The first two questions can be covered quickly, but it is important to slow down a bit with questions 3 through 6. The clinician might use the Life Path and Turnaround Worksheet (see the appendix) and ask the client to make some notes about personal values and barriers the client experiences when trying to pursue more meaning in life. When asking questions 5 and 6, the clinician should encourage the client to get present with any emotional responses or other private experiences that show up. The clinician should help the client complete all aspects of the Life Path and Turnaround Worksheet and either hold onto it until the first group session or instruct the client to bring it to the session. The first group session will largely consist of a review of each member's life path exercise.

The Life Path Protocol

In this section, we will describe a very brief, highly portable three-session FACT protocol that can be used with all comers. Typically, group or classroom sessions are sixty to ninety minutes in length, with groups for children typically being limited to sixty-minute sessions unless their parents are also participating in the group. Groups or classes may be led by one or two clinicians.

Table 4 provides an outline of activities for each of the three sessions, along with estimated times for their completion. Some of the activities are self-explanatory; those that aren't are described later in the chapter.

Table 4. The Life Path Class

Session	Task	Method	Time
1	Build group cohesion.	Ask participants to introduce themselves and say something about their family, occupation, or studies.	2-3 min. per participant
	Identify values, strengthen the connection with values, and create a functional view of struggle and avoidance behaviors.	Ask participants to respond to the *life path questions*, displayed on a whiteboard.	4-5 min. per participant
	Assign homework to help participants gather information and practice observing.	Ask participants to monitor their experience of struggle and do nothing but observe their experience.	15 min.
2	Review homework.	Ask clients to describe their experience with the monitoring homework.	15 min.
	Teach mindfulness and promote defusion, or stepping back from painful private experiences.	Conduct a guided imagery exercise that invites participants to a place where they can observe painful experiences and learn to hold them more lightly.	10 min.
	Train participants in taking the observer, or self-as-context, perspective.	Conduct such exercises as having participants write down sticky thoughts on sticky notes, drawing pictures of feared content and sharing them with a partner, or developing physical representations of feared content as seen from an observer perspective.	15-25 min.
	Promote acceptance.	Have participants give a major barrier a tender name (or, for younger children, have them draw a picture of it). Conduct the mirroring exercise.	10-20 min.

	Teach skills for interacting interpersonally while being aware of painful psychological experiences.	Ask participants to wear a piece of paper with the tender name or picture on it and to interact nonverbally with other participants while doing so.	5 min.
	Assign homework.	Ask participants to plan to do a valued activity and to practice accepting a barrier that is likely to come up when doing that activity.	10 min.
3	Review homework.	Ask participants to describe their experience with the valued action and acceptance homework.	10-15 min.
	Promote the ability to make public commitments and learn from direct experience.	Have each participant walk a metaphorical life path, encountering and coping with obstacles.	40-60 min.
	Assign homework.	Ask participants to continue to make intentional choices, pursue valued directions, practice self-compassion, and learn from their experiences.	10 min.

At the book's website (nhpubs.com/23451), we've included outlines of sample session-by-session FACT group protocols for children, teens, and adults, along with full-page copies of all the assessment, case formulation, and treatment planning tools we've described in earlier chapters. If you peruse the group protocols, you'll see that, for the most part, each three-session protocol is the same regardless of the target population. The clinician simply makes adaptations when discussing FACT principles to address the developmental level of the target group. The other major adjustment is to the wording and focus of homework assignments.

Applying Core FACT Interventions in Groups

In this section, we will demonstrate how to organize and deliver FACT interventions in a group format. To aid your understanding, we will examine each group session individually. Later, we will introduce a case example to show how to carry over intervention themes from one session to another.

Session 1

The goal of the first session is to help participants develop a new perspective on struggle and avoidance and help them recognize the similarities in the predicaments of all group members. The life path questions and participants' answers to them provide a framework for the first session. The group goes through all of the questions sequentially, and the leader encourages each member to disclose his or her responses. Often, the avoidance strategies of participants may seem different on the surface; for instance, one member might be sleeping eighteen hours a day, while another may be getting high. However, the group leader reframes these seemingly different responses as examples of a bigger agenda that everyone in the group is pursuing: how to control or eliminate distressing and unwanted thoughts, feelings, memories, physical symptoms, and so forth. The leader brings participants into contact with the negative results of avoidance strategies and suggests acceptance as an alternative. When going over the homework assignment, it is important for the leader to emphasize that there is no need to do anything when the urge to engage in a struggle shows up—that, while difficult to do, the assignment is to practice just noticing painful private experiences.

Session 2

The goal of the second group session is to teach participants to adopt an observer perspective that will allow them to take a more accepting stance toward distressing private experiences. The leader helps members understand that taking the perspective of an observer will enable them to pursue valued directions even when they experience difficult private events and their mind is telling them to go to war with those experiences. The leader begins this session with a review of participants' experiences with the homework assignment. There are usually some participants who haven't followed through on the homework. It is important that the leader avoid making a big deal of this and instead just acknowledge that engaging in new behaviors can cause anxiety. The problems that bring people into therapy often produce shame related to repeated failures in trying to overcome those problems. There is no benefit in rubbing it in when participants don't complete an assignment. Those who haven't done the homework will learn from the experiences of those who have. By the third session, most participants will be engaging in the homework assignments.

After a brief review of the homework, the leader conducts a guided imagery exercise to help participants remember and fully experience times when they struggled with painful private events during the past week. Following this, the leader may have participants make a few written notes describing their struggle. Children and adolescents, and perhaps some adults, may want to draw a picture to characterize their struggle. Another approach is to ask group members to represent the struggle with a physical posture; asking members with different postures to relate to each other without talking can be illuminating and also provide some humor that helps participants hold their struggle more lightly.

Another technique to help participants hold their suffering lightly is to have them give it a tender name or describe it in terms that promote self-compassion. The group leader might use the example of renaming "damaged, ugly girl" as "vulnerable child." Another useful exercise is to have participants write painful content on sticky notes, then put the labels on their shirt or other clothing and walk about the room talking with others or engaging in some type of valued action (for example, making and holding eye contact even as the other person looks at their painful stuff). These exercises help participants learn to experience their thoughts and feelings in an open, accepting way. These kinds of physical exercises and metaphors also create an opportunity for voluntary exposure to negative content, implicitly teach perspective taking, and, perhaps most importantly, offset the tendency to make acceptance and openness intellectual concepts.

Participants of all ages will benefit from exercises that help them physically enact the dialectic of acceptance versus struggle. An experiential mirroring exercise is an excellent way to accomplish this. In this intervention, participants work in pairs, taking turns acting in two roles. First, one person tries to watch and verbally describe negative private events (for example, "hurt feelings," "getting mad," or "punishing myself for mistakes") and then adopts a posture in response to this stuff (for example, screaming at it, pushing it away, or running away with a frightened face). That person freezes in place for about one minute just to experience the physical pose. The second person stands in front of the first one and watches all of this in an accepting way. Then the group leader cues the first person to in some way soften the pose to make it reflect the accepting stance of the second person, who just stands there, watching and accepting. After the first person finds a new posture, the second person mirrors it by assuming the same posture. They freeze for a moment, and then talk with each other about what each person experienced during the exercise. The exercise is repeated with the two partners reversing roles.

Session 3

In the third session, the leader begins with a review of homework. This typically generates a variety of possible directions for the session, including both educational and experiential interventions. The leader is less active in this session and elicits more feedback from group members. A key exercise for this session is having group members walk a metaphorical life path. In this exercise, one group member describes a valued life direction that he or she is headed toward, and something in the room is chosen to represent the valued destination, perhaps a window or door in the room. The other group members stand along the path, and the walker asks individual members to portray painful stuff that tends to surface when he or she has tried to move in this direction in the past. Other group members are free to offer suggestions on how to handle these barriers when they arise. The walker physically acts out each suggestion (for example, "Take that thought and bring it with you, "Embrace that painful emotion," or "Put your arm around it and keep walking"). When each member of the group has had a chance to walk his or her life path, the leader asks everyone to write down the next steps they are willing to commit to. For some, the next steps may include graduation from the group; for others they might include repeating the three-class protocol to further increase their flexibility and get clearer about valued life directions. Prior to the close of the group, each participant stands up and makes a public commitment to a key action step. Other participants listen, and if they choose to, they can offer a comment or word of encouragement.

Case Example: Jenny

Jenny is a twenty-three-year-old woman who has attracted a lot of labels over her short life: bipolar disorder, bulemorexia, post-traumatic stress disorder due to sexual abuse, addiction to cannabis, and borderline personality disorder. Her therapist has been concerned about the level of risk associated with her sexual activities. Jenny has participated in therapy for many years and is currently taking four psychotropic medications: a mood stabilizer, two antidepressants, and a benzodiazepine. She has moved recently and is seeking care at a psychiatric center that offers a FACT group for clients with any kind of problem.

Pre-Group Orientation

During her pre-group orientation visit, Jenny revealed that her boyfriend had committed suicide nine months ago, that she blamed herself for his death, and that she was 100 percent sure that she would kill herself one day. She explained that she had a gun at home and that it was only a matter of time before she would shoot herself. The group clinician therefore needed to explore Jenny's motivation for attending and participating in a group therapy experience.

Clinician: Okay, so what's the point in seeking help if you're 100 percent positive about committing suicide?

Jenny: (Looks at the clinician for a while before answering.) You aren't supposed to say that. You're supposed to try to convince me not to do it. That's what therapists do.

257

Clinician: Which therapists did that?

Jenny: My former therapists, and also my doctors.

Clinician: Did it work?

Jenny: (*Laughs.*) No, for sure not.

Clinician: If you could choose, what would you want to see happen in your life, if you didn't end up putting a bullet in your head?

Jenny: I would like to be normal and not feel like every day is a struggle.

Clinician: What are you feeling that's so painful that you would choose death to get away from it?

Jenny: I am constantly sad and angry. I have a lot of anxiety and I just lie awake at night trying to get my mind to stop churning. Sometimes I try to figure out how to get my courage up so that I can kill myself.

Clinician: What else are you doing in life besides struggling with your mind?

Jenny: I work full-time as a caregiver for an old woman in my neighborhood. She's disabled and can hardly get around without help. My schedule varies—sometimes nights, other times days, and also some weekends. The thing is, I like my job. It's the only thing that gives me any relief from my anxiety... besides smoking pot.

Clinician: Okay, it sounds like your pain isn't constantly at ten on a scale of zero to ten. It sounds like you feel a little better when you're working.

Jenny: Yeah, I guess you could say that.

Clinician: You mentioned smoking pot as another way you escape or numb the pain inside.

Jenny: Yes. It's the best anxiety reliever in the world.

Clinician:	How often do you smoke pot in order to calm yourself down?
Jenny:	Well…almost every day, unless I'm working.
Clinician:	Okay. I have no idea if joining this group is going to work for you, but what do you think? Do you want to try it?
Jenny:	What? Why should I try it if you don't even think it's going to work?
Clinician:	I didn't say I think it won't work; I just said that I didn't know if it would. I kind of like acknowledging the uncertainty. Seeing into the future isn't part of my tool kit. You said that you'd like to be normal. For the record, I don't know what normal is. I've never met a normal person, and I'm including myself here.
Jenny:	I'm not functioning. I have an eating disorder. I exercise an hour and a half at the gym every day and take laxatives. I have five boyfriends that don't know about each other. I smoke pot on a daily basis and I want to kill myself. I can't sleep without pot, and I'm taking all kinds of drugs that don't do shit for me. You call that normal?
Clinician:	Yeah, we can call it anything you want to call it. It's just a word. Say it backward for me.
Jenny:	(Pauses.) Lamron! (Laughs.)
Clinician:	I like the sound of that; it fits the situation here much better. But there is one thing that I will not negotiate about, and that's the gun. The gun bums me out, and when I'm bummed out, I'm not at my best. Can we agree to put your death on hold while we try something different?
Jenny:	That's not a problem. I have a friend who can store the gun in his garage. I want to try the Life Path Class.
Clinician:	Why do you want to try it?
Jenny:	I don't know. I just want to do it. I'm sick of being me right now.

Clinician: Okay. In the group, we'll try to help you get back on track and headed in a life direction that means something to you. If you start moving in a better life direction and you still decide to commit suicide, that's your choice. For now, let's just see if we can find some other avenues for you to take so that you don't make that choice any earlier than necessary.

This was a challenging pre-group orientation visit, yet the clinician was able to assess the risk involved and determine that Jenny could benefit from the Life Path Class. After all, committing suicide is the ultimate expression of walking in the direction of no meaning. Jenny is walking in a direction, even while talking about terminating the walk altogether.

Group Therapy Process

Jenny didn't do very well in the first two sessions. She was late for the first session, appeared nervous, and was reluctant to open up in front of the group. Jenny arrived at the next session under the influence of LSD, which she had taken the night before. Just prior to the session, she'd taken several benzodiazepines, and she dozed off several times early in the group session. She was taken to a holding room and placed under observation for the day and was sent home that evening. The group leader asked the other group members if they were willing to let her come to the third class, given her difficulties participating in the first two classes, and they agreed to allow it.

At the third session, Jenny was the last participant to talk during the homework review. She sidestepped talking about the homework and instead told the group that she was going to kill herself because she couldn't take it anymore. She said this in a calm manner with a steady voice. Everyone was quiet and looked back and forth between Jenny and the group leader. The leader sat down in a vacant chair by Jenny and began a conversation with her.

Clinician: I want you to work with me on a short exercise, Jenny. You have nothing to lose since you've already decided what you're going to do.

Jenny: Okay, but I don't really want to.

Clinician: (*Looks at the group.*) I want you all to participate in this exer-
              cise, along with Jenny. First, I want you to close your eyes and
              just notice how your body moves as you breathe in and out.
              Notice the sensations of breathing. Scan your body from the
              top of your head down to your shoulders… Work your way
              down to your toes, just noticing the sensations. (*Pauses for a
              long time.*) Now I want you to picture a little girl, five or six
              years old, standing in front of you. She's sad and afraid. This
              is you when you were young. Can you remember a time when
              you were small and vulnerable, Jenny?

Jenny: Yes, when my dad raped me the first time. I felt so totally
              alone and couldn't talk with anyone about it.

Clinician: Okay, Jenny. I want you to listen to this little girl. She wants
              to tell you exactly how she feels. (*Pauses.*) What is she telling
              you?

Jenny: She says that she's in pain, that she's all alone and scared.
              She's hurting, and she's bleeding.

Clinician: Ask her what she needs right now.

Jenny: She needs to know that it isn't her fault, that she's okay. She
              needs to be loved and cared for.

Clinician: Could you give her that? Could you give her reassurance that
              she is perfectly okay and she has done nothing wrong?

Jenny: (*Cries.*) Yes. I can provide her with that. I can hold her hand
              and give her what she needs.

(*Several group members watch intently, and some start to cry.*)

Clinician: What would you want for this little girl in her life, Jenny?
              What would you like to teach her about living?

Jenny: That she doesn't have to be alone. She can be with friends.
              She is so beautiful.

Clinician:	Would you show her how to live a beautiful life? Would you show her how to love and to be loved?
Jenny:	(Sobs.) Yes, I will do that. I will show her.
Clinician:	Now I want you to connect with all of the other people who are here with you right now. They want the best for you, Jenny. They want you to have a good life. What can they do to help you take those first steps toward a beautiful life?
Jenny:	(Cries.) Tell me they believe in me even if I struggle at first.
Clinician:	Okay. Now let's just get back into the room. Picture what you will see when you open your eyes again, and when you have that picture, just open your eyes.
Jenny:	(Sits with her head down, staring at her lap and refusing to make eye contact with any member of the group.)
Clinician:	Jenny, can you look at me for a moment?
Jenny:	No.
Clinician:	Just raise your head a bit and look at me. Just raise it a little bit, if that's okay. Come on.
Jenny:	(Raises her head and looks at the clinician.)
Clinician:	Okay, what showed up for you, Jenny?
Jenny:	It was like I was being kicked in the stomach, but I can't kill myself after this. I need to give this a chance. Thanks for doing it.
Clinician:	How do you feel right now?
Jenny:	Ashamed. I don't cry in front of other people.
Clinician:	Do you think these people think that you're weak now?
Jenny:	Yes.

Clinician: Take a look around. Start with Madeleine over there. Just take a look into her eyes. Then go around the circle and look in each person's eyes and tell me what you see there.

Jenny: *(Slowly raises her eyes to meet Madeleine's and keeps eye contact for a while. She then smiles, cries a bit more, and moves on to make eye contact with the person to Madeleine's right, and continues in this way around the circle.)* No, they don't think I'm weak. They're nice. They're on my side. You are all so kind.

This group intervention helped Jenny stay present during a highly vulnerable moment and opened the door for self-acceptance and self-compassion to begin to replace self-loathing and blame. By the end of the session, Jenny made a commitment to start individual therapy to work on some of the issues that had surfaced during the group intervention. The exercise also had a positive impact on other group members. Several talked about experiencing an increased sense of self-compassion as they were experiencing compassion for Jenny.

Treatment Summary

In the weeks that followed, Jenny made significant strides toward building a better life. She continued to attend group sessions and was far more involved with group interactions. She exhibited genuine interest in the welfare of other group members and did not seem so self-absorbed. She stopped engaging in promiscuous sex, and her behavior around eating began to improve. She still exercised regularly, but not to excess, and she stopped using laxatives. She continued to smoke pot occasionally, but much less often than before. Her suicidal ideation also diminished significantly over the course of the group.

On a Final Note

FACT groups or classes may offer a variety of clinical benefits above and beyond those produced by individual, couples, and family treatments.

They can be used as a primary treatment modality, as a supplementary treatment, or, as Jenny's case demonstrates, as a springboard for entering into more productive individual therapy. FACT principles can be easily understood by children, teenagers, adults, and the elderly. These principles are easy to teach in a group or classroom format. FACT groups may also be helpful at the community level with people who might be at risk for negative health or mental health outcomes. This might include groups for people who are dealing with chronic disease, people who are trying to address health risk factors such as obesity or tobacco use, or people dealing with social challenges, such as living in a violent neighborhood. As an intervention model, FACT need not be confined to just one population, problem, or life arena, because the combination of acceptance, mindfulness, and living according to personal values is a universal formula for living well.

Appendix

Interview, Case Formulation, and Assessment Tools

I n this appendix, you'll find blank versions of all of the worksheets and assessment tools discussed in the text. Due to the page size of this book, we are unable to offer full-size, user-friendly versions, so the material here is just for your reference. Feel free to design your own versions based on what you see here, or visit the book's website (nhpubs .com/23451), where you can download full-page versions of all of the forms.

Focusing Questions

As a reminder, the four focusing questions that can yield maximal information in the limited time available in brief interventions are as follows:

1. What are you seeking?

2. What have you tried?

3. How has it worked?

4. What has it cost you?

A fifth key question increases motivation to change and helps clients identify valued life directions that are within their reach:

- What kind of life would you choose if you could choose?

Structured Exercises to Help Clarify Valued Life Directions

The Life Path and Turnaround Exercise and True North Exercise create a visual metaphor of clients' life direction and help them identify new behaviors in keeping with those directions. In the pages that follow you'll find blank worksheets for both exercises:

- **Life Path and Turnaround Worksheet:** This version is designed for use in individual brief intervention sessions. A version of this worksheet for use in groups is available at the website address given above.

- **True North Worksheet:** This worksheet can be used for either individual or group sessions.

Case Formulation Tools

Because FACT is so effective, clients often respond quickly, making formal case formulation unnecessary. With some clients, however, it may be helpful to evaluate their strengths and weaknesses in a more structured way. The information thus obtained can then be used to craft more tightly focused interventions to promote radical change. We've included two tools to aid in case formulation:

- **Flexibility Profile Worksheet:** Use this worksheet after each session to rate the client's flexibility in each core area, where 0 = minimal strength, and 10 = a great deal of strength. In the notes section, include your ideas about which core area or areas to target in your next visit with the client.

- **Four Square Tool:** This tool helps you analyze clients' workable and unworkable behaviors. It can be used to just describe the client's strengths and weaknesses, or it can be used as a treatment planning tool in which you identify behaviors you want to increase (workable behaviors) or decrease (unworkable behaviors).

Life Path and Turnaround Worksheet

← —————————————————————————————— →

More Control	**More Meaning**
What do you want to control, avoid, or get rid of and how are you trying to do that?	What type of life would you choose if you could choose?

1. Draw an arrow above the line to indicate where you are on your life path these days and which direction you're moving in.

2. What, if any, are the costs and benefits of pursuing control?

3. What behaviors would tell you that you're moving toward more meaning in life?

4. When you get stuck, how can you help yourself keep moving toward more meaning?

5. Who or what helps you move in the direction of more meaning?

True North Worksheet

What are your values?

What are your current strategies, and are they working?

What skills will you need to make the journey?

Clinical Issues

1. **Openness** (Accepts private events without struggle? Notices and lets go of unworkable rules?)

2. **Awareness** (Able to be present? Aware of private experiences? Able to take perspective? Shows compassion for self and others?)

3. **Engagement** (Clear values? Can organize for effective action? Can obtain reinforcement? Sufficient interpersonal skills?)

Flexibility Profile Worksheet

Openness	Awareness	Engagement
Able to detach from distressing private experience and associated rules	*Able to experience the present moment*	*Exhibits strong connection with values*
Able to take a non-judgemental, accepting stance towards painful material	*Able to take perspective on self and self-story*	*Able to sustain values-consistent action*

Today's Rating   Today's Rating   Today's Rating

_____ _____ _____

0   1   2   3   4   5   6   7   8   9   10

Low Strength   High Strength

Notes (core areas to target in the next visit):

Four Square Tool

		Workability	
		Not working (do less)	More workable (do more)
Behavior	Public		
	Private		

In-Session Assessment of Problem Severity, Confidence, and Helpfulness

In-session assessment strategies take only minutes and can help the clinician determine whether the intervention is working, detect possible barriers to change, and assess clients' perceptions about the helpfulness of each session.

Problem Severity

At the beginning of each session, ask clients to rate the severity of the problem that is bringing them in for help using a scale of 0 to 10, where 0 = not a big problem, and 10 = a very big problem. Over multiple visits, you can use a graph to track changes in problem severity ratings as a way of assessing the client's response to the intervention, as illustrated in the case examples. If problem severity scores don't change over time, this is a signal that you need to change intervention strategies.

Confidence

Near the end of each session, ask clients to rate their level of confidence that they will do what was planned in that session using a scale of 0 to 10, where 0 = not at all confident, and 10 = very confident. Generally, a rating of 7 or above is the target. Ratings below that should trigger an additional interaction about barriers to action that might be showing up for clients. There might be a need to either identify a new plan or to reduce the scale of the original plan.

Helpfulness

Near the end of each session, ask clients to rate how helpful the session was using a scale of 0 to 10, where 0 = not at all helpful, and 10 = very helpful. Generally, a rating of 7 or above is the target. Low ratings (0 to 4) signal that there is a major disconnect between the goals of the therapist and the goals of the client. Midrange ratings (5 to 6) might trigger a conversation about what the therapist and the client could do to create a more helpful approach for the client.

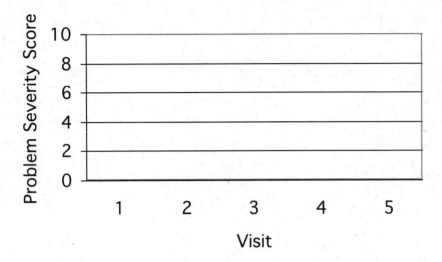

References

Aderka, I., Nickerson, A., Boe, H., & Hoffman, S. (2012). Sudden gains during psychological treatments of anxiety and depression: A meta-analysis. *Journal of Consulting and Clinical Psychology, 80,* 93-101.

Baker, A., Lee, N., Claire, M., Lewin, T., Grant, T., Pohlman, S., et al. (2005). Brief cognitive behavioural interventions for regular amphetamine users: A step in the right direction. *Addiction, 100,* 367-378.

Baldwin, S., Berkeljon, A., Atkins, D., Olsen, J., & Nielsen, S. (2009). Rates of change in naturalistic psychotherapy: Contrasting dose-effect and good-enough level models of change. *Journal of Consulting and Clinical Psychology, 77,* 203-211.

Bateson, G., Jackson, D. D., Haley, J., & Weakland, J. (1956). Toward a theory of schizophrenia. *Behavioral Science, 1,* 251-264.

Blackledge, J. T., & Hayes, S. C. (2006). Using acceptance and commitment training in the support of parents of children diagnosed with autism. *Child and Family Behavior Therapy, 28,* 1-18.

Bond, F. W., Hayes, S. C., Baer, R. A., Carpenter, K. C., Guenole, N., Orcutt, H. K., et al. (2011). Preliminary psychometric properties of the Acceptance and Action Questionnaire–II: A revised measure of psychological flexibility and acceptance. *Behavior Therapy, 42,* 676-688.

Brown, G., & Jones, E. (2005). Implementation of a feedback system in a managed care environment: What are patients teaching us? *Journal of Clinical Psychology, 61,* 187-198.

Bryan, C., Morrow, C., & Appolonio, K. (2009). Impact of behavioral health consultant interventions on patient symptoms and functioning in an integrated family medicine clinic. *Journal of Clinical Psychology, 65,* 281-293.

Budman, S., Hoyt, M., & Friedman, S. (Eds.). (1992). *The first session in brief therapy.* New York: Guilford Press.

Caffo, E., Forresi, B., & Lievers, L. S. (2005). Impact, psychological sequelae, and management of trauma affecting children and adolescents. *Child and Adolescent Psychiatry: Current Opinion in Psychiatry, 18,* 422-428.

Cape, J., Whittington, C., Buszewicz, M., Wallace, P., & Underwood, L. (2010). Brief psychological therapies for anxiety and depression in primary care: Meta-analysis and meta-regression. *BMC Medicine, 8,* 38.

Chaffin, M., Silovsky, J., Funderburk, B., Valle, L. A., Brestan, E. V., Balachova, T., et al. (2004). Parent-child interaction therapy with physically abusive parents: Efficacy for reducing future abuse reports. *Journal of Consulting and Clinical Psychology, 72,* 500-510.

Christensen, A., & Jacobson, N. S. (1998). *Acceptance and change in couple therapy: A therapist's guide to transforming relationships.* New York: W. W. Norton.

Covey, S. (2004). *The 7 habits of highly effective people: Powerful lessons in personal change.* New York: Simon and Schuster.

Crits-Christoph, P., Connolly, M., Gallop, R., Barber, J., Tu, X., Gladis, M., et al. (2001). Early improvement during manual-guided cognitive and dynamic psychotherapies predicts 16-week remission status. *Journal of Psychotherapy Practice and Research, 10,* 145-154.

Deacon, B., & Abramowitz, J. (2006). A pilot study of two-day cognitive-behavioral therapy for panic disorder. *Behaviour Research and Therapy, 44,* 807-817.

De Shazer, S. (1985). *Keys to solution in brief therapy.* New York: W. W. Norton.

De Shazer, S. (1988). *Clues: Investigating solutions in brief therapy.* New York: W. W. Norton.

De Shazer, S. (1991). *Putting difference to work.* New York: W. W. Norton.

Doane, L., Feeny, N., & Zoellner, L. (2010). A preliminary investigation of sudden gains in exposure therapy for PTSD. *Behaviour Research and Therapy, 48,* 555-560.

Erikson, E. H. (1968). *Identity: Youth and crisis.* New York: W. W. Norton.

Frankl, V. (1992). *Man's search for meaning.* Boston: Beacon Press.

Gingerich, W., & Eisengart, S. (2000). Solution-focused brief therapy: A review of outcome research. *Family Process, 39,* 477-498.

Gottman, J. M., & Notarius, C. I. (2000). Decade review: Observing marital interaction. *Journal of Marriage and Family, 62,* 927-947.

Grant, B., Dawson, F., Stinson, S., Chou, M., Dufour, M., & Pickering, P. (2004). The 12-month prevalence and trends in DSM-IV alcohol abuse and dependence: United States, 1991-1992 and 2001-2002. *Drug and Alcohol Dependence, 74,* 223-234.

Grilo, C. M., Masheb, R. M., & Wilson, G. T. (2006). Rapid response to treatment for binge eating disorder. *Journal of Consulting and Clinical Psychology, 74,* 602-613.

Haley, J. (1993). *Uncommon therapy: The psychiatric techniques of Milton H. Erickson, M.D.* New York: W. W. Norton.

Hayes, S. C., Barnes-Holmes, D., & Roche, B. (Eds.). (2001). *Relational frame theory: A post-Skinnerian account of human language and cognition.* New York: Plenum Press.

Hayes, S. C., Luoma, J., Bond, F., Masuda, A., & Lillis, J. (2006). Acceptance and commitment therapy: Model, processes, and outcomes. *Behaviour Research and Therapy, 44,* 1-25.

Hayes, S. C., Strosahl, K. D., & Wilson, K. G. (1999). *Acceptance and commitment therapy: An experiential approach to behavior change.* New York: Guilford Press.

Hayes, S., Strosahl, K., & Wilson, K. (2011). *Acceptance and commitment therapy: The process and practice of mindful change.* New York: Guilford Press.

Howard, K., Davidson, C., O'Mahoney, M., Orlinsky, D., & Brown, K. (1989). Patterns of psychotherapy utilization. *American Journal of Psychiatry, 146,* 775-778.

Howard, K., Kopta, S., Krause, M., & Orlinsky, D. (1986). The dose-effect relationship in psychotherapy. *American Psychologist, 41,* 159-164.

Howard, K., Lueger, R., Maling, M., & Martinovich, Z. (1993). A phase model of psychotherapy: Causal mediation of outcome. *Journal of Consulting and Clinical Psychology, 51,* 1059-1064.

Hoyt, M. F. (2001). *Interviews with brief therapy experts.* Philadelphia: Breuner Routledge.

Hoyt, M. F. (2009). *Brief psychotherapies: Principles and practices.* Phoenix, AZ: Zeig, Tucker, and Theisen.

Jacobson, N. (1985). Family therapy outcome research: Potential pitfalls and prospects. *Journal of Marital and Family Therapy, 11,* 149-158.

Kim, J. (2008). Examining the effectiveness of solution-focused brief therapy: A meta-analysis. *Research on Social Work Practice, 18,* 107-116.

Lackner, J., Gudleski, G., Keefer, L., Krasner, S., Powell, C., & Katz, L. (2010). Rapid response to cognitive behavior therapy predicts treatment outcome in patients with irritable bowel syndrome. *Clinical Gastroenterology and Hepatology, 8,* 426-432.

Levin, M. E., Hildebrandt, M. J., Lillis, J., & Hayes, S. C. (in press). The impact of treatment components in acceptance and commitment therapy: A meta-analysis of micro-component studies.

Lock, J., Agras, S., Bryson, S., & Kraemer, H. (2005). A comparison of short- and long-term family therapy for anorexia nervosa. *Journal of the Academy of Child and Adolescent Psychiatry, 44,* 632-639.

Lowe, B., Unutzer, J., Callahan, C. M., Perkins, A., & Kroenke, K. (2004). Monitoring depression treatment outcomes with the Patient Health Questionnaire–9, *Medical Care, 42,* 1194-1201.

Lutz, W., Stulz, N., & Kock, K. (2009). Patterns of early change and their relationship to outcome and follow-up among patients with major depressive disorders. *Journal of Affective Disorders, 118,* 60-68.

Meyer, J. (2001). *Age: 2000. Census 2000 Brief (C2KBR/01-12).* Washington, DC: U.S. Census Bureau. http://census.gov/prod/2001pubs/c2kbr01-12.pdf. Retrieved July 3, 2009.

Miller, S., Hubble, M., & Duncan, B. (Eds.). (1996). *Handbook of solution-focused brief therapy.* San Francisco: Jossey-Bass.

Molenaar, P. J., Boom, Y., Peen, J., Schoevers, R. A., Van, R., & Dekker, J. J. (2011). Is there a dose-effect relationship between the number of psychotherapy sessions and improvement of social functioning? *British Journal of Clinical Psychology, 50,* 268-282.

Nathan, P. E., & Gorman, J. M. (Eds.). (2002). *A guide to treatments that work*. New York: Oxford University Press.

O'Hanlon, W. (2009). *A guide to trance land: A practical handbook of Ericksonian and solution-oriented hypnosis*. New York: W. W. Norton.

O'Hanlon, W., & Weiner-Davis, M. (2003). *In search of solutions: A new direction in psychotherapy*. New York: W. W. Norton.

Olfson, M., Mojtabai, R., Sampson, N. A., Hwang, I., Druss, B., Wang, P. S., et al. (2009). Dropout from outpatient mental health care in the United States. *Psychiatric Services, 60,* 898-907.

Öst, L. G. (2008). Efficacy of the third wave of behavioral therapies: A systematic review and meta-analysis. *Behaviour Research and Therapy, 46,* 296-321.

Osterholm, C., & Mansdorff, M. G. (2009). [A functional analytic group therapy for persons with self-harming behaviors: A randomized controlled study in a psychiatric clinic for open care.] University of Stockholm, Department of Psychology. Unpublished manuscript.

Parkerson, G. R., Broadhead, W. E., & Tse, C. K. J. (1991). Development of the 17-item Duke Health Profile. *Family Practice, 8,* 396-401.

Powers, M. B., Vörding, M., & Emmelkamp, P. M. G. (2009). Acceptance and commitment therapy: A meta-analytic review. *Psychotherapy and Psychosomatics, 8,* 73-80.

Pull, C. B. (2009). Current empirical status of acceptance and commitment therapy. *Current Opinion in Psychiatry, 22,* 1, 55-60.

Renaud, J., Brent, D. A., Baugher, M., Birmaher, B., Kolko, D. J., & Bridge, J. (1998.) Rapid response to psychosocial treatment for adolescent depression: A two-year follow-up. *Journal of the American Academy of Child and Adolescent Psychiatry, 37,* 1184-1190.

Robinson, P., & Reiter, J. (2006). *Behavioral consultation and primary care: A guide to integrating services*. New York: Springer Science+Business Media.

Roozen, H. G., Boulogne, J. J., van Tulder, M. W., van den Brink, W., De Jong, C. A., & Kerkhof, A. J. (2004). A systematic review of the effectiveness of the community reinforcement approach in alcohol, cocaine, and opioid addiction. *Drug and Alcohol Dependence, 74,* 1-13.

Rosen, S. (1991). *My voice will go with you: The teaching tales of Milton H. Erickson*. New York: W. W. Norton.

Ruiz, F. J. (2010). A review of acceptance and commitment therapy (ACT) empirical evidence: Correlational, experimental psychopathology, component and outcome studies. *International Journal of Psychology and Psychological Therapy, 10,* 125-162.

Sedlak, A. J., Mettenburg, J., Basena, M., Petta, I., McPherson, K., Greene, A., et al. (2010). *Fourth National Incidence Study of Child Abuse and Neglect (NIS–4): Report to Congress, Executive Summary*. Washington, DC: U.S. Department of Health and Human Services, Administration for Children and Families.

Sijbrandij, M., Olff, M., Reistsma, J., Carlier, I., de Vries, M., & Gersons, B. (2007). Treatment of acute posttraumatic stress disorder with brief cognitive-behavioral therapy: A randomized controlled trial. *American Journal of Psychiatry, 164,* 82-90.

Smyrnios, K., & Kirkby, R. (1993). Long-term comparison of brief versus unlimited psychodynamic treatment of children and their parents. *Journal of Consulting and Clinical Psychology, 61,* 1020-1027.

Strosahl, K. D., Hayes, S. C., Bergan, J., & Romano, P. (1998). Assessing the field effectiveness of acceptance and commitment therapy: An example of the manipulated training research method. *Behavior Therapy, 29,* 35-64.

Talmon, M. (1990). *Single session therapy: Maximizing the effect of the first (and often only) therapeutic encounter.* San Francisco: Jossey-Bass.

Tan, L., & Martin, G. (2008). *Taming the adolescent mind: A pilot study of mindfulness-based group program for adolescents with mixed mental health presentations.* Poster session presented at the Association for Contextual Behavioral Science World Congress, Chicago, IL.

Tang, T., DeRubeis, R., Hollon, S., Amsterdam, J., & Shelton, R. (2007). Sudden gains in cognitive therapy for depression and depression relapse/recurrence. *Journal of Consulting and Clinical Psychology, 75,* 404-408.

Tani, S., Hyougo, E. K., Gakuen, S., & Kitamura, K. (2010). ACT workshop for the parents of children with PDD. Association for Contextual Behavioral Science World Congress, Reno, NV.

Tjaden, P., & Thoennes, N. (1998). *Prevalence, incidence, and consequences of violence against women: Findings from the National Violence against Women Survey.* Washington, DC: U.S. Department of Justice.

Vromans, L., & Schweitzer, R. D. (2010). Narrative therapy for adults with major depressive disorder: Improved symptom and interpersonal outcomes. *Psychotherapy Research, 19,* 1-12.

Walker, E. A., Torkelson, N., Katon, W. J., & Koss, M. P. (1993). The prevalence of sexual abuse in a primary care clinic. *Journal of the American Board of Family Practice, 6,* 465-471.

Watzlawick, P., Weakland, J., & Fisch, R. (1974). *Change: Principles of problem formation and problem resolution.* New York: W. W. Norton.

Weakland, J., & Ray, W. (1995). *Propagations: Thirty years of influence from the Mental Research Institute.* New York: Haworth.

Werner, E., & Smith, R. S. (1992). *Overcoming the odds: High risk children from birth to adulthood.* Ithaca, NY: Cornell University Press.

White, M. (2007). *Maps of narrative practice.* New York: W. W. Norton.

White, M., & Epston, D. (1990). *Narrative means to therapeutic ends.* New York: W. W. Norton.

Kirk Strosahl, PhD, is a cofounder of acceptance and commitment therapy, a cognitive behavioral therapy that has gained widespread adoption in the mental health and substance abuse community. He is the author of numerous articles on the subjects of primary care behavioral health integration, using outcome assessment to guide practice and strategies for working with challenging, high-risk, and suicidal clients. Along with Patricia Robinson, he coauthored the highly praised self-help book, *The Mindfulness and Acceptance Workbook for Depression*. Strosahl currently works as a primary care psychologist at Central Washington Family Medicine, a community health center providing health care to a large medically underserved population. He is well-known nationally for his innovative approach to the integration of behavioral health and primary care services. Strosahl lives in Zillah, WA.

Patricia Robinson, PhD, is a director of clinical services at Mountainview Consulting Group, Inc., a firm specializing in providing consultation for health care systems seeking to integrate behavioral health services into primary care settings. She was a member of a pioneering research team that explored primary care-based behavioral health care in the 1990s. She then moved on to refine the primary care behavioral health model and apply it to delivery of health care services to underserved people in rural America, including migrant farm workers and members of the Yakima Nation. Robinson has consulted with numerous public and private health and mental health care systems, including the United States Air Force and the San Francisco Department of Public Health. She is the author of numerous articles, book chapters, and six books, including *Real Behavior Change in Primary Care*, and is coauthor of *The Mindfulness and Acceptance Workbook for Depression*.

Thomas Gustavsson, MSc, is a licensed psychologist and one of the founders of Psykologpartners, a company providing psychology and psychiatry services in Scandinavia. He has worked as a consultant for several community-based services, social workers, treatment centers, schools, and primary care clinics. In addition, he is one of the pioneers in building an integrated, evidence-based psychiatry program within a large primary care system in Helsingborg, Sweden. Gustavsson resides in Rydeback, Sweden.

Index

biomedical approach, 51, 53

black-and-white statements, 87

blaming others, 72–73

Body Scan intervention, 169–171

Box of Stuff intervention, 172–173

breathing, Present-Moment, 148–149

brief intervention, 12

brief therapy, 11–25; criticisms of, 23–25; defining the concept of, 12–13; Erickson's contribution to, 18–20; historical evolution of, 18–22; managed care linked to, 23; myths and misconceptions about, 13–18; narrative therapy as, 22, 25; problem-focused, 20–21; scientific studies of, 24–25; solution-focused, 4, 21–22, 24

C

Camus, Albert, 105

Carlin, George, 155

case examples of FACT: with an adult survivor of sexual abuse, 180–201; with a couple, 231–242; with a depressed elderly woman, 204–225; with a poly-substance-abusing adult, 155–178; with a sexually abused child, 129–153; with a therapy group member, 257–263

case formulation process, 98–103, 266–267; assessing flexibility, 98–100, 266–267, 270; examining workability, 100–103, 267, 271

case formulation process (case examples): adult survivor of sexual abuse, 191–192; childhood sexual abuse victim, 142–143; depressed elderly client, 213–214; substance-abusing adult, 166–167

categorization and comparison, 35–36

change: accepting in others, 244–245; couples and, 242–245; experimental approach to, 59; FACT perspectives on, 54–57; focusing on the process of, 244; low-cost, 242; myths and

misconceptions about, 13–18; phase model of, 16; positive valence around, 60–61; process of radical, 49–65; pursuing in others, 244; setting the stage for, 80–82; short-term, 243; small behavioral, 60; vague theories of, 24; values-based, 242

childhood abuse/trauma: pointers on using FACT for, 152–153; protective factors relating to, 129–130; stages in treating, 130–131

childhood sexual abuse case example, 131–152; awareness-promoting interventions, 145–149; case formulation process, 142–143; engagement-promoting interventions, 149–150; focusing questions, 132–138; life direction exercise, 140–141; openness-promoting interventions, 151–152; radical change discussion, 139; treatment summary, 144–152

choice, 121–122

classroom therapy format. See group therapy

clients: focusing on willingness of, 63; in-session assessments by, 272; myth on therapeutic desire of, 13–14; relationship of therapists to, 61–64

clinical hypnosis, 18–20

clinician-client relationship, 61–64

Clouds in the Sky intervention, 151

cognitive-affective scripts, 37

colloquialisms, 87

committed action, 122–123

comparison and categorization, 35–36

compass heading metaphors, 94

confidence ratings, 272

confusing language practices, 19

consciousness, 30

context of behavior, 30–31

contingency-based learning, 244

contingency-shaped behavior, 33–34

and, 46, 119–125; openness and, 45, 113–119; three pillars illustration, 45

public behaviors, 101, 102

QRS

questions: focusing, 70–80, 265–266; pre-group orientation, 250–251; skillful use of, 63–64

radical change process, 49–65; adult survivors of sexual abuse and, 187; childhood sexual abuse victims and, 139; depressed elderly clients and, 209–211; setting the stage for, 80–82; substance-abusing adults and, 162–163

rating scales, 272

reframing problems, 82–83

rehabilitation phase, 16

relational frame theory (RFT), 32–33

relationship counseling. See couples therapy case example

remediation phase, 16

remoralization phase, 16

reorienting interventions, 120–121

resistance, encouraging, 19

retirement party exercise, 120

revolving-door problem, 16

river analogy, 55–56

role modeling, 62

rule following, 40–41, 54, 87

rule-governed behavior, 34–35

rumination, 101

Say It Slowly intervention, 198

Scales of Choice intervention, 174–177

schizophrenia, double bind theory of, 20

scripts, cognitive-affective, 37

self: distinguishing from mind, 114; Little Self, Big Self intervention, 145–148; observing, 30–31

self-narrative, 36, 109–110

self-reflexivity, 35

sense making, 36

serendipity, 60

sessions. See therapy sessions

sexual abuse case examples: adult survivor of sexual abuse, 180–201; childhood victim of sexual abuse, 131–152

short-term changes, 243

short-term therapy, 12

single-session therapy, 14

small behavior change, 60

social labeling, 51

social skills training, 153

sociocultural context, 30

solution talk, 21

solution-focused brief therapy (SFBT), 4, 21–22, 24

speaker-listener relationships, 115

speech: rule following indicated by, 87. See also language

sticky thoughts, 114

storytelling, 109–111

stress, coping with, 51–52

substance abuse: addictive behaviors and, 177–178; challenges to treating, 155–156; pointers on using FACT for, 177–178

Substance Abuse and Mental Health Services Administration (SAMHSA), 3

substance-abusing adult case example, 156–177; awareness-promoting intervention, 169–171; case formulation process, 166–167; engagement-promoting intervention, 173–177; focusing questions, 157–161; life direction exercise, 163–165; openness-promoting intervention, 171–173; radical change discussion, 162–163; treatment summary, 168–177

suffering: behavioral rigidity and, 44; FACT technique for describing, 255; language related to, 28–29